John,

America Matters

Keep the Faith

COMING TO AMERICA

COMING TO
AMERICA

Stories of the immigrants who make America

*"You Don't Know What
You've Got 'Till it's Gone"*
—Joni Mitchell, "Big Yellow Taxi"

Kathleen S. Roos Ph.D.

Charleston, SC
www.PalmettoPublishing.com

Coming to America
Copyright © 2022 by Kathleen S. Roos Ph.D.

Hardcover ISBN: 978-1-68515-745-6
Paperback ISBN: 979-8-88590-304-2
eBook ISBN: 978-1-68515-747-0

INTERESTING AND RELATED QUOTES

"Give me four years to teach the children, and the seed I have sewn will never be uprooted."
—Vladimir Lenin, circa 1918.

"If we lose the kids, we lose the country."
—Ann Coulter

"It's easier to fool people than to convince them that they have been fooled."
—Mark Twain

"Facts don't care about your feelings."
"There is no such thing as 'your truth'. There is truth and your opinion."
"Without a clear moral vision, we devolve into moral relativism, and from there into oblivion."
Ben Shapiro

"If you believe a lie, even though it's a lie and not really true, it becomes true for you because that is what you believe."
—Life Point via Joyce Meyers

"The problem with socialism is that you eventually run out of other people's money."
—Margaret Thatcher

"Socialism is a philosophy of failure, the creed of ignorance, and the gospel of envy, its inherent virtue is equal sharing of misery."
—Winston Churchill

"Nothing would be more fatal than for government of the states to get into the hands of the experts. Expert knowledge is limited knowledge: and the unlimited ignorance of the plain man who knows only what hurts is a safer guide, than any vigorous direction of a specialized character. Why should you assume that all expert doctors, engineers, etc. are drones or worse?"
—Young Churchill writing to H.G. Wells

"Socialism states that you owe me something simply because I exist. Capitalism, by contrast, results in a sort of reality-focused altruism: I may not want to help you, but if I don't give you a product or service you want, I will starve. Voluntary exchange is more moral than forced redistribution."
—Ben Shapiro

"The Inherent vice of Capitalism is the unequal sharing of blessings: the inherent virtue of socialism is the equal sharing of miseries."
—Winston Churchill

"Optimism is the faith that leads to achievement. Nothing can be done without hope and confidence."
—Helen Keller

"Capitalism: the worst economic system, except for all the others. Capitalism is no different than anything else in this world. It is imperfect because imperfect men created it. Humans are not perfect, nor are they capable of perfection. Avarice and greed are not unique to capitalism. They were present in the USSR, and they will present themselves in any man-made system."
—Matt Barnes, *The Pitt News, 2014*

"You were given a choice between war and dishonor. You chose dishonor and you will have war."
—Winston Churchill

"*If you win, you need not have to explain, if you lose,
you should not be there to explain!*"
—Adolf Hitler

"*He alone who owns the youth, gains the future.*"
—Adolf Hitler

"*To conquer a nation, first disarm its citizens.*"
—Adolf Hitler

"*The great strength of the totalitarian state is that it forces those
who fear it to imitate it.*"
—Adolf Hitler

"*Humanitarianism is the expression of stupidity and cowardice.*"
—Adolf Hitler

"*If war is horrible, servitude is worse.*"
—Winston Churchill.

"*To build may have to be slow and laborious task of years. To destroy can be
the thoughtlessness of a single day.*"
—Winston Churchill.

"*Attitude is a little thing that makes a big difference.*"
—Winston Churchill.

"*If you are not liberal at 20 it is because you have no heart. If you are not
conservative at forty, then you have no brains.*"
—Winston Churchill.

"*Why do our enemies see us as Americans and we
Americans see each other as the enemy?*"
—Kathleen Roos PhD.

"We have met the enemy and it is us."
—Walt Kelly's comic strip *Pogo and Politico 2021.*

"The United States is the last best hope of Earth."
—Abraham Lincoln

"Only America can hurt America."
—Eisenhower

"Mostly is it the loss which teaches us about the worth of things."
—Arthur Schopenhauer

"Experience outweighs your opinion."
—Candace Owen and John Rich

"You don't know what you've got till it's gone"
—Joni Mitchell, *"Big Yellow Taxi"*

"How do you tell a Communist? It's someone who reads Marx and Lenin. And how do you tell an anti-Communist? It's someone who understands Marx and Lenin."
—Ronald Raegan

"Government is not the solution to our problem: government is the problem."
—Ronald Reagan

"The Liberal/Marxist Machine in our Country demands that Equity of Outcome be mandatory. Be that as it may, I have to admit…I cannot wait for these idealists to discover that ultimately, they too, would wind up being controlled by the very machine they built."
—H. G. Goerner

"Government's first duty is to protect the people, not run their lives."
—Ronald Reagan

"As government expands, liberty contracts."
—Ronald Reagan

"Government does not solve problems. It subsidizes them."
—Ronald Reagan

*"The best minds are not in government. If they were,
business would steal them away."*
—Ronald Reagan

*"We don't have a trillion-dollar debt because we haven't taxed enough: we
have a trillion-dollar debt because we spend too much."*
—Ronald Reagan

*"We must reject the idea that every time a law is broken, society is guilty
rather than the law breaker. It is time to restore the American precept that
each individual is accountable for his actions."*
—Ronald Reagan

*"Socialism only works in two places: Heaven where they don't need it
and hell where they already have it."*
—Ronald Reagan

*"Politics has become so expensive that it takes a lot
of money even to be defeated."*
—Will Rogers

*"Everything is changing. People are taking their comedians seriously
and the politicians as a joke."*
—Will Rogers

*"If you want to be successful, it's just this simple. Know what you are doing.
Love what you are doing. And believe in what you are doing."*
—Will Rogers

"Because someone repeats something over and over and louder and louder, still does not make it true."
—Kathleen S. Roos, PhD

"Science is never settled. It is probationary and with new information and new technology it can change." Thomas Kuhn. Basis: "Science is taken from the Latin word 'siens' 'to know'. It is the intellectual and practical activity encompassing the systematic study of the structure and behavior of the physical and natural world through observation and experiment."
—Oxford Dictionary

"There are but two ways of forming an opinion in science. One is the scientific method; the other, the scholastic. One can judge from experiment, or one can blindly accept authority. To the scientific mind, experimental proof is all important, and theory merely a convenience in description, to be junked when it no longer fits. To the academic mind, authority is everything and facts are junked when they do not fit theory laid down by authority"
—Robert A. Heinlein, "Life-Line."

"Freedom Is never more than one generation away from extinction. We didn't pass it to our children in the blood stream. It must be fought for, protected, and handed on for them to do the same, or one day we will spend our sunset years telling our children and our children's children what it was once like in the United States where men were free."
—Ronald Reagan

"Let us not seek the Republican answer, or the Democratic answer, but the right answers. Let us not seek to fix blame for the past. Let us accept our own responsibility for the future."
—John F. Kennedy

"Death is the solution to all problems. No man, no problem."
—Joseph Stalin

"It is enough that the people know there was an election. The people who cast the votes decide nothing. The people who count the votes decide everything."
—Joseph Stalin

"Education is a weapon whose effects depend on who holds it in their hands and at whom it is aimed."
—Joseph Stalin

"We don't let them have ideas. Why would we let them have guns?"
—Joseph Stalin

"If a government is big enough to give you all the stuff you need, then the government is big enough to take it all away."
—Mark Brnovich, Arizona attorney general

PRAISE FOR COMING TO AMERICA: YOU DON'T KNOW WHAT YOU'VE GOT TILL IT'S GONE IN CITIZEN'S JOURNAL

"This project is a worthwhile read for those of us who are appreciative of what we have, where we are and the opportunity and freedom to pursue our goals and dreams. Hopefully these personal histories are shared with others who may not have received this gift of learning how many of our fellow countrymen have overcome challenges to their very existence and stand as examples of how perseverance and spirit have created heroes."
—Mary Matera

"This is a fantastic article and interview! I look forward to reading more of these interviews from Kathleen Roos. Hopefully more people will read these interviews and realize how lucky we are to have been born and living in the USA!"
—Joy Swift

"This article provides tremendous insight to the drive and motivation of these immigrants who put their lives at risk to escape their government. It definitely evokes a greater sense of appreciation for this great country we live in. I particularly like the nonpolitical approach which allows for an open mind. This work speaks to Kathleen's compassion and commitment to bringing immigration to a whole new light. I look forward to reading more interviews and gaining an even greater perspective!"
—Donna Matera

"This may be the beginning of one of the most important books of these terrifying times we live in. It is well written with great intelligence and a sincere desire to help the sleepers wake up to the reality of what is happening to our once great country. I implore everyone to share this article far and wide, especially with our younger generations. They have been lied to and manipulated from every

side. I look forward to reading and sharing Ms. Roos' book. A MUST read."
—Maggie Kennedy

"There are so many parallels in India's history and current culture to what we are experiencing in America today. The agenda of many of our US politicians is to create the new structure of those who maintain control over our lives and those who perform as directed with most of our earnings going to enrich the select few. What is most scary is how slow many of us Americans are to assimilate these parallels and actively voice our objections to have our autonomy taken away. How ungrateful we must seem in the eyes of someone like Zulfi, who has done everything he can to fight for independence and a safer way of life!"
—Mary Matera

"I read this article several times. Zulfi sees the issues many want to obscure or ignore. Thanks for posting."
—Sheryl Hamlin

"Very inspiring article showing the evil roots of the CCP and communism. It really helps illustrate what's at risk with the current evil regime in D.C."
—David Lunn

"Wonderful write up and so appreciative to live in the USA!"
—Maria Finney

"I love reading these stories! They make me feel so lucky to have been born in the US. The Khmer Rouge were horrific!"
—Joy Swift

"What a great uplifting story about this wonderful country and it's immigrants! I look forward to reading more from Kathleen Roos!"
—Joy Swift

"Very good read & nostalgic."
—Marilyn

"Thank you so much for this article! Mark's insight is right on as to what is going on in the USA Today!"
—Maria Finney

"Maybe it would also be a good article about how many people are leaving blue states for red ones, and why."
—William Hicks

"Great article. really makes you appreciate the US under Trump not the current train wreck of a president. It's amazing how so many are like frogs in soup, your series really highlights the changes going on in the US and the people who immigrated legally to have a better life are seeing the kind of stuff in the US that they were running away from."
—David Lunn

"Dems read this and take notes. Their open borders plan satisfies their need for masses of ignoramuses to complete the job."
—Michael A.

"This article highlights comparisons of life in Iraq with that offered to a young woman in the US. For example, while Iraqi women have little power to make their own life choices (own her own home, marry whomever she pleases) she cites the more extensive priority on education in Iraq versus her assessment of education in the US. While she finds America offers more opportunities for jobs and careers, she misses the closeness she attributes to her family in Iraq. To be able to choose her life in the US speaks volumes about the gift of freedom many of us take for granted!"
—Mary Matera

"I think it is important for people living in the US to take time to listen, and read stories from people like Angela who migrated to the US with a background like hers. Regardless of where we stand, (left or right) we can all gain a new

perspective on events happening in the US that we are currently living through, based on someone else's experience in a country like Chile during that time."
—James C.

"It is frightening to note the comparisons between Angela Bond's recounting of the violence and lack of consequences for criminal behavior under Allende and the subtle changes in our basic freedoms. Because our elected leaders don't always have our best interests in mind, we may find ourselves powerless to pursue opportunities and make individual choices that US citizens currently take for granted."
—Mary Matera

"Excellent interview. The parallels that Ms. Bond observes between the Chilean communists and US Socialist Dems are eye-opening. Forwarding this interview to others."
—Neil Jordan

"A true reality check. I appreciate Angela's story and wish EVERYONE had her insight. It is sad to watch America fall. Our beautiful Republic is worth fighting for."
—Erin

"Had a student from Chile. Wonderful country. Incredible diversity. Thanks for this story."
—Jack Cameron

"Thanks for this report. Especially the part about the woman who stuck her tongue out at Allende. (Isn't it ironic how the Left accuses Pinochet of the very things Allende did? (Apparently, dictators like Pinochet are malo, but dictators like Castro are bueno.)
"As the Left revises history, it is difficult to find the truth about what life was really like back then. The kids have been indoctrinated by the schools and don't know the truth. They weren't taught that the Chilean Supreme Court had ruled that Allende's election was invalid.

"I know a business woman in Chile, also in her midfifties now, who has similar stories and sees Communism returning to her country. Her $3 Million USD business is all but over."
—GringoMike

"Her discussion of the education system parallels the description in "The Smartest Kids in the World" by Amanda Ripley which details this and how it mattered to a US student who studied there."
—William Morris

"In these two interviews, Mony Toch and Olivia Roeun describe their struggles with communist repression in Cambodia that eventually brought them to America. They plead with our complacent citizens to actively avoid socialism and communism and to appreciate our country's gifts of freedom, resources and opportunity."
—Mary Matera

"One of the best. You didn't have to work, it was just going to be given to you, and you would be taken care of. You will be given one to two meals a day. This is the beginning of socialism when they start offering you things for free. That everything will be taken care of by the government. The gratitude, the appreciation for the opportunities she has here after her family's experiences under socialism, the emotional swings that occurred time and time again, the riches to rags to…I think it was the ups and downs she and her family experienced that touched me more…I just cannot imagine going through all that and still having my sanity."
—John Vogt

"Amazing stories! Her (Dr. Roos) adventures are so exiting. Real world history!"
—Linda Miller

TABLE OF CONTENTS

COMING TO AMERICA
Kathleen S. Roos, PhD

"You Don't Know What You've Got 'Till it's Gone"
—Joni Mitchell, "Big Yellow Taxi"

INTRODUCTION

These are the stories of immigrants to the US who have experienced firsthand varying degrees of socialism or communism and forms of government that differ from the USA. Many of these immigrants have lived through conditions and horrors that most Americans thankfully will never experience. Knowledge of these stories may lead persons both young and old to do more research into history and educate themselves on some of the promises and rhetoric made by politicians and activists today in this country.

The historian Forest MacDonald said that George Washington is an "indispensable man." Americans have given up commemorating George Washington's February 22 birthday in exchange for a three-day weekend. One of the downsides, according to Gary M. Gillis (Feb 19, 2021), is that we are now more likely to overlook the wisdom Washington has to offer us. That is particularly unfortunate following an intensely uncivil and partisan election, whose subsequent "unity" has continued to be uncivil and partisan. My point: the civility and knowledge coming from history is being trampled by the very same people who once insisted it was imperative. The tearing down of statues, burning books, silencing opinions and classical music, and eliminating one's history is not the answer. Just look to the Taliban destroying greater than three-thousand-year-old Buddha statues against the entire world's pleas. We need to learn from the past and build upon it. Ignorance should not be allowed to destroy existing knowledge for future generations. Allow them to figure it out on their own. Preservation of knowledge will allow future generations to have their most prosperous existence.

My purpose in writing this expose is to alert those who may have little knowledge of the past or the damage caused by socialism, communism, and other forms of rule such as dictatorships, monarchies, and "military democracies." The individual histories portrayed in these pages still exist in the hearts and minds of those who experienced them firsthand. Many still live under such rule as the people of Cuba, under the totalitarian rule of Communist Party of Cuba communist rule since 1958 and so timely demonstrated. Unfortunately, even today, many university professors and their impressionable students and many politicians are denying our history! I come from parents and relatives who fought in World War II or worked in industry proudly on the home front. I have friends, living and deceased, who served in Korea, Vietnam, and the Gulf Wars. I am of the generation who understands that people left Europe to escape the cruel and inhumane policies and actions carried out by Mussolini, Tito, Lenin, Stalin, and Hitler. We are all immigrants to some extent unless we are Native peoples and believe that America matters.

When I started to see friends of thirty-plus years never speaking to each other again and close-knit families avoiding sharing holidays together, I felt I had to do something. To me that was so "not American." Today many do not appreciate the damage caused by socialism and communism and are easily led by emotional blogs and suggestive media that do not provide all the truth. To make this point, I will share several examples: I shared with an acquaintance a rather horrific story, included in this expose, about the actions of Josef Stalin during one of his speeches. The reaction was laughter, and he said young people today would say, "Who's Stalin?" Another example comes from one of my interviewees whose niece denied her experiences in Santiago, Chile, stating she knew because of what her professors told her. And yet another where I shared the story of Edgar Harrell, the last surviving marine of the *USS Indianapolis*. I had seen his amazing story televised on Memorial Day on David Barton's *WallBuilders*, where it was noted that in the US today, our educational system from first grade to K12 in advanced placement history consisted of a single page devoted to World War II, and that was almost entirely devoted to coverage of Japanese internment camps. I was relaying Edgar's emotional story to a very successful, educated young woman. She was moved by his story and said, "what is this *Indianapolis*?" This response startled me. The lack of knowledge of history today is destructive to future generations. Though socialism may appear on paper as harmless and even glorious and beneficial to some, that could not be further from the truth. As I read in a recent post on Next-door.com (a neighborhood social media website), "so what's wrong with wanting free stuff!" which points out that having knowledge is critical to enjoying freedom and having liberty. There is no free anything. Someone is paying somewhere. And when it comes to liberty, it may be in lives lost, as in the *USS Indianapolis* episode. Yes, there are many different types/levels of socialism, and I will address these options, but just know it is a slippery slope. Often and possibly unknowingly, some describe other nations as being successful socialist countries; for example, Sweden. The problem is, they are not socialist countries. They have some socialist programs, as does the US, such as Social Security. Often their citizens are paying taxes ranging from 30-45 percent, and this information is never conveyed.

I have traveled a great deal during my career, and little did I realize at these times, how much those experiences would impact me and help contribute to this effort. I have personally had several encounters with socialism and communism and other forms of government during my work. I will include my story at the end. However, it was when I was talking to a Vietnamese colleague one day and he related his experience as one of the boat people escaping from Vietnam that I thought this information had to be made public. That was years ago. I never pursued it until now. We are becoming less American and more like the places many people wanted to escape from.

Few Americans are aware of these experiences and how common and universal they are. The reader will note these similarities—I call them common threads—throughout these stories. Most immigrants, legal or not, appear more appreciative of American values than many Americans who have the great opportunity to have been born here. You will hear this sentiment time and time again throughout these interviews. Ask yourself, Why is it that our enemies see us as Americans and we Americans see each other as the enemy? America, the place where thousands of peoples from more than 145 countries are trying to enter! America matters!

Yet another anecdote. I mentioned to a friend that I was interviewing people from socialist/communist countries as to why they had come to America and how they felt about their experiences in their native countries compared to the US. Her immediate and rather defensive response was "Well, I certainly hope you are interviewing someone from Sweden or Norway." I have made every effort to interview someone from Nordic countries and unveil the progressive "halo" of Sweden and other Norwegian countries being the answer to our governmental and societal woes. To address comparisons, provide balance, and let the reader decide, I have conducted interviews with those from countries considered by some to be socialist (Sweden, which is not) or have socialized programs such as health care in the United Kingdom. My purpose does not include comparatives such as geographical size, demographics, or gross and net GDPs, but when space and focus allow, I elaborate. When this concern was shared, my interviewee from India agreed that Finland is a paradise, but then he said but it is mostly Finns and the size of California. It doesn't have fifty states with their version of states' rights and thousands of people from more than 145 countries trying to invade its borders. A friend just returned from an October 2021 trip to Italy and relayed they had been hard pressed to find any Italians, obviously depending on locale, due to Italy's open border policy. The population noted were Syrian, Iranian, Turkish, and so on. And just look to the young man Enes Kanter Freedom, the Boston Celtics basketball player speaking out about human rights and comparisons to China and the companies who do business there! He is from Turkey and is Muslim, and his family is paying a price for his decision to speak out. He is also taking a lot of heat from others here in the US to risk his career to take such a stand. A very decent guy who makes a great reference when describing well-known people who appreciate the US and our freedoms and deplore the atrocities in China and other parts of the world relative to abuse and lack of human rights.

My qualifications for writing this expose are none. I am not a sociologist, psychologist, political science major, or historian. My degrees are in biology, marine science, and environmental engineering. I am, however an avid reader of history, stay current with civic events, and consider myself a patriot. My favorite authors growing up and remain today are William Manchester, Barbara Tuchman, Ayn Rand, James Clavell, Alan Moorhead, Winston Churchill, George Orwell, Alex Huxley, Richard Feynman, Michael Crichton, Carl Sagan, Thomas Sowell, and Victor David Hansen, and I enjoy the imagination of Gene Roddenberry. As stated, when I saw friends and family never talking to each other again, I felt a need to communicate that something is very wrong and find a way forward. That America with our Declaration of Independence, Constitution, and Bill of Rights is the place where change can and has come about for the betterment of all. We have our history, as do all other countries, but we have, I would say, progressed toward the positive. We are the only country in the world where our armed forces, police, and sheriffs swear allegiance to the US Constitution and the people, not some president, monarch, dictator, or parliamentarian.

In my past, I avidly tried to avoid using social media sites such as Twitter and Facebook. I recall my niece telling me "It's just social engineering" and think, how little did she realize how correct her observation was? I have long thought many are being socially engineered to a single mindset and not one of your own choosing. I know I will not get friends back, but I am attempting dialogue.

My method for interviews varies based on the situation. In some instances, it was more comfortable for the story teller to just talk, especially if some translation was necessary. At other times I conducted a more formal interview. Most interviews were in person, and as word spread about this effort, interviews were conducted via phone and internet due to location. Whatever method is used, my input and clarifications are italicized. Otherwise, all the stories are exactly from the those being interviewed, other than some reorganization for flow. I did not take on "cleaning anything up" to make it more palatable to some or politically correct to others. That is not my right or intent.

Most stories are presented in the order they were conducted. Originally, installments (chapters) were published in *Citizen's Journal*, a Ventura County online newspaper. The order in that online publication may not be the same as presented herein. No prioritizations of stories are made or opinions added, though some wanted to. I rejected including others' opinions or perceptions. Comments in the *Journal* provide these. These are their stories. I have added quotes prior to each chapter, as I believe they may be of historic interest to you, the reader, and often relate to common threads (see index) seen throughout this compilation.

Views presented in this book are those of the interviewees. Their opinions will give the reader varying perspectives. Although the original intent was to interview those from socialist or communist countries who came to the US, with increased interest and my effort to interview those from countries that have socialist programs such as health care (and many do not consider themselves socialist countries), my effort was expanded to include Sweden, Finland, and the UK. My questions, elaborations, and clarifications to interviews, are italicized in bold for the reader.

"If we lose the kids, we lose the country."
—Ann Coulter

CHAPTER 1

To conquer a nation, first disarm its citizens."
—Adolf Hitler

CAMBODIA AND THE KHMER ROUGE
Interview with Vanchhat Toch conducted on Feb 7, 2021.

Mr. Toch, with the former Cambodian army known as the Freedom Fighters, fought against the Communist Party attempting take over the government of Cambodia.

Photo depicting absolute cruelty of the Khmer Rouge

Vanchhat was born in Cambodia in 1941. He had four brothers and two sisters and practiced Buddhism.
From 1970–1975, I was in the Cambodian Military and fighting with the Freedom Fighters against the Communist Party of our government. I lived in the Battambang region of Cambodia. I was 30 years old when I escaped with my family to a camp along the Thai border. I do not remember the name of the camp. There were many camps that were stood up by the United Nations.

During these years Cambodia was an agrarian society of peasants living off the land. We farmed and raised our own food. There was no market economy. We raised primarily rice and when the

Communist entered into the region in 1970, they formed labor camps where our children from ages 5 and up were taken to work and grow rice. The money went to China.

Money was borrowed from China by Cambodian leaders. All our children were taken from our homes. *Mony, Vanchhat's second son was taken when he was 5 years old and worked in the camps until about 9 years old. They stayed in the camps and ate primarily wet rice daily. Vanchhat's family of 2 boys and two girls were separated during this time.*

The King of Cambodia, Pram Norodom, a despot wanted power and was influenced by Communist China. If you left Cambodia and went to US, you were considered a traitor and many were killed. The famous prison of Tael Slung is where many where sent. Others left early to go to France for study and were killed when they returned. All those with educations or professional jobs were considered 'intelligencia' and were imprisoned or killed. Even the simple act of wearing eyeglasses was considered a sign of studiousness and **was enough to justify the execution** of the transgressor.

The times were very confusing. The ethnic Vietnamese were also Buddhist and they were executed along with the Cambodians. However, it was the Communist Chinese and Vietnamese who entered Cambodia and attacked local citizens.

Vanchhat's brother, Vanthang was disappeared by Khmer Rouge in 1973. This was when Vanchhat knew he had to get out of Cambodia to get his family to safety. (Photo left of Vanchhat and his brother Vanthang, provided by Vanchhatt (June 2021)

Vanchhat said it was very confusing as to who they were fighting— communist Chinese or communist Vietnamese. Vanchhat fought Pol Pot's army in 1974.

I was a member of the Freedom fighters and fought with Lon Nol. Communist Pol Pot lied to us, his people, and no one believed what Lon Nol was telling us about not trusting what the communists were telling us (regarding giving up our guns or leaving valuables in a single place) as to what was to come. Marshal Lon Nol was Cambodia's politician and general serving twice as Prime Minister. He also served as defense minister and provincial governor.

Freedom Fighter General Lon Not was exiled to US., and US helped him escape or he would have been executed.

The Communist government lied to us *(the people)* and told us when they were taking our guns that we would be safe and there would be no more wars. They told us to collect all our valuables, gold and jewelry and put it in one place so it could be kept safe by them. I saw them going home to home and stealing these caches of our possessions.

This is when Vanchhat was in military and knew what was happening, and he draws parallels to what is happening in US today regarding gun confiscation efforts.

Catholic churches and Buddhist Temples were destroyed. No religious practices were allowed. Schools were closed. All the children went to camps to prepare the fields to produce for the Communist Chinese.

Pol Pot and the other leaders never worked or created anything ever in their lives, yet they felt they were born to be Kings and could take anything that belonged to us.

Cambodia wanted to destroy Tuol Sleng prison but we Cambodians fought to maintain it as a museum so people would never forget the Khmer Rouge or what they did to the people of Cambodia. I wanted to get my family out. My brother and a nephew had been executed. Others just 'disappeared'. I knew of the camps along the border with Thailand. The Communist

Vietnamese did not want we Cambodians or ethnic Vietnamese to get out. Many were captured. I spilt my family up for survival in case one of us would be caught. My family walked for a full day and night, hiding in the jungle, avoiding the Khmer Rouge and mines placed by the Communist to get to the border. I had to separate the family to escape. I took Mony and his brother and sister while my wife and other brother and sister went into hiding. Mony, my younger son had no shoes, only slippers while in the Camp. He walked all the way to the camp bare footed. My remaining family came later. The camps were almost like prisons themselves. If you tried to leave there was razor wire around the camp. It was known as the 'Prison of No Walls'. Many would try to escape to get food for their families only to be executed.

According to Vanchhat, China was instrumental in the development of Pol Pot's Khmer Rouge, and the Cambodian General Lon Nol attempted to fight them. Lon Nol tried to tell Cambodians what the communists were trying to do: taking our weapons, valuables, our food crops going to China. He was not believed. General Lon Nol had demanded that all communist Vietnamese leave Cambodia. These events marked the start of the Cambodian Civil War, pitting Lon Not against the Khmer

Rouge and North Vietnam. After a protracted conflict, the communist Khmer Rouge took control of Cambodia in 1975.

In 1973 Vanchhat's son, Mony's brother-in-law, escaped to become a marine in US and then go back to train Cambodians. He spoke French fluently and was a member of Cambodia's version of US. FBI. He had no family left and escaped to US. and lives in Pomona, CA.

On January 7, 1979, the Vietnamese communists marched into Phnom Penh and replaced the Khmer Rouge with a more familiar brand of tyranny. It is estimated that between two and three million were either executed or died of disease and starvation from 1975 through 1979.

Photo (above rt) taken from *Tuol Sleng Genocide Museum* (www.websitesrcg.com)

I was 30 years old at the time of our escape from Cambodia. My family and I remained in the Thailand border camp for almost 4 years before we were moved to the US. We stayed in many camps in Thailand before we reached the US. The camp is similar to the photographs included below. We could have gone to France but we wanted to go to the USA.

CHAPTER 2

*Give me four years to teach the children, and the seed
I have sewn will never be uprooted.*
—Vladimir Lenin, circa 1918

CAMBODIA: THE NEXT GENERATION
Mony Toch interview, July 15, 2021

*Background: Vanchhat Toch (chapter 1) is the father of the following
subject, Mony Toch. I will explore the generational impact the Khmer
Rouge has had on families. I have known Olivia Roeun (now Toch) and
Mony Toch, Vanchhat's son, for over sixteen years. They operate a small
business in my area. These are hardworking Americans whom I have
known to work 364 days a year for all those sixteen years. They often put
in twelve-to-sixteen-hour days to provide a better life for their family,
just as his dad did escaping Cambodia for his family years earlier. I recall
when they decided to extend their one day off on Jan 1 to three days so
they could get some rest and share time with their children. I have always
been taken by their work ethic compared to many Americans born here.
That work ethic very much reminded me of my mother. I shared that
information in letters with family and friends over the years about the
Tochs. Mony was the young child taken from his family at five years of
age to work in Communist Chinese labor camps. On their escape to the
Thai refugee camps, Mony was barefoot. He was given some slippers at
the camp but mostly remained barefoot until they left the camp, when
he was given plastic shoes made in China! They stayed in the refugee*

camps for almost four years. Olivia is younger, and her story is different. Yet her mom experienced many similar atrocities and fears. These are their stories.

Mony, tell me about your life in Cambodia, your escape with your dad, and coming to America.
I was born in Cambodia in 1970. When I was 5 years, I was taken from my parents along with my brothers and sisters to work in rice paddies to provide money for the Communists. I stayed in a camp located near the working fields and did not see my parents. We ate wet rice every day with some long green leafy vegetable that grew in the rice paddies. We drank dirty water.

My Dad was in the Cambodian military and he knew what was happening. His brother had already been disappeared. We kids didn't know exactly what was going on but we knew things had changed and it felt very wrong. My dad split the family up as people were being kidnapped, raped and killed. All families did this so if someone was captured at least part of the family would hopefully survive.

We left the camp and walked through the jungle all night. We started first thing in the morning when it was still dark. We had to move in and off trail when we thought someone is coming. We would walk in the tracks of others before us to avoid the mine fields that had been placed by the Cambodian and the Vietnamese Communists. I had no shoes. I walked all the way there barefoot. It was dry season so rains were not the problem, dried broken grass, bamboo and stones were. Your feet get tough.

Mony Toch, Cambodian refugee transfer in Thailand.

I asked Mony if they carried any supplies: a backpack, jacket for rain, or anything.

No, we carried only what we had on our backs. I had on a T-shirt and cut off pants. We had no jackets and no such thing as rain gear for us. We carried a rice pot for cooking rice and a small rolled up rattan mat for sleeping. I had no shoes. I was given slippers at the Thai camp but they wore out fast, then I was back to bare foot. Walking on dried bamboo is very sharp like glass and cuts your feet up, but they toughen up.

It was summer season when we left. It was very hot. There was no water and I remember being very thirsty. We had to travel at dawn and dusk not only because of the Communists trying to catch us but because of the heat.

The UN had dug some wells and these were used to get water. When we got to the border camps along Cambodia/Thai border we saw many others. There was UN, Cambodian and Thai troops guarding the border and the camps. The Red Cross and UN brought in rice and dried fish from Thailand so we got some protein. The World Health Organization (WHO) was there also. I remember that big 'WHO' logo. USAID was there also but many of us assumed all were Americans. We didn't know other European nations were there as well. All were white so we didn't know and assumed they were Americans. Many photographers were there who were mainly European, again we did not know who was helping us. All looked the same.

I was given those slippers I told you about. We were given some clothes from Thailand. I was barefoot the entire time I was at the refugee camp. When leaving after 3 years and 8 months, I was given a pair of black plastic shoes from China. When you showed me those pictures from Tuel Slung prison, I had chills and the hair on my arms and up my neck stood up. I remember seeing those pictures and hearing about the museum. The Cambodia government wanted to shut it down but the people wouldn't let them.

From the refugee camp at the border, we were transported to Chong Khao Phlu and then to Chanthaburi and stayed there for another 4-5 months. At these locations the Thai and other countries had built temporary houses for the refugees. Wells were dug by UN and often water trucks came in the pumped water to containers stored on the roofs. I remember the WHO logo on the water trucks also. There was a school where the kids could play games. From Chon Buri we went to Bangkok and then were flown to the San Francisco in US. From San Francisco we were flown to LA *(Los Angeles)* where our sponsor was located in San Dimas. Our sponsor was my sister's in-laws who had immigrated to the US prior to the war in 1972 or 73. My brother-in-law had come on a visa to train with the US Marines, Ur Ram. He was from a relatively rich family and could afford to be sent to US to be military trained to go back to Cambodia and train their troops. He never went back to Cambodia and worked for NASA for many years.

I asked Mony how he met his wife.

Our mothers knew of each other and met in Pomona, California. They set us up on a blind data. It was not an arranged marriage. We had moved from San Dimas due to high cost of living there to Pomona which was less expensive to live.

When I first arrived in US I did all sorts of odd jobs, from Nordstrom packaging department in Ontario to a medical assistant in Rosemead. I also worked security for a while. I was in Fresno for 8 years and got into the

baking business with my uncle in 1990 to 1991. It is good to develop a business in the US. Not true in Cambodia.

I met my friend Emmeraud 'Simon' Sok at one of the refugee camps at the Thai border. We played as kids do. Simon had been through a lot and he was the type of kid who could stand up for himself. His wife Pavi, though from Cambodia, they met in the States. Simon found Pavi on the streets living a starvation life in Los Angeles.

Years later Mony and Simon met again in the US. Mony and his wife Oliva ended up purchasing Simon's bakery.

CHAPTER 3

Socialism is a philosophy of failure, the creed of ignorance, and the gospel of envy, its inherent virtue is equal sharing of misery."
—**Winston Churchill**

CAMBODIAN/THAI BORDER
Interview with Olivia Roeun, July 2021

I was born at the border of Thailand and Cambodia. My Mom was Yeng Nhep. My Mom would not use my dad's name Roeun back then as he had been executed and she was afraid what would happen to her. My Mom told me my dad was taken, blindfolded and executed. She was always in fear for her family so she kept no pictures or family records that could identify her with her husband. I was only 3 months old when my dad was killed.

Do you know who killed him?

The Khmer Rouge killed my dad. They were killing everybody. My Mom did not get to see him after he was taken away. They were separated and my mom went to Thai border as did many. After my dad was killed, two of my sisters died also primarily from illness and starvation. My oldest sister got married through an arranged marriage by the Pol Pot regime. That is common practice even today. These regimes decide who you will marry and how many children you can have. It is all about control.

We were just there. I do not recall a lot. Just what my mom told me. I was born in the camp. Don't know where or which camp. My brother is older by 13 years and we were all separated by age in the camps, not by families. You would be separated even in the camps from your own family. Everyone ran to the borders just trying to stay alive. The Vietnamese were also fighting the Khmer Rouge.

My second sister, brother and mom are in separate camps from each other. My mom knows my oldest sisters are already dead. Another older sister is already married off by the Khmer Rouge. They do this all the time for control. Who you will marry, who you can have a baby with?

Mony's aunt was also married off by the Khmer Rouge.

It sickens me to think about. All the control, that is what they want. If you found a potato in the forest and you ate it and were caught, you would be killed for not sharing it.

I am amazed that people in the US do not realize how blessed they are. People who live in third world countries would trade places with you Americans in a heartbeat. I am forever grateful and feel very blessed to be an American citizen. America is not perfect but America is the best country in the world. Let's keep America from socialism and communism. My family left Cambodia for this very reason. Please don't bring socialism and communism to America. Those of you who want to tear down America have not had experiences like mine or my family and you pass judgment and tell others how they should live and what type of world they should want to live in. They sound like the people we escaped from.

CHAPTER 4

Optimism is the faith that leads to achievement. Nothing can be done without hope and confidence.
—Helen Keller

OAXACA, MEXICO
Interview with Tony Galicia on Feb 15, 2021.

Tony was born in a small town near the Guatemalan border with Mexico called Oaxaca. He came to the United States about thirteen years ago.

Why did you want to come to the US?
We were very poor. There was no food, no money, no work. Every day was hard just finding something to eat. I did not have a family. I was on my own. I did not know this until I was about 8 years old. I was staying with a family but I did not know they were not my *(biological)* family. It was not a good life.

When did you realize the family you were living with was not your real family?
About 7 or 8 years old I sensed something was wrong, that things were different. I was always hungry while others in *'my'* family ate. I found out I was adopted at about 1 year old.

There is no formal process.
They said my parents went north for work. There were jobs in the fields, just like here *(in US)* in Mexicali and Sinaloa. I stayed with the older son but didn't feel I was wanted. I felt I had to leave. I was always hungry, always thirsty. I told my older brother but he didn't get it. He, nor this family gave me any love. I was told to go play but I would say I am hungry. We don't care. I ran away when I was about 8.

How did you know you had to leave and how did you get to the north?
I just knew I was hungry and felt there was no love. There was no food, nothing to drink. I had to leave and maybe find my parents in the north where there is work. In Mexico the large trucks that transported fruits, and vegetables and other products are all open in the back, not closed like here in US. I hung out at truck stops and when one stopped, I would jump in the back and hide. I did not know how far way the north was!

Food was sold in carts and open stalls along road ways. This is how I sometimes got food.

Did you pack clothing or supplies to help you run away?
I had old cracked shoes and very dirty clothes. I never had new clothes.)
There were no back packs. I ran away with what I was wearing and was in the trucks for 4 plus days with no change of clothes. I stayed on the first truck for about 2 hours.

Tony had no watch, so he is estimating times and going by what he heard when he overheard the drivers talk.
I got to a little city and jumped out. I asked where I was and was told "Little City." I told drivers and people traveling that I wanted to go to Tijuana and was told over and over that that is very far away. I was 7 or 8 and had no idea. I was sleeping on the ground for weeks at a time. I kept asking people if they were going to Tijuana and they said it was very far. I jumped into another truck that I had heard the driver say he was heading towards Tijuana. I was not sure what he was delivering. I think it was fruit.

I waited for this driver, hiding, for almost 5 hours. I kept listening to the drivers trying to figure out which one was headed closest to Tijuana. After several hours in this truck, I jumped another one still heading north, **hop scotching my way north**. Maybe I could find my parents working to the north. I was very young. I did not know.

So, what happened when you got to Tijuana?

Tijuana was very bad life for me. I lived in Tijuana from about 8 to 16 years old. I lived under a bridge with others kids like me. They found me and showed me where to hang out. They were all about 8, 9 and 10 years old. Lots of boys living under the bridge. Some were experienced and knew how to find food. I would follow the experienced kids out early. Found food in trash, and some people gave us food. Outdoor food stalls were everywhere in Tijuana. We would ask if we could do some type of work or help to get one taco. Some people had good hearts and would give us a taco and others would say 'get away'. One taco was a big deal! We had only dirty clothes, no shoes and smelled bad. This is why I love America. There were many American tourists in Tijuana and they were the kindest and would walk around asking" you want to eat"? They were very generous. None of us spoke any English yet we could understand the Americans would help us. Mainly buying tacos, but 3-4 tacos made us very happy as most of us would not get anything to eat later on. We did not know when we would eat again. Next day, nothing. Sometimes two to three days would go by with no food.

I went to sleep often with no food, no drink. When I was 10 years old, I got very sick. I don't know what it was, maybe flu but I could not get warm. I was so sick I could not get up to get food in the morning. The other kids would keep me warm and go get food. I kept asking where is my mom and dad? Where are you?

Tony never found his parents.

It was the same life every day. When I was 11 after about 3 years living under the bridge, maybe I was 12 a lady came by. She looked rich. She was Spanish and asked me my name and where I was from. Are you hungry? She bought me food from the outside vendors. I asked her if she would buy food for my friends, about 7-10 kids. They would split off and go in different directions every morning and come back to the bridge at night. It was many kids and maybe more than that. She bought them all tacos. I showed her where we were all sleeping. Where is your mom, she asked? I am looking for her.

'Do you want to go with me'? I said no because I didn't feel I could leave my friends. She came back again after a couple weeks. She asked again do you want to come home with me where you can live and eat and have a shower and go to school? I said no.

She asked him what he really wanted and he said a bicycle. She said 'I will give you good life and nice clothes. Tony felt too bad to leave his friends. Finally, he agreed to go live with her under one condition. That condition was that he could come back every day with food for his friends.

I came every day with food for my friends. She lived close by. Her name was Angelica and she was a teacher. After a few months she said she could no longer keep going every day to bring food to my friends. She had to work. She would continue every week or two but not every day. She picked me! I don't know why. There were many kids but she picked me. Made my life better. I stayed with her until about 16 years old. She gave me a very good life. She was single and maybe 30- 32 years old when I knew her.

Just went to school until I was about 16. My relationship with her changed when I was about 14 years old. She wanted a romantic relationship. In Mexico it as OK. Here you would go to jail. She molested me. Her mind was different than before. She bought me everything. I stayed until I was 16 and just left, working small jobs and going to different places looking for work, a place to stay and food.

My thinking was to come to the US. I had learned from many in Tijuana how to get into the US. I found a sponsor. I saw everything in Tijuana. Drugs, shooting up, asked to sell drugs, human trafficking, mules, people killed because they didn't pay. Saw most of this especially at night. It was bad.

I worked for a company in San Diego and would travel back and forth across the border. I tried to find out who my parents were. To get a Green Card or residence in US you have to know where you are from and who is your family. I will never know that. Immigration came while I was working construction in San Diego and asked for papers. I had to go back to Mexico.

Tell me why you think the US is such a great place.
US is the best place. There are lots of opportunities if you are willing to look and work hard. Opportunities to go to school and if you want, to work. I have never understood graffiti. With so many opportunities to make a good life, they just must not want it. I don't know why these people *(born here)* do not want to use these opportunities they are born with. They are born here and can make money, go to school and they want to live on the street.

In Carpinteria I was working construction for a very nice family. All my customers are really nice people and treat me with respect. They had just constructed a new wall around their place and within a month it was totally covered with graffiti. I feel so bad for them. I don't know why people do this.

If I were a citizen, I would only want good things. Very big opportunity to get here and make a good life. I cannot make this opportunity as I don't know where I am from *(born)* or who my parents are.

In Tijuana I met an older lady, about 50 years old. She treated me like a son. The first time I ever felt love like a son. I was looking for a job after I left Angelica. I met Regina and she said I could stay at her home. She said she was poor and it was a poor home but I would have food. I told her I don't have any money but I work jobs. I lived in her poor home for about 6-7 months buying food that she would prepare for us. The home flooded and I left to find a better life. I told her I would come back for her. I promise I will come back for you Regina.

I brought her to Oxnard, California. She was like a mom to me. I felt loved. She was like my mom or what I wished my mom was. She was the only mom I really know. We were very happy in my apartment in Oxnard for 7 years. She had family still in Tijuana. Three daughters but she felt I was her only son. She got sick, went to St. John's hospital. She remained in touch with her daughters. She died several years ago (in 2017). She ended up back in Tijuana.

I did not get whether Regina died at St John's or was sent back to immediate family earlier. I could tell Tony greatly misses Regina and feels intense loneliness when he comes home from work every night. Tony is a very hard-working man. He tells me of all the opportunity here if you are legal. He tells me it is always over his head that he may have to go back, so he remains connected to Mexico.

CHAPTER 5

Facts don't care about your feelings.
—Ben Shapiro

There is no such thing as "your truth."
There is truth and your opinion.
—Ben Shapiro

Without a clear moral vision, we devolve into moral relativism, and
from there into oblivion.
—Ben Shapiro

Experience outweighs your opinion.
—Candace Owen and John Rich

SANTIAGO, CHILE
Interview with Angela Bond, conducted Feb 21, 2021

Background: Salvador Allende was the founder of Chile's Socialist Party
in 1933. He contested a presidential election in 1952. Allende gained
power in the 1970s. Mining companies owned by the USA were nation-
alized without compensation. Large agricultural estates were expropri-
ated to be transformed into peasant communes. Wages were raised and
prices frozen. Money was printed, and inflation rose. Strikes prolifer-
ated. Local banking suffered. There was a hostile response from the US,
and economic aid ended. The CIA had links to senior officers within
the Chilean army. To keep the army on his side, Allende appointed
generals to his cabinet. One was Augusto Pinochet, whom Allende made

commander in chief of the army in 1973. Pinochet led a violent coup eighteen days later, on Sept 11, 1973, and Allende was murdered—or some say committed suicide—in the presidential palace.

Angela started with her recollections from when she was seven to nine years old.

I was born in Santiago, Chile June 12, 1964 when Salvador Allende held leadership of Chile. When Pinochet took control of my life and that of my family, our lives were much better. Some call him a dictator; I call him my hero. He saved us.

When I was 7-9 years old, we were starving. We would get up every morning early and my mom and dad would take us to different places to try to get food. We would stand for hours and wait in lines all day long to get even a piece of bread and maybe some oil. We would be on line at 8 am and not return home until 10 pm. My brother would wait on one line and my mom and me would go to another. My dad, if not working, would attempt another location. We were in hopes that one of us would be lucky enough to get some bread.

During Allende's time, all of the people who were not in Allende's network were starving. There was constant violence. Criminals walked the streets and there was no protection for the people. Criminals would open car doors and pull you out of your car and rob you of whatever you had. I see parallels in this country with the far left and what is happening in our cities. The lawlessness and no consequences for people who injure others or destroy their businesses is out of a horror novel.

My dad who worked near the palace often could not get home. There were tires burning every night. The violence in the US during the summer especially in Seattle and Portland *(summer of 2020)* reminded us of these times. It was frightening to see this, especially here.

The level of violence was extreme *(in Santiago, Chile)*. We were told to stay home. Could not go to school. My Dad still had to go to work.

Something I will always remember; I was out with my mom. We witnessed an Allende motor cade going by and a woman on a bus stuck her tongue out at the motorcade. The motor cade with Allende's body guards surrounded the bus and we saw her dragged off of the bus. Allende's guard exited one of the vehicles and grabbed the woman by the neck choking her. We were watching all this! I was 8 years old. It was horrifying and remember I was 8 years old. He joked her and said 'I am going to kill you if you do not apologize immediately, I will kill you'. We all could hear this. I will never forget. You don't forget things like this happening especially when you are only 8 years old. It was very scary.

As I said violence was daily, especially at night. Women could not walk around without being molested or robbed. There were many rapes. Tires burned constantly and the air smelled and it burned your lungs. We had no food available to us. Shelves in stores were empty. I remember standing in line every day trying to get some food. Maybe one of us would come home with some bread and some tea. That is all there was. I was scared to go anywhere. We all were.

There was a card issued by Allende's group. It was known as a JAT. I do not recall what the letters stand for but if you promised this group to go along with Allende's party in power, you would be issued this card to get food and supplies. Agreement with the party in power determined whether you go food or not.

This is a parallel Angela relates to what she is seeing in US today.
You have to go along or be silenced. Allende's supporters would go house to house and if you agreed with their policies', you could get a card issued. My

mother slammed the door in their face. You have to realize this is the only way you could get something to eat. If you refused like my mother did, you were put on a list. I can tell you all about Blacklists! I see this happening in the US and I can't believe it.

It was impossible to go anywhere. The poverty was so extensive.

The day before September 11, 1973 the owner of a beautiful house near us was owned by an Air Force Officer who knew my dad. He came to our house. My dad was at work. He was a really nice guy. He said to my mom to tell her husband "Do not go to work tomorrow. Keep your children home. That is all I can tell you".

My dad just decided I can't stay home from work so he went anyway. His work was near the Palace.

On September 11 we heard radio news and planes overhead. We did not go to school that day. It was surreal, like out of a movie, with the plans overhead and bombs dropping.

It was surreal to see downtown Santiago being bombed. But we were so happy to see Pinochet take over. He was our salvation. The town of Santiago was closed for 3 days as there were dead people laying in the streets.

My dad could not get home that night as he was driving, he had to walk around all the unrest to get home to his family. He walked for miles. We stayed home for several weeks. It was hard. You could hear machine guns every night. When Pinochet's Army located Allende's caches' they found huge munitions caches and tons of food and supplies. Their people had everything you could have wanted and no shortage of food. In these caches and storage areas, numerous "blacklists" of people were discovered: list of people targeted to be killed. Allende's supporters had everything, while we were starving.

I asked about any gun confiscation. Or do you recall religious practices being curtailed or attending church being banned in Chile?
I do not recall that except no one went anywhere during the violence of Allende's reign.

My dad was retired from the Air Force. We had no weapons and I do not know about any confiscation of weapons just that we did not have any.

My dad continued to work in communications at a government building near the palace. He died at 82 years old.

I left Chile when I was 24 years old. I never intended to leave. I lived under Pinochet's rule from 9-24 years of age. He opened investments and we had the best economy in South America with Pinochet. He implemented a great plan for retirement and medical coverage. Everything changed for us. I invested in these plans in Chile and did very well. The economy boomed.

I was studying law and in Chile and you can practice law after three years doing civil suits. I was successful and doing very well with a good job and going to school. Chile is a beautiful country with beaches and mountains and deserts. I love Chile.

Then I was introduced to an American via a relative. He loved Chile and came to visit often. We fell in love and married. We lived in Chile for a while but then he wanted to return to the US. He convinced me that I would have even more opportunities in the US and could continue my education in law. My parents did not want me to go but they felt I would be better off with him. I really didn't want to go at first but I did. Very bad mistake as he became very abusive.

We were managers of a building at this time and I was working for a physical therapist. This is when he broke my jaw and nose. He beat me. I told my husband to leave. I asked the building owner if I could stay and he said yes while I recovered.

What did you tell your parents?
I did not tell my parents until years later. I was too embarrassed to tell them.

Did he beat you while you were in Chile?
No, only after we returned to the States.

My viewpoint when I see what is going on in the US right now I relate back to what I have been through. People here are very spoiled and claim they are entitled. The black community plays the same card, that they are owed something. They did not go through what I have been through. I see it after 21 years.

I had a few small jobs at first. I worked at the Dollar Tree Store, then Bank of America and El Pollo Loco. I trained to become a phlebotomist and worked in a Physical Therapy Department where I met my current husband. I am blessed with a wonderful child. I found this company on my own and now am in a supervisory position and doing well again. I have 12 wonderful people working for me. I observe their attitudes. Some of them, even with good jobs always complain. I tell them "You don't appreciate what you have".

I studied law in Chile. After 3 years one can handle cases. I wasn't planning on coming to the US. I had a great future in Chile. I was seen as a success. I could help my mom and dad. Met cousins' friend as I told you and we married.

I went through a lot here too, with my husband beating me and all the abuse. More than that though, I enjoy the freedom America offers. When I saw the violence here this summer, I could not believe it. It took me back to those days in Chile under Allende with fires in the streets every night. I just couldn't believe it was happening here. The destruction parallels what I experienced growing up In Santiago, Chile.

I like Trump. I call him my favorite jerk. I think he did good things for this country. There is no integrity in the new government now. When you see people destroying property while wearing $200 Nike's and telling us they are owed. I remember having a single pair of shoes and in the rainy season I remember my feet being wet all day. There was no change of shoes. I am very appreciative of what I have here in the US. I came as a resident and after 3 years I got a green card, then citizenship. I am proud to be here.

I get angry with all these ungrateful American's who are lucky enough to be born here. You are ungrateful and there is a lot of ignorance about your history. I cannot stand the complaining about entitlements and wanting reparations when they have achieved nothing. You are so fortunate and you don't get it!

Pinochet is considered a dictator by many but for me and my family he saved our lives. Even one of my nieces denied my experiences in Chile, saying that is not what she learned in school. Now there are many parties in Chile and open elections.

CHAPTER 6

How do you tell a Communist? It's someone who reads Marx and Lenin. And how do you tell an anti-Communist? It's someone who understands Marx and Lenin.
—Ronald Reagan

AFTER THE KHMER ROUGE CAMBODIA (YEARS LATER)

Interview with Leroy Carson, DDS, conducted March 2021

Background: Although Dr. Carson is not an immigrant, he experienced the lives and atrocities many Cambodians were subjected to, especially those with a higher education or professional career. He experienced first-hand stories during his professional work as an adviser in Cambodia's dental schools and as a practicing dentist working throughout Cambodia and with NGOs within the Cambodian prison system.

As an addendum to this interview and Installment 1, and keeping this a living document, Mr. Vanchhat (Chapter 1) got in touch with me through his family to tell me he had forgotten to relay how the Khmer Rouge would tell the public to gather up all their possessions such as jewelry and gold and the like and keep it in one place for safekeeping. The same had been done with guns. While the people were out working the fields, Vanchhat said, he saw the Khmer Rouge party go door to door and confiscate any wealth, be it gold or jewelry. He knew, being military and seeing what had happened with the gun confiscation, what was going to happen. His family hid what they could.

This interview is conducted with Leroy Carson DDS, a medical professional who visited Cambodia years after the Khmer Rouge rule. At first a tourist, he became enamored of Asia. Then, with his advanced practices in dentistry, he found he could help train Cambodian dental schools in the more advance practices such as IV (intravenous) sedation. During his long-term work with Cambodia's top dentists and dental schools, he experienced many amazing stories, especially while volunteering to work in the prisons. He was taken by how much the Khmer Rouge regime and the communist mentality still pervaded much of Cambodia.

I met Dr. Leroy Carson though my own dentist, Dr. Derek Carson, his son. I mentioned to Dr. Derek Carson the project I was working on to interview immigrants and share their stories, the horrors and impacts suffered by peoples who escaped communist and/or socialist countries. I told him I don't think many Americans were aware of what many of our legal immigrants had experienced and why they wanted to come to the US. This is my purpose. These real stories seem to be often jaded by today's politics and often manipulated by the press with their own agenda and a news media cycle that competes with a gerbil on an exercise wheel!

I had just conducted a rather emotional interview the night before with Vanchhat Toch from Cambodia (Chapter 1). He had shared some the horrors of fighting the communists in Cambodia, the camps, the tortures in the prisons, the children being bayoneted or swung overhead like a toy until their head hit a tree, and the relatives who had been disappeared. While under the influence of nitrous oxide, I shared some of that interview with my dentist. This is all while I was reciting the Pledge of Allegiance. I think that was my subconscious patriotism being shared while under the influence—that these things could not have happened here. Derek was puzzled and told me, "My father can tell you all about Cambodia and what happened there. He has been there many times and shared many of his stories with me." I asked if I could possibly interview his dad, Leroy, and he said he would ask. Dr. Leroy

Carson agreed and called me, and this is his story. Several names have been changed to protect any professionals still remaining in Cambodia.

Dr. Carson immediately began his story without my asking questions. It was 1970 and I was a dental school graduate. Though I loved dentistry I really loved to travel and wanted to help others in the world. I had studied the history of China, Asia and Japan and fell in love with that part of the world. I volunteered to go into the Air Force as a practicing dentist and so I could travel. I traveled to Thailand first as part of the military, then onto Vietnam, the Philippines and then Taipan. My wife was pregnant at this time.

After my military service and to continue my service to help in Asia, I got in contact with a Dental Facility in Cambodia and invested a great deal into the A&Z Royal Bank which had ties to banks in Australia and New Zealand. I felt this was an opportunity to provide dental assistance to areas in great need.

I gave two weeks' notice to my kids and informed my current established dental practice that I was going to Cambodia. I gave my family everything I had. I gave my son, also a dentist, half of my dentistry practice.

I had made contact with a Cambodian named Samut. Samut was his first name. The agreement was that I could practice dentistry with him and be able to teach. Cambodia did not have experienced dentists especially in anesthesiology and other more advanced dentistry techniques. I could bring my Intravenous (IV) sedation license, something they were really interested in learning about.

While over there *(in Thailand)* I would fly to Hong Kong and transfer to Dragon Air. This was 2008. I didn't know if Samut was meeting me at the airport or not. Communication was difficult. It was hot and very humid. I stayed in Korat (Nakhon Ratchasima) Thailand, the palace where my wife Beverly and I would go frequently.

Asia was ingrained into my system. I wanted to stay in this part of the world. I wanted to do more than just make money. My wife Beverly felt the same way and wanted to go with me. She was told she could teach English, which *(Beverly told me she never got to do).*

I loved the history of the Thai and Thailand as well. The Thai had been squeezed out of South China. They came about the time of Christ. They had an aggressive culture, were good fighters and dominated many kingdoms. This is a major reason Thailand has never been invaded by another country.

(Author's note: While I lived in Thailand (1984–86), I asked the Thai about never being invaded or taken over by any country. They were very proud of this fact. The Thai, with their typical sense of humor, would say to me, the Vietnamese communists would get lost in traffic!)

Photo (above) *The Killing Fields*, taken from *Tuol Sleng Genocide Museum.* (www.websitesrcg.com) Photo of the 'Killing Fields' in Cambodia. Taken from Tuol Slung Prsion archives)

In Cambodia, I helped set up all the dental school meetings to create the teaching facility and did most of the teaching on anesthesiology. We all did lectures on other parts of dentistry as well.

During the Khmer Rouge reign, the party in power wanted to destroy all intellectuals. The results of this "cleansing' were evident while I was there and Samut, and others, would share their stories which were rather frightening. Samut was a Chinese born Cambodian. He was not favored by the Khmer Rouge and he and his family experienced the Khmer Rouge Regime.

He was almost put to death. He was a professional and most often anyone in a professional career or considered an intellectual, even wearing glasses, was justification to be put to death.

However, Samut was put to work by Khmer Rouge to guard and maintain cattle. He is a professional dentist, not a cattle man. The cattle he was in charge of destroyed crops and he was charged of this as a crime. He came very close to being put to death. When the Khmer Rouge was going to sentence someone to death or punish them, the observers would all clap their hands. They would clap! The louder they clapped the more chance your sentence was death. If the Chinese Communists knew he was a dentist he knew he was dead.

Samut's father escaped and survived the Khmer Rouge also by hiding in the Mekong Delta. He was sentenced to death primarily because he was Chinese/Cambodian and not communist.

Many in Cambodia prior to the Khmer Rouge ate French food. The French had a major influence in this part of the world. When the Khmer Rouge came to power, they killed all the French chefs, lawyers, doctors, teachers and anyone who wore glasses were put to death. The wearing of glasses, as mentioned in Vanchhat's story (Chapter 1), designated that one was educated and immediate grounds for execution.

Vietnam went to war against the Communist Vietnamese. During the Vietnam War, the Khmer Rouge was liquidating anyone who had western contacts. They were so cruel. They would take little children by the legs and twirl them around until their heads struck something, a building, a tree anything to kill them. Photos of this practice exist in the Tuol Sleng Prison, in Cambodia to this day. The Vietnamese could not stand this level of cruelty either. Nor could the Communists Vietnamese stand the Khmer Rouge's cruelty. Khmer Rouge stands for Khmer (Cambodia) Rouge (Red). I admit because of this I was upset when Trump chose the color red for his MAGA hats. It is just that some these things stay with you. Kaleem, another dentist, invited me to go to many dentistry trainings events and lectures throughout Asia. I would get letters of appreciation since I would lecture on a yearly basis. I became well known. I did lectures on implants, aspirations, and taking skin cells from hips to use in grafts so you could avoid people having to wear dentures. This was all beyond 'state of the art' for the Cambodians.

I often went alone to Cambodia, without Beverly, from 2008 to 2011. By this time, there was a lot of stealing. They steal from you all the time. At first it seemed not a big deal as only minor things were stolen. But then it got to be frightening. Their approach was to only steal half of what you had thinking it was OK that they left you with half. It was their unwritten law that it was OK. *(I experienced this same practice in Thailand)*.

I saw a huge change in behaviors and attitudes towards foreigners from 2008-2011. In Cambodia they use a method of transportation called Tut Tuts *(similar to Tuk Tuks in Thailand)*. It was more a carriage than Thai Tuk Tuks and they could spin on a dime.

Against this oak, Khmer Rouge soldiers bashed the
skulls and bodies of infants and children.

Australians, Malaysians and many from Singapore travel to Cambodia so English is a required language. Americans do not go as often to Cambodia. To Cambodians, Australians are the equivalent of Americans.

***Author's note: In Thailand we are known as Forangs)*.**

I would see cops standing on a corner. None wore helmets. Often you would see a family of five riding on a small motorcycle driving by grassy meridians where many were practicing Thai Chi. Traffic moved both ways on both sides and was very scary and confusing.

People were friendly while I first was going to Cambodia on a regular basis, however the longer I stayed, as communism spread throughout the country, it was feeling less and less safe. **(*Similar observations were made by Rolando Chinea in Cuba in Chapter 8 and Vanchhat Toch in Cambodia in Chapter 1 years earlier as communism began its reach in those countries*).**

The European Union sent people to help Cambodia. German dentists came there and I was invited by Samut to join them. The Dean of the International Dental School was helpful to me. He actually helped get me out of trouble. Kalam the director who helped me, was gay and that is not accepted in Cambodia. I accompanied him to the Dental Angel Project. The Project consisted of a bunch of NGOs (Non-Governmental Organizations) working in the Cambodian Prison System. They would enlist people from all the dental schools to help out in shifts. The prisons made up of cinder block buildings surrounded with chain link fencing and barbed wire. There were steel steps you had to step over and the prisoners were all in chains so that made it impossible to escape.

Early in my time there in Cambodia, I had no dental drills to practice dentistry. We were provided only the bare bones in materials. I would attempt to lean the chairs back so I could work on a patient. The Cambodians refused any sit-down dentistry. All had to be done while standing up. They just all stood up. It was difficult to practice and have any leverage which one needs in dentistry.

The Cambodians would freak out if you turned them upside down or tilted them back even slightly as we practice in the states. I used elevators and forceps. We would use a spoon to scrap out decay and cement for a temporary restoration. As I said I did not have access to more current tools of the trade especially while practicing in the prisons. In the prisons, you were forbidden to take photographs. I snuck in a camera once. When I went to the bathroom, there was a swarm of mosquitos and while dealing with them, I dropped my camera into the toilet. Though I tried to hold onto it, it slipped out of my pocket. The Camp director, Kaleem, got the camera back for me. Good thing this it was an Asian toilet and not a western flush style!

I visited and practiced in many prisons. The prisoners would tell me all these stories of how they got there. One guy was a devoted Christian. He was a missionary and he was imprisoned for that! He was in an awful room. They paid him a meager salary as a dentist, and fed him even less. He shared a lot with me. I volunteered to help him in training. A large portion of the prisoners were European or from Singapore and ran into the Cambodian system, through often through no fault of their own. One guy didn't have his seat belt on and was imprisoned for it. If you didn't pay a bribe or know what was happening, as many westerners did not, you often went to prisons until you could pay up. If they considered you wealthy, that bribe could be very high! One time I didn't have my seat belt on and that is exactly what the cops were looking for that day. My friend gave the cop $10 US. dollars which is a lot of korona in Cambodia. Cop just pocketed it and I didn't go to prison.

If you have connections you can afford to stay in Cambodia at a local hotel rather inexpensively. It is very expensive otherwise. For example, with connections you can stay at the best Cambodian hotel for $70 a night. If you aren't connected it would cost you $200 a night. They have their own version of the 'Mafia'. This is common knowledge for those who traveled here. Corporation was the big term used at this time. You were part of 'the corporation! The corruption (*like syndicate*) became more and more rampant.

One night someone set off a bomb at a hotel where I was staying. It was at a Vietnamese hotel. Every hotel in Cambodia has girls. Prostitution is big business. Cambodia built factories so the girls would have a place to work and stay during the day, thus the sweat shop. The girls had the choice to either work in the rice paddies or in the factories or as prostitutes at the hotels and restaurants and bars. The rural areas flood badly so working in the rice paddies can be very unhealthy.

Beverly and I went everywhere in Asia. We finally stopped going to Cambodia in about 2011 There was a very severe influenza virus outbreak

KATHLEEN S. ROOS PH.D.

at the time. It was bad. I was invited back to lecture. But my wife got very sick and I told them I could not come.

When I did return, I started feeling this aura of 'Mafia' again, as though I was being watched similar to all the people in the prisons. There were doctors, lawyers, pharmacists all in the prisons and they were extorted for money. They would remain in prison for the rest of their lives if they could not find someone to pay. Even when some did pay, they did not get out.

I had brought drugs legally into Cambodia to support my dentistry practice and teaching. I did this for many years with no problem. I had to disclose all this and I always did. I gave this information to Samut. The medication I brought in included oral sedation, IV (intravenous) sedation, and each time I had to go through customs. Each time I disassembled all my dental carts to travel. The Chinese got a hold of these dissembled carts and thought they must have thought they were bomb making equipment. I became a marked person after that. I could just feel the change.

At one time I went to the airport to retrieve my equipment. There was an international fight going on between Thailand and Cambodia. There was no one at the airport. I mean no one! I identified my suitcase, grabbed it, and flew the first Business Class flight I could find out of there. I used every mile I could to get out. I was that frightened.

The Cambodians wanted to split Beverly and me up on travel back; to take different flights. She would fly one day, me the next. I didn't want that to happen. I knew I was being targeted. Many Chinese said I was a drug dealer. Many had no knowledge of sedation so this was their perception. No education or sharing knowledge seemed to change their perspective.

There were only about 200 dentists for the entire country of Cambodia and about 2/3 either just did not use sedation or felt it was wrong to use. Samut stopped answering my phone calls. We had used Skype all the time, but all that stopped suddenly. That is when I knew for sure I was a target. I had invested $200K in their banks. My calls were monitored because this is a Communist Country. Using my cell phone one time I pick up a police officer. They were tracking my calls even when in the US.

The situation was not limited to the police. They aren't wearing helmets or shields. Now no one is talking. Cops take money as pay offs to not send you to jail or prison. Tut tuts are removed from transporting people so there is no way to get around. They don't want people to get around or communicate. The police want taxes back on the transportation so they can get their kickbacks. Very convoluted but all about corruption and bribery.

I stopped going there. The Opposition Party was outlawed. Total dictatorship now that China has bought out the Country. South Korea tried to help but they were bullied out by China also. You see much of this going on in the South China Seas as well as in Australia.

I got the Cambodian dentistry schools set up with their first digitalized system. You could take x-rays digitally. This was a huge benefit to them. My name was on the door. The Cambodian dental technique was called the Australian Injection (Goo Gals) hitting the nerve that goes directly into the brain. If you needed to have all your teeth removed, Cambodian practice took them out the side of your mouth. Common to have dry sockets by extracting all wisdom teeth in less than an hour. These were the barbaric practices I tried to educate them to change with proper techniques, medicines and equipment.

Did you hear about temples or churches being destroyed?
I do not know of the Khmer Rouge destroying temples but they made it unpleasant to attend while I was there.

Vanchhat Toch, in Chapter 1, stated churches and temples were destroyed during his time in the 1970s.

CHAPTER 7

The Liberal/Marxist Machine in our Country demands that Equity of Outcome be mandatory. Be that as it may, I have to admit…I cannot wait for these idealists to discover that ultimately, they too, would wind up being controlled by the very machine they built.
—H. G. Goerner

ALIGARH, INDIA
Interview with Uddin Tareen Zulfiqar on April 9 and July 4, 2021

Background: The following interview was conducted with Uddin Tareen Zulfiqar, of Aligarh, India. Zulfi, as we call him, is a local Ventura County businessman. This is the sixth installment in **Coming to America,** *and it's Zulfi's story. Zulfi was born, through no fault or choice of his own or his parents, into a class in India called "the untouchables." Though many may consider this an actual term of low class or just the poor, it is actual telling these people that they do not exist. For many Americans, this is almost impossible to conceive. Though the government of India is moving forward and eliminating these practices, the beliefs remain.*

Where are you from, Zulfi?
I was born in Aligarh India. I came from a very poor family. I was born in one of the most racist countries in the world. India gained its independence in 1947. Even so India still practices the caste system. People are divided into 4 castes, brahmin, Rajput, middle business caste and lower castes based on parts of the god Brahma's body. The untouchables don't come in any

class. They are Dravidians who were conquered by Aryans and turned into untouchables.

The Aryans came from north of Caspian Sea about 3,500 years ago or 1500 BC. these Aryan hordes came from north of Caspian Sea, Destroyed Davidians civilization, the first Indians who were the first migrants from Africa. Aryans conquered them and pushed to the southern parts of India. Dravidians could not fight back because they had no weapons to fight with. Most of them were killed. The rest were turned into untouchables. *Upper caste Hindus* do not want to accept this history. They claim that upper caste has been living in India from beginning of the time.

There was just too much discrimination in India for me to establish a business or get work. The whole system is dependent on religion one way or another. I was Muslim but I have renounced Islam.

I thought India had moved away from the caste system?

Yes, the government is working to eliminate the caste system, but it is too engrained into the people's psyche. There is lots of discrimination especially towards Christians and Muslims. This is often misunderstood by others. Christians are treated the worse. Even as we speak their villages are being burned throughout India. India is a hell hole for the poor, the weak and to women not of the upper caste.

What did you do for work in India?

I had nothing in India. there was no work for me because I was Muslim and in India, Muslims are worse than untouchables. There was no employment for minorities. Today unemployment in India is 70-90% for minorities depending on where you are.

I applied to over 400 companies in India for work. I have a degree in biology from Aligarh University. Aligarh is east of Delhi. I never heard back even one company. The reasons I believe are; 1) there are no jobs due to overpopulation and congestion. You have to establish your own work to be employed. 2) hate is so intense that Muslim youths are being mob-lynched every day. No one relies on police because they are corrupt. Woman are raped all over the country and no one cares and, in most cases, rapists don't get arrested or punished. This happens all the time. A famous woman named Phoolan Devi from poor family reported to police that she had been raped by upper-caste Hindus. The poor girl was then raped again in the police station by the police. She became famous outlaw and killed her rapists.

Minorities cannot fight back. They have no guns even to protect themselves from thieves, and home invaders. They have no political power either. Their poverty is their weakness. They whole society is brutal towards poor, women and minorities. Police are allowed to use 'third degree torture' on poor to extract confession or make them pay bribe to police. People pay local government officials to take have their problems solved, if they have the money. Paying government officials and police is also used as a tool to settle scores with opponent. The government and police are enemies of poor.

Is the military like the police or how are they different?
The military is neutral most of the time, but not all the time. Military is committing crimes against Kashmiris who wants to be autonomous, and India does not want this. That is why Indian government is using army to brutalize Kashmiris. On the other hand, Muslims are doing exact same to non-Muslims in Middle East and other Muslim countries. Muslims have been killing Christians and other minorities in Islamic states. Muslims are as brutal as the Hindus are in India. Both are especially brutal towards Christians.

Why did you want to come to the US?
I left India for fear of being killed. I felt I had no value and no human dignity. In India, people of my class have no security of job and no security of life. you just do not exist. This is hard for Americans to understand. On paper the government of India wants to change the discrimination but in real life it does not happen. It is extremely difficult to change thousands of years of hateful and discriminatory cultural and traditions.

How did you manage to come to the US?
Before partitioning of India after its independence from the British, some land was given to farmers. My family had this small portion of land which

I inherited from my father. I sold it to get a ticket to go to Saudi Arabia to find a job.

There, I saved money to get a VISA to visit the United States. In 1997, I married an American citizen and got green card.

United States is the best place. Now it is being turned into hell by democrats. They want to turn USA into third world hellhole by letting millions to flood in. In LA, your car and your property are not safe because criminals roam around and take everything from people and nothing is done about it. Homeless fill parking lots and streets. I can't believe this is happening here in USA.

I got robbed four times in my businesses here in US by the same people who are calling all others racist. Who is promoting this you ask? The democrats who are hungry for power and money.

China continues to persecute Muslims as India does. Pakistan is persecuting Hindus and Christians. Pakistanis call Christians "choora" which means filth. Did you know Native Americas have no rights in Mexico?

With 70–90 percent unemployment of minorities, how do the people survive?

They do menial jobs, they sell fruits and crops off carts, they have turned their homes into stalls to sell textiles, make socks, and sell produce. Whatever they can. It is still very bad.

Christians are the worse off. They are gathered like cattle behind fences to get protection from Hindus. The government has been taken over by extremist national party called RSS. They are wreaking havoc on minorities in India. The poor are being crushed. Thousands of Hindus are converting to Christianity to be treated as equal in the society, which is very frightening to Hindu clergy because Hindu masses are the source of income for Brahmins. The more people convert to Christianity the less money for Brahmins and temples. The temple money goes straight into the pockets of Brahmins. It all comes down to money and power. Christians are a threat to the Brahmins' income, influence, and power.

Many Americans don't realize that life outside of America is not easy. Americans are spoiled. What I see happening in America is that minorities committing crimes against the majority. Democrats using lawlessness created by minorities to their benefit. If a white man runs a red traffic light, he's called white supremacist. If a minority person in the US kills someone, he is considered a victim who is simply trying to feed his family and whites are accused of discriminating against him.

I find Congresswomen like AOC and Omar Ilhan extremely hateful of America and white people. Everything I have now, I owe to America. I am grateful to the entire country and specifically white people for creating such a wonderful country. I see democrats as vengeful and wanting to support illegal immigration to exploit them and exploit the system. The democrats know that all these illegals will vote for them. The illegals still vote for democratic candidates even if they know they don't have the right to vote. I support legal immigration. I carry the US Constitution in my pocket everywhere I go. People get angry with me when I defend the US.

Non-whites control the vote in California, New Mexico, and parts of Texas. The wealthy don't see it but the blue-collar working people do. The illegal gangs in Los Angeles now harass all communities.

In the US, I see whites becoming oppressed in this country. Everybody wants to come USA. You don't see anyone wanting to go to China, India, or Russia. And they could not get into Australia because it has a point system to get into their country. If you come to USA, then contribute to the economy. Do not become a burden on the system, always looking for welfare. I feel I contribute to America. Canada is setting a bad example by letting masses in without checking their qualifications or background.

I experienced great fear and anxiety throughout my life in India and in Saudi Arabia. I was always under the threat that I would be killed. It was that bad. I kissed the ground when I got onto the tarmac in Los Angeles in August of 1981. With what is happening now in the US, I feel the same way I did in Saudi Arabia and India. Two of my friends have been killed here in downtown Oxnard by Mexican gangs. One was working at a 711. He was killed in 2008. The other a business owner who was coming out of a bank was shot in 2008.

It saddens me to say but I feel America is turning into the hellhole like any third world country, thanks to democrat's policy of open borders and unrestricted immigration. I came here legally and am proud to become a US citizen. We learned the English language and adopted American values. You may remain connected to your past if we choose so. Nobody is against it.

I mentioned to Zulfi about Finland and Sweden and how many say their system of government is the answer.
Zulfi stated yes, Finland is a paradise for Finns and people of the European Union. The Finns pay up to 45% in taxes for that heaven. I know of a young Indian man in his early 20s who corresponded with a Swedish woman in her thirties. She said get to Sweden and she will marry him and then he will be a Swedish citizen. He bicycled his way from India through numerous countries stating he was just touring but his end goal was citizenship in Sweden.

You mentioned Finland and Sweden before and I said Finland was a paradise if you could live there. Not as easy as they say. Finland does not speak much English, most speak Finnish. Only Sweden is where many speak English as well as Swedish. Now things are changing in Europe and many, up to 98% are studying English. In India we have Computer Centers where people can go to use Internet. Many do not have computers or Internet in their homes.

Author's note: As of this writing (March 2022) two Finnish citizens; Paivi Rasanen and Bishop Juhana Pohjola are facing imprisonment on criminal charges for tweeting Bible verses questioning their church's sponsorship of an LGBT pride event in 2019.
I think this is one reason why America is so great. You have 50 states, and they all speak English. The method of communication and common language attributes much to America's greatness. Different ideas are shared with all 50 states work as on unit. No other Country could have produced the likes of Google, Facebook, Twitter, Instagram nor sharing of all the brain power from all these varying states. You don't have to export to or from Texas, or Illinois. You have a huge market that you share with each other. You have a universal postal system. China is our biggest threat. They are trying to close the gap through theft of Intellectual Property.

How do you feel about Britain and its past history with India?

When the British arrived, Indians were burning widows and killing female infants to avoid paying dowry. The British stopped both evil practices. Britain united India and gave India its military, justice system, Navy, police system, and a Parliamentary system of government. India owes much to the British. All government building like Parliament House and Prime Minister House were constructed by the British which provided jobs to all Indians from Kashmir to Kerala (*the expression means* "*throughout India*").

How do energy companies and water distribution function in India?

In the larger cities there is electricity. In many cases the electricity is limited to only certain hours. Due to load shedding. Out in the country there are generators only. Many places in India do not have running water. One third of the houses in the country have no toilets. People go to jungle.

What are women's rights in India?

Women can drive and they have equal rights, but women are not safe in the country. India is among the top 10 most dangerous countries for women to live. It ranks with Afghanistan, Pakistan, Sudan, and Yemen when it comes to safety and security of women.

Author's note: As of 2022 India has ranked as one of the most dangerous countries for women according to the Travel Industry Association.

What is the major industry or basis of India's economy?

Agriculture and farming are largest industry exporting beef, wheat, rice, fruits, cotton, and tea. Yes, we make cars but mainly for local market as few are exported. India is self-sufficient in oil, approximately 90% of energy is derived from petroleum. India gets some of its oil from Saudi Arabia and Iran. Also, India is not like China. Everything does not come from China there. Most commodities that US imports from China are made in India. India is opening their markets to China. Remember 1% of 1.3 billion people are super rich in India. Of that 1.3 billion about 10-15% are considered rich and the remaining 80% plus are dirt poor!

I feel if you want to come to America, then come here but do it legally. Don't fake it and get here and want to keep your own customs and language. If you want that stay where you are. Adopting American lifestyle and the freedom and liberty it offers is what you came here for. You can maintain your own traditions and customs, just don't try to change us because now you got here!

CHAPTER 8

SANTIAGO, CUBA
Interview with Rolando Chinea, May 2021

MY AMERICAN DREAM

*Background: I spoke with Rolando about his perceptions of Cuba in the
past and comparisons to the America he is seeing now. He told me that
where he came from, one had to have a passport to buy eggs, tires, gas.
Events are unfolding in Cuba as we speak. People are fighting for their
freedom. Now that news has been overshadowed by the ever-changing
and "hungry" news cycle, one must ask why, if Afghanis and Haitians
and too many to identify peoples from South America, Africa, Europe,
and the Middle East are literally pouring across the southern border
of the US, why are Cubans directed by US State Department not to
come? Also ask why all these peoples with no masking or vaccines are
allowed to be disseminated within the States with no warning or information as to their whereabouts to local authorities or the citizenry.
I travel a great deal for work and require vaccinations to travel to*

South America, Africa, and many Middle Eastern countries. These vaccines are for cholera, yellow fever, measles, smallpox, tuberculosis, pertussis, and hepatitis, to name a few, and the reason these vaccines are required is that these locations still have major outbreaks of these diseases. These were long-standing requirements (from US CDC and State Department) prior to COVID, yet people from these locations can enter the US and subject its population to all these diseases, not to mention disease-carrying parasites they may also carry.

Rolando, tell me what Cuba was like.

You had to have a card stamped and were limited as to how much or what you could buy. In Cuba during my time everything was socialized and mandated by the State. If you had an emergency or accident and needed emergency care you had to go to a clinic. These clinics are not like medical clinics in the states. They did not have the equipment or expertise to care for these emergencies and people were not allowed to go directly to the hospitals.

The clinics or dispensaries as they were known were transfer places for you to get to a hospital. They would have no medications and sometimes the hospitals didn't either. Many Americans make so many assumptions because they have always had everything.

The education system in Cuba they say is the best. Everyone was brought out of having no education to be educated. The government had good intentions to increase the education level but it became and is an indoctrination tool.

My mother was a dentist in Cuba. When the Communists took over, the State forced her to close her practice and work for the State.

What I see happening here in US during the COVID crisis with all the empty shelves in stores is identical to what happened in Cuba. It is happening yet again and I see it as a means of control over the population. I came home one afternoon, when the COVID pandemic had just started, after going to the market. My wife Gloria looked at me in shock. She said I was white as a ghost and asked what happened? I said "It's happening here!" The Russian Communists destroyed all of Cuba's history. They burned all the books. They silenced communication amongst the people. If you don't see the comparisons with the progressive left and the Big Tech censorship of differing views, you are blinding yourself.

The following is taken directly from the writings of Rolando Chinea: Definition of the American Dream.

The idea that every US citizen should have an equal opportunity to achieve success and prosperity through hard work, determination, and initiative. "She or him could achieve **the American dream** only by hard work." A happy way of living that is thought of by many **Americans** as something that can be achieved by anyone in the US especially by working hard and becoming successful. With good jobs, a nice house, two children, and plenty of money, they believed they were living the **American dream.**

The **Real Meaning of the "American Dream"** …The term "**American Dream**" was apparently invented in 1931 by historian James Truslow Adams; he was referring to "That **dream** of a land in which life should be better and richer and fuller for every man, with opportunity for each according to his ability or achievement."

What does it really mean if you are not US born? Can we achieve the Dream as well? We all know that everything is possible if you set your mind properly, follow some steps and move forward; it is the Universal "law", in some cases harder to achieve than imaginable, but not impossible.

I was born in an Island in the Caribbean, Cuba. I am the only son of a married couple also from Cuba, Rosa and Rolando. They both were very accomplished individuals back in our land. My father, an Electrical Engineer, was the Head of the Power Generation and Distribution Office for the Island. My mother was a Dentist MD with her own medical practice as well as a job in a local medical facility back in Havana. The year was 1959-60, I was five years old. Life in Cuba was rapidly changing. The country faced a new reality, Cuba became a communist and socialist country. Both of my parents did not approve or like the changes; they were willing to put everything on the line for me and my future. It didn't matter to them, they were focused and determined to protect me and my future from both communism and the socialism regime. They moved forward with the decision. They requested permission to relocate the family – "leave the country"- and at the same time requested permission to come to the United States of America (USA). What happens next is hard to imagine, but it really happened. My father was removed from his post (position) and banned from work anywhere. He was 39 years old, on a top his professional career path…suddenly terminated. My mother's private practice was taken away from her, "closed out" by the government and on top of that she was mandated to work in a clinic every night, 60 miles away from home. At the time we didn't know it, but for the next 7 years she became the head of the household.

The Government really tried hard to break the family apart, but once again they both were determined to reach their goal. Finally, seven years later the waiting was over. The Cuban Castro regime and the US Government granted permission to leave the country via Madrid, Spain. My parents agreed, I was six months away from reaching another communist ideological milestone. At age twelve (12) especially for Cuban males, the indoctrination is moved into a higher gear. Kids are considered "STATE" property; in other words, your new family is the "STATE" and not your biological parents. The government removed the kids away from family nucleus and place them on "pioneer camps" for heavy duty indoctrination camps. As a family we all went together to Madrid, Spain. What a relief!!!!!!

Madrid, Spain was what I am going to call now the LIMBO LAND. Why? We had to wait until the vetting process by USA was done and completed. We knew the law from the beginning and my parents agreed to the terms. During our temporary staging process in Madrid, we couldn't work in any capacity, we couldn't get any help from the local government or any government agency and we were 100% dependent on our US American sponsors, period. In our case they were my uncles who were already citizens of the US living in Puerto Rico. To emphasize, if for any reason, any of the agreed conditions were broken by any family member, the contract between us and the governments was considered not valid anymore (BROKEN) and for that reason the complete family was mandated to return to the country of origin, in our case, Communist CUBA. Can you imagine, or even better, do you have the courage to give up everything you previously earned in your life, your wealth, your career, your home, your savings, your securities. Everything, just for a DREAM. The future of your soul made reality through your son or daughter. That is for me what I call the ultimate SACRIFICE. It is PRICELESS. The good news arrived; our vetting was completed and we were able to come to the States. WELCOME TO AMERICA.

No, I did not have any idea at that time, of what they both did for me, but now I know. I also know for certain my parents are my HEROES and what they represent is PRICELESS. I think everything in life happens for a reason and sometimes is not obvious. My father's birthday was July 4, 1920...July 4. THE INDEPENDENCE BIRTHDAY. Why do they choose the United States of America as our final destination? The new beginning, the new journey? You Tell Me. I call it "INDEPENDENCE."

After arriving to USA, about three months later my father suddenly passed away. Who said life is fair? My mother, again took control of the household role and did what she had to do. It was not easy for her, as you can imagine, not a time for grievances, no time for vacation, no time for rest. She re-invented herself on a different career path, and in a nutshell, she pulled me over the hump into our new life. One more time, nothing was given to us – nothing was free. Everything came about due to the hard work and dedication that she invested. the way I believe it should be.

In about mid 1971 I met somebody very special, very special. We became friends, good friends, sweethearts, we dated for several years and in 30 Dec 1976 we became one. By the way she also was my Citizenship Sponsor around 1972-73. She also was instrumental in my college education; she invested in me, just because. Together we have two beautiful daughters and two grandchildren.

After 40 plus short years and one more time we came together to a critical crossroad. I would say that for over 25 years or so, I had mentioned to her, our kids and some limited number of friends that this Great Nation of US has been under attack. I am sure, that they looked at me and probably they thought, what are you taking about? They did not have a clue on my message, because they never were exposed to what I was exposed to in my childhood. They had no idea.

My Friends, the Socialism, wanted or not is here *(in Unites States)*, infiltrated in our own blood; is almost like a terminal type of cancer, and is up to us to cure America, our America, our USA. We know it. It has been proven over and over again, Cuba, Venezuela are the latest victims of the socialism. These countries have collapsed. Their broken, corrupted, anti-humanity political social system is not the answer to a better USA.

I invited every US citizen to join the movement, I call the FREEDOM MOVEMENT, to protect our legacy, our US Constitution and what it represents for generations to come. Our rights, freedoms and the abilities to pursue happiness are at grave risk.

The current situation in Cuba as of this writing in July 2021 is dire.

Socialism states that you owe me something simply because I exist. Capitalism, by contrast, results in a sort of reality-focused altruism: I may not want to help you, but if I don't give you a product or service you want, I will starve. Voluntary exchange is more moral than forced redistribution.
—Ben Shapiro

CHAPTER 9

Government's first duty is to protect the people, not run their lives.
—Ronald Reagan

JALISCO, MEXICO

ARNULFO MARTINEZ'S STORY
Interview with his daughter Maria Finney

June 2021

Arnulfo Martinez, known as Arnie to most, was born in Mechoacanejo, Jalisco, Mexico on July 3, 1933. Mechoacanejo was a very small town about 2 hours from the city of Guadalajara. Arnie's parents were farmers and from a very poor family. He had an older brother and younger sister. Dad's childhood was very happy, surrounded by friends and cousins because in a small town everyone knows each other. At five years old, he worked in the fields and only completed the third grade. Arnie lost his mom when he was 15. His dad was sick and the kids had to take care of everything especially after the loss of their mother.

His first job was as a builder and then took classes to become a tailor. In January 1953 at the age of 19, he married Teresa Ramos who was 16 years old. Teresa was born in Monterey Park, California but moved back to Mechoacanejo as a child. Arnie and Teresa had 3 daughters, Maria (11/9/1953), Luisa (8/4/1955) and Mary Lou (3/7/1958) in Mexico and later on had 3 more children in Los Angeles, CA.

My dad wanted a better life for his family, so they moved to Tijuana where they waited to get my dad a green card to enter the US. During this time, Teresa, who was a United States citizen, worked as a seamstress in Los Angeles while Dad stayed home (Tijuana) caring for the 3 girls. I remember my mom would bring home Campbell soup when she could get a weekend off of work in Los Angeles and would visit us (would take a bus) in Tijuana.

I was born in Mexico in 1953 and I remember my dad receiving his Green Card in 1960. We moved to Los Angeles where my mom continued to be a seamstress and dad struggled to find work. The people who treated Arnie the worst were surprisingly other Mexican. He would do menial jobs, tearing down houses and similar work.

Arnie worked several odd jobs and then learned how to lay brick which he was able to make better money. He found a job with Mr. Bill Barnes of Blue Champagne Pools. He worked there for 12 years. He continued to develop his trade, saving money when he could, and when the company owner retired, Arnie was left with no work so he decided to go out on his own. Arnie went out and got a contractor's license in 1981 and, started his own Company: Arnie's Masonry, Company.

My dad was a very industrious man. Family was together and meant everything to him. He saved enough money to take the family on road trips and vacations. It all went bad when my mom developed cancer. She was

diagnosed with stage 4 cancer and she died Easter Sunday 1989. Dad started developing Parkinson's disease in 1985 and became worst around the time of Mom's death. We don't know what caused it. Arnie's Masonry failed when there was no one able to take on the responsibility of running the business. He re-married Rufina Escobedo from Mechoacanejo on January 1991 and he also filed an application to become a US Citizen.

I was at my Dad's US Citizenship Ceremony. He was so proud and emotional. I was also emotional because the ceremony was beautiful. He was so proud to be a US Citizen. I don't think many Americans realize the

number of hours it takes to study for the test and pass it. They don't know how beautiful the ceremony is conducted. Being from Mexico with an American mom, myself and two sisters were naturalized in about 1965. On 8/23/61 another sister Norma was born; on 10/9/64 my brother Arnie was born and last on 8/17/71 my brother Daniel was born. I remember how proud my dad was of all his family and proud that his dream of giving us a better life materialized! He made the right decision to work hard to come to the United States to give us a better Life! I'm so proud to be his daughter! He passed away February 7, 2013!

CHAPTER 10

Politics is when you say you are going to do one thing while intending to do another. Then you do neither what you said nor what you intended.
—Saddam Hussein

If you win, you need not have to explain, if you lose, you should not be there to explain!
—Adolf Hitler

BAGHDAD, IRAQ
Interview with Vian Barker, June 18, 2021

Where were you born and raised, and what was it like growing up in Iraq?
I was raised in Baghdad, Iraq but was born in the United States, in Gulfport Mississippi. My parents traveled to study abroad. I was brought to Iraq when I was less than 1 year old. I was in Iraq from about 1983 to 1999 when Saddam

Hussein was in power. Boys and girls went to separate schools. If someone wants to be with you *(dating)*, they must ask the entire community.

What does that mean? Does that mean to be just a friend or date?
No, not really to date, it means if a man wants to marry you, he has to

meet with the mother and sisters of the clan first and if approved by them, then the men will meet. They will then decide if the man can marry the woman. It is very strict for women and remains so.

My cousin, Zainb got married in Iraq and was pregnant in 2001 when she was sent to US. Her husband intended to follow her to the US. Since her husband was a dentist and thus considered wealthy, he was kidnapped and had to pay his own ransom. He paid and just days before he was to leave Iraq he was found cut into pieces in a ditch.

Was it because of his faith, Shia or Sunni?

No, it was just about money. It does not matter if you are Shia or Sunni. It is all for the money.

My Mom left her home to visit me abroad. An Iraqi citizen came to visit Vian and told her mother that her home was being taken over. She was notified by local neighbors that other Iraqis were moving in and taking over her home. Anyone can take your house especially if you do not have a husband. My mother and father were divorced and my dad lived in Australia. My Mom returned to Iraq and had to go through laborious efforts to prove she owned the home. While my *(Vian's)* grandparents were there everything was OK, but when you are women alone people will take what they want through, what is the word: intimidation.

My mother was told they could take her home as she was not married or they would marry her to whomever they chose for her. She had to pay to have fake marriage papers drawn up to say she was married to another man just to keep her home. My Mom is still having a hard time. I want to get her out of there. My Mom's health is bad and it is just hard for her.

Iraqis in power told my mom she has to have a boy. She gets what you call social security from my grandparents. My Mom told them she cannot have a boy. She told them she is in her 60s!

Medicine is very expensive, more than here *(in US)*. You often don't get the right medication; the dosages are not correct or they are fake medications. Pharmacies are located in strip malls.

I have been trying to get my mom out of Iraq since her Green Card expired. The Iraqi government uses fake documentation against you. You are required to stand in long lines to get papers. Often you cannot get them without paying someone off. This is how my mom's Green Card expired.

I don't really like Saddam Hussein but growing up there I did not see the kind of things that are happening now. The assassinations for money would not be happening if Saddam was there. No one is strong enough to be in charge. There is no system for anything.

What did you experience growing up in a war-torn country?
I remember in kindergarten; a missile was dropped onto the school. It did not explode. Was a major panic to get the kids out. My mom came and got me. Schools were totally open, not enclosed buildings like here. You sit on top of layers of red sand. Ricochets were common cause for injuries. Electricity as intermittent. You had to study during daylight as there is minimum lighting available. You weren't allowed to have lights on as they could be sighted.

Everyone sleeps on the roofs of their homes in Iraq since it is so hot. I would remember roaches flying all over, got into your hair and your ears. It was awful. I would pull the covers over my head to keep the roaches away. My cousin got one in her ear.

Sand storms are common and then the rains would make conditions even worse. We always had problem with water availability. Turkey would shut off flow of the rivers and Iraqis downstream would suffer. My Mom is half Turkish.

How were you impacted by the government during these times?
This is true even today, the government controls hours you can be out. At 5 o'clock they say you should be in your home. Certain hours are specified that you can shop or be out and about. It is very restrictive.

I asked if there was a reason for the restrictions.
No, just regulations and control. Sometimes when the religious people came into town, there were more restrictions put on everyone. You had to be in your home by 5 o'clock unless there was an extreme emergency.

How did you meet your husband?

My husband is in the Coast Guard and we met in Maryland where much ship building and maintenance is done. I was a hotel manager where the Coast Guardsmen would be put up. We met through other people.

My dad stopped talking to me when I get married because my husband is non-Muslim and non-Kurdish and an infidel. Though my dad has been married multiple times when he was younger, had 4 wives and wanted to keep them but Australia would not allow. My dad threatened my mom that he was going to kidnap me. It is written in Muslim law that the father must take care of his daughter/s until she is married and then her husband takes on that role. My dad didn't take care of me, he thinks he is Noah!

He stopped talking to my mom also when I got married. That I married a sinning person and my children that are 4 and 6 are from a sinner. My cousin stopped talking to me for almost 5 years when I ate a piece of bacon in a sandwich from Panera. I told them to remove the bacon but it was not taken off and I just ate it. My cousin got upset and then the argument escalated out of control.

I am both Sunni and Shia. Iraq is all about the family and the clan's name you are from. It is really all about money. All of my family go out of Iraq. They are in Syria, Jordan, or Germany. My mom has to go to Yemen, Bahrain or Turkey to complete paper work. I could help and go there to help my mom when I was single. Now as an American with children and a husband I do not feel safe to go.

I have been trying a couple years to help Mom come to the states. COVID put another year delay in all this.

I asked if her dad would or could help her mom.

He could but would not. He has the finances to help. If he got me to Australia that he had planned I would be married to a Muslim Kurd by now.

What do you see or value here in America?

In American we have electricity all the time for the Internet etc. I would say the schools are better but the education is not. In Iraq all we did is go to class and study. We just studied more in Iraq. When I was in US I was told by Army recruiter when less than 20 years old I could be an officer due to my education.

I was learning English in first grade! We only had 30-minute lunch period then it was class time from 8-4. Most schools had Muslim classes as well. I had many Catholic friends and I would go to their church services with them.

I don't think the US has 'crazy freedom' but though health care is expensive I have it. There are many more opportunities here especially for work and especially for young women and teenage girls. Teenage girls cannot work in Iraq unless they work for the family. Iraqi women, especially teenagers don't get to go out and do whatever or go wherever they want. The families have approved a male driver who will take the girls to school, or shopping but he is known an approved by the men of the clan.

Can women drive in Iraq?

Yes, women can drive but not younger women. Not teenage girls.

How do the US and Iraq compare?

I miss the hominess of Iraq. Family was always together for tea or coffee. Iraq is much more family oriented. You are always surrounded with family. I miss that. I don't think Americans have that closeness.

When I first came here, (to US) I experienced some pretty mean people in school. I was called a 'sand crab' and much worse. In Iraq we didn't have bullies like you have here. I am a fun person and not hateful so I did not let it bother me.

Are you glad to be in America?

I am glad my mom got me out of Iraq because of the wars and all that has happened. She got me to Jordan first. My mom was told she got me out because she knew the war was coming. My mother did not know any wars were coming, she just thought the US was a better place for me.

My grandparents raised me as my mom was always working and my dad was in Australia. I was with my grandfather when he passed a short time after my grandmother passed in 1994. Funerals in Iraq are in the home and continue for 40 days of mourning. The body is wrapped and placed on the kitchen table. Plain wood, closest to the earth, coffins are used. Prayers are said over the body. Mattresses are laid throughout the home for people to sleep during the 40 days. All wear black clothing. I remember wearing black for 40 days. The women and the men do not mix. They come together only at the burial.

I miss these cool traditions but I don't like many middle easterners who have come here. They change when they come here.

I told her she has a "bubbly personality and is very outgoing."

I am bubbly here but I could not behave this way in Iraq. I would be much more reserved. I was asked to marry many men mainly to get them out of Iraq. I could have married my cousin. I thought this was weird.

I am sometimes told I think weird, or am not compassionate. I am very compassionate but I tell them I was brought up in a war-torn country. That makes me a little less emotional about things. I don't get all gooey or 'oh poor you'. I hate the victim stuff so prevalent in US.

I love Babylon and I loved to go there. There were beautiful schools, one the oldest in Baghdad. Was just beautiful. My uncle is a famous archaeologist and told me all about its history. When I am asked what the difference is between Allah and our God, I tell them it is the same God. Ours is just in Arabic. She thinks these people are not very bright.

CHAPTER 11

Humanitarianism is the expression of stupidity and cowardice.
—Adolf Hitler

To build may have to be slow and laborious task of years. To destroy can be the thoughtlessness of a single day.
—Winston Churchill

GHANA, WEST AFRICA
Interview with Johanna Anim July 16, 2021

Accra is on the Atlantic coast. I grew up not far from the beach.

I was born and raised in Ghana until I was 22. Growing up my family lived outside of town in the Ashanti Region and moved to the Capital when I was 6. My dad worked for the YMCA in the regions and when he was promoted to National General Secretary that is when we moved to the city. He stayed at the Capital until he retired in 2012. My Mom and dad spent half their time in Ghana and half in the US.

We were a family of six with two brothers and a sister. I am the second of four children.

This is a picture of dad and colleagues visiting one of the vocational training institutes of one of the 77 branches of the YMCA that my dad administered.

I asked what the major industry or agriculture is in Ghana and about water and power availability.

Ghana is mostly agrarian with Gold, cocoa beans, timber, and oil the major exports crop. Ghana has the largest dam in the area and thus gets all its power from Hydro power from the Volta River. Ghana provides power to the surrounding area. There still are power outages and sometime power is rationed.

There really isn't a drinking water availability problem due to the rivers. Many wells are dug and all outside the city use generators if they can afford them.

This is an image of meeting with a local chief

Growing up we had access to many things because of my dad's job. Many were not as fortunate. Trucked water was often brought is when wells could not supply enough water. Trucked water was often pumped up to tanks located on the top of roofs. This is still a common practice.

I was educated in Ghana and taught school for a little over 1 academic year before I left to continue my education. I found teaching very rewarding, but I wanted to do more than just teach.

When did you come to the US?

I left Ghana for school. I had the opportunity to study hospitality management in a program that my sister had already completed so I was familiar with it. I applied and received a full scholarship. This was my opportunity to leave Ghana. I was teaching 3rd grade and Jr High English. I just didn't see myself living in Ghana for the long haul.

What is the government of Ghana like?

Ghana in the early 90s, was ruled by a military government led by JJ. Rawlings. There had been several coup d'états since independence from the British in 1957 but in 1992, Rawlings resigned from the military, founded a political party, and became the first President of the 4th Republic. Rawlings was a Lieutenant in the Ghana Air Force. He said Ghana needed to be more modern. I voted for him during his re-elections in 1996 because he was cute. I was young. My father voted against him.

Ghana, like most sub-Saharan nations has always been very corrupt. I went to a Presbyterian College. Even with good grades, it is very difficult to gain admission to secondary and tertiary institutions because of fewer schools. You had to know somebody and even so, you still had to pay bribes to gain admission. It was very competitive to get into the college I attended so my family paid the bribe in Deutsch marks, not Ghanaian currency to get an edge.

Nothing happened without bribes. All the police took bribes. I don't think they even have tickets; they just take your money. It is just that way. *(I found this true in South Africa and Botswana also)*. I don't think I will see a non-corrupt Ghana in my lifetime; sadly.

Photo of a traditional council where they adjudicate disagreements such as family and property disputes.

Asante Chieftains. These are my tribe's people – A lot of disputes are still adjudicated through the chieftains. The Legal framework doesn't have much trust.

I wanted to be anywhere but there. Most of my friends went to Canada, the UK, or the US for higher education.

When I got accepted into the school in Colorado, I knew it was my chance to get away, so I worked hard. However once here I did not feel this was my calling either. Many who attended this school in Colorado did not end up in the hospitality field. I did love Colorado, the weather, the change of seasons, the beauty and especially the people. Colorado is a beautiful State.

I was a very sickly kid growing up. For a long time, they thought I had sickle cell anemia, common in Africa. But I was tested many times and I did not have this trait. I would just faint sometimes, so my parents never wanted me to drive. I learnt to drive as soon as I got to the US. I was a terrible driver at first but the freedom to try it kept me motivated.

You can have a business here and make yourself into something. I enjoy that I can be free to do those things and not have to have a man or have children. My mother pressured me to be married and have kids. In Ghana a woman could become a third wife to a man just to get her married. There, a woman is considered useless unless she is married with children.

What is the most prominent religion in Ghana, and did you see government interference in religious practice?

There are three main religions in Ghana; 75% are Christians, 25% are Muslim and 100% African Traditional Religion. Christians and Muslims coexist side by side and there are no tensions between them. Many people come to Ghana because we have a stable government compared to other African nations. Ghana's first language is English however there are 66 other languages, so most Ghanaians are multi-lingual.

Did you ever feel racism or animosity toward you when you came to the US?

Not really. The school I attended was very International and there were students from all over the world: Japan, India, Brazil, Thailand, Columbia etc. The staff, faculty and the locals were all very accommodating and welcoming. I remember failing my first driving test and the examiner being very consoling and encouraging. I told her my parents wouldn't let me drive but it was my something I really wanted to do. She encouraged me to go practice more and come back in a month.

Also, when I finally got my license, I was going back to campus one night with a friend. It was dark and we were following an SUV (sport utility vehicle). My friend, from Zimbabwe thought it might be a police vehicle. I was skeptical because it was a very nice car. I said no way, the police don't drive such nice cars. We decided to get a lot closer so we can verify. The car pulled off to the shoulder to let us pass then they pulled us over. Sure, enough it was a police car. The officer came over to ask if we knew why we were being pulled over. I said no. He said it was because we were following too closely. I told him I didn't believe that the police had such a nice car so I wanted to get a closer look. He told us about safe following distances and told bade us good night. I have since had a lot of interactions with police officers. All have been good. The couple times I did get a ticket, it was fair. Like I said, I was a terrible driver. I hit a lot of cars.

Were they parked cars or moving in traffic?
Both! If it was in my way, I hit it. I just seemed to hit everything. I am much better now.

What is the medical system in Ghana like?
In Ghana any medical treatment is cash only. If you did not have cash, you do not get treated. I wore eyeglasses since 4th grade. I went to the 37 Military Hospital in Accra because my father could pay, I was treated. If you had the cash, you got the treatment. Medications were a good example. To get Chloroquine a very common medication due to malaria and jaundice, one would have to pay in cash. Same for Paracetamol, similar to Tylenol.

I never had any problems seeing Doctors. I saw a small group of them regularly, so we became friends. Sometimes they'll send a nurse to our house with my medications or even come visit me at school to make sure I was I was doing well.

Traditional medicine was and still is practiced. Animals can be sacrificed if one is very sick. These could be chickens, goats, and sheep. Lots of people would go to traditional "doctors" to get herbal medications. Some still saw Witch doctors who can expel evil spirits and use special leaves, tree barks and roots to heal. There is still a strong belief in the national culture that not all health issues are meant to be treated by western medicine.

If people could not get chloroquine from doctor, they would boil the leaves of Neem and use that herbal remedy.

Image of a traditional Ghana festival.

What did you do after you completed your schooling in the US?

I went back to Ghana and applied to come back to the US. I went to IT (Information Technology) school in Denver. For work I became a data entry person for a Telecommunications company. They were looking for people with IT knowledge to move up in their company. I went to night school to be better able to get promotions. I worked hard and looked for opportunities. If I was not sufficient in something, I would go back and take classes to fill in my deficiencies. I went to night school after work for 3 years. I would work from 5 am to 2:30, then go to school from 4-11.

When I met my husband Mark, I was working as a Tier 3 technical support specialist. Mark wanted to get married but he was going to move to Oklahoma and wanted me to quit my job and move with him.

I never wanted to be a dependent wife or dependent on anyone. I wanted to work and be successful. In Ghana having a man is critical. My parents would not let up, especially my mom. In Ghana the mentality is a woman's place is in the home. Mark knew I was an independent woman. He asked me to quit and move with him but I would not go until I knew I could be employed in Oklahoma. I wasn't able to transfer within my company as a technician, so I got a job as a program manager. I managed the data and IT accounts for the City of Oklahoma City which included the police and fire departments.

My clients were wonderful and even though I eventually left the job to start my own business, I remain friends with some of them.

I never felt or experienced racism in my company or with my clients. As a matter of fact, I felt just the opposite. The only time race was an issue was when 3 of my Black co-workers who were frequently late to work and took a lot of time off due to family issues wanted me to join them in filing a class action lawsuit against the company because they were being disciplined for their lack of work ethic. (1 had been fired; the other two were facing other disciplinary actions they construed to be unfair). Due to high skill nature of what we did, it was a small group so any unplanned absence meant the rest of the crew had to work longer hours to cover the shortage.

Calling in sick once in a while is one thing, constantly calling in sick was another. Eventually the company had had enough. They turned and immediately sued the company filing a class action lawsuit saying the company was racist against them. They wanted me to join their discrimination lawsuit. I was working just fine and disagreed with them and told them their work ethic was the problem. I didn't join them but they assumed I would because I am black.

As far as racism, if I went for a promotion and didn't get it, I worked harder or went back to school to get the education required. I never felt any prejudice regarding me being black, let alone a black woman.

The only time I disagreed with a job I was qualified for but lost to someone else was regarding a job opportunity In Irvine California. One guy had moved to Irvin a year or so prior so he got the job as the company would have had to pay to move me. I was upset about that for a while.

The only animosity I received was sometimes from my customers. Because of my accent as soon as I answered the phone, they would inquire as to where I was from and not very politely. As an IT specialist I worked closely with the Fire and Police Departments on managing their data. These guys did initially test me but as soon as they realized I knew what I was doing I got earned their respect. The police even gave me a tour of the city a police helicopter.

I also had a few incidents of what could be perceived as discriminatory treatment in a very wealthy store in Oklahoma City. I was going to purchase a very expensive purse and decided not to buy there but I did go to another store and purchased the same purse. My take is that they had probably had bad experiences with African Americans shoppers, so they were not nice to me when I walked in. The reason I gave them that benefit of a doubt was my sister had opened a clothing store in Cherry Creek Colorado. The African Americans shop lifted everything. She eventually had to close her store. They came in pairs or threes. One would distract her while the others shop lifted. It destroyed her business. She felt victimized because she was African and not African American.

I look at America as a place of opportunity. If someone like me can come here and make something of myself, I wonder why a person black or white or purple born here can't do the same. A few of my black friends talk about how the system is rigged against blacks in America. I tell them just show up to work on time. And when the boss tells you to do something, maybe just do it?

I did not come from a poor family or a poor part of Africa. I was very fortunate in that but in America, I took whatever part-time job I had to way, get me to my next goal. They weren't glamorous but they afforded me independence.

Hard work wins in this country. I would like anyone to challenge me on that assertion. Perhaps if people actually went to work on being productive and self-reliant, they will have less time to feel victimized and not allow themselves to be used in a political narrative that they themselves have contributed to its corruption.

Elmina Castle is one of a few well-preserved slave trade castles. I believe history should be preserved. ***Photo removed due to copyright issues.***

CHAPTER 12

Let us not seek the Republican answer, or the Democratic answer, but the right answers. Let us not seek to fix blame for the past. Let us accept our own responsibility for the future.
—John F. Kennedy

UNITED KINGDOM
Interview with Laurence Cree, July 19, 2021

I use to love to read the morning newspaper with a nice cup of coffee. Looked forward to it. Now newspapers are so extreme as though we cannot think for ourselves. I cannot read them. I continue to read the Wall Street Journal.

Where were you born? And tell me about your life education and career in the UK.
I was born in London in 1943. I am 78 years old and was there during the Blitz when London was heavily bombed. My father was away fighting the war and my mom, left caring for her children, was always totally very self-reliant. Mom took me and my brother away from London to the safety of a farm located to the north of England to stay with a farmer and his wife. My dad was in France driving an ambulance. At the end of the war my dad ended up in Holland where the troops were honored for liberating the people. Many years later we continued to get Christmas and thankyou cards from the Dutch my father befriended during the liberation. They were forever thankful, probably until their deaths as I always remembered receiving those cards.

My dad was an old-fashioned doctor where he had patients come into his office set off on the side of our house. He had a black bag and was always ready to travel. After office hours he would go out and do at home visits to those who could not make it to our house. Primarily the patients he saw at home were those who could not make it to his office that he termed 'the surgery room'. The house calls were in the afternoon and late morning often in Wembley. He made house calls to anyone who could not make it to our home. He delivered many babies. People did not go to the hospital to have a baby. Most stayed in the local area and my dad ended up delivering generations of babies into the world. I truly admired him and he loved his work. We had what is called the National Health Care Service and it worked well for us. My dad worked very hard was paid well. He would take off two weeks a year.

During those two weeks it was idyllic. We would tour Brighton Beach on the south coast of England. We had wonderful parents and a beautiful upbringing. We would cruise the English Channel and in the 50s go to the Mediterranean. It was beautiful and there was very little tourism during these years. In Spain we would go to Costa Brava along the Mediterranean Sea. It was covered with vineyards and the wine was free. The women elders would prepare the fishing nets early morning for the young men to go out and catch fish. It was beautiful. These were happy times with my brothers. I remember the first phot we ever had taken was here and I still have the photo. Probably because of the times I always wanted to live near the coast and look it took me until now to be in Oxnard to live that dream.

My parents sacrificed a great deal for their kids. I had two brothers: Jonathan and Anthony. Anthony was the older. We were sent to very good schools. The Priest at St. Paul built in 1500 and started our school located adjacent to the cathedral. Even before it became a school, it was a teaching church and lessons were given by the priests. Lessons consisted of Latin, Greek, Ancient history, and they did keep lessons relevant. Later the school was relocated and the curriculum expanded to many subjects becoming a private school. Upon graduation you would earn a silver fish made of real silver. These are still issued today.

Saint Paul is a building of beautiful Victorian architectural design of old brick. It is located close to central London. The lessons were divided by children's ages. The old level exams were prepared for those 14 and 15 years old. You had to decide early what you wanted to be. (I think that became problematic). Old Level Exams consisted of Old English Literature, French, geography, physics, chemistry, math and biology. At 14 or 15 you had to pass difficult exams to get to A level exams given to 18-year-old. These were college and University entry exams and one had to demonstrate academic excellence. There were very high standards and my brothers flourished. Both got into Oxford University which is no easy task.

Both Anthony and Jonathan were studying to be doctors, following in my dad's footsteps. On Anthony's 20 birthday old friends were visiting. A driver having an epileptic fit drove into a crowd of people and Anthony was killed. I do not think my mom ever got over it. Johnathan completed his MD at Christ Church. I too wanted to stay in the medical field and follow my dad's tradition. I was good with my hands and I passed in all the 3 A levels in physics, chemistry, and math. I planned on being an engineer. This is where I think the school systems was problematic. If you changed your mind later on you would be without adequate education. I changed my mind and thought going to dentistry school would be the best of both worlds for both use of my hands and pursuing a medical degree. I thought dentistry would be great as you are not often confronting life and death. I had to go back and take biology for another year. This put me at a disadvantage. You had to decide what you wanted to do with your future at 15! You couldn't change your mind. You could go directly into anesthesia school or dental school; we had no premed or pre-dental schools

In the UK you are giving a GAP year because there is so much pressure to achieve. Europe really pressures the students. I understand this is becoming more common practice in the US as well. During my GAP year I went to Israel, learned to speak and write Hebrew and attended a Kibbutz School. In Kibbutz School you learn to work the land, grow your own food and be self-reliant. My parents loved it. The School I attended was within a mile of the Syrian border but this was a time when things were peaceful. My parents are Jewish and considered Young Zionists as this was before the State of Israel existed. My mom was one of the many speakers at Hyde Park's Speakers Corner speaking out about needing our own Country. As Aliah, meaning going up, exalted, rising to an ideal level of living, it is fulfilling an ideal. My friends now were lifelong friends with my mom and they traveled to Israel. England is a beautiful Country and there was always a great deal of diversity.

I believe both the UK and the US are wonderful countries and treated people of my grandparents' generation very well. They took in refugees from all over the world. My grandparents are from Plotz in Poland surviving the Russian Pogrom was the killing of all Jews in Russia and Poland.

My grandparents had the courage to leave. They came to UK in 1905. It was challenging for them. They had to learn a new language, which they did and sent their children to school. This had to be daunting. On my mother's side, the folks settled in UK and established their roots there. My grandfather was very religious from Poland.

I celebrated my Bar mitzvah at 13 and you have to sing in Hebrew. This had great meaning for my grandfather. On the Sabbath he would walk everywhere and would never take a car. That devotion seems to dilute with each generation. We have a very nice Rabbi here in US. There is a loss from old traditions but we still believe.

Larry Gelbart, creator and producer of the TV series MASH and a co-writer of "A Funny Thing Happened on the Way to the Forum" were close friends with my mom. His wife Pat is a cousin of my mother and they came to America. America and England treated people of that generation very well. We all met in England in the 60s and had a warm family reunion, discussing all the persecutions, history and memories.

In London was my dental school named Guys Hospital Dental School had developed anesthetic medicine and oral surgery during WWII due to all the dental injuries incurred during the war. US dentist would come to England to learn from East Grinsted Hospital under Terence Ward to learn dentistry. But Americans had better dental schools.

I graduated from GUYs which is part of the bigger hospital. They had strong academics and difficult exams. It was a good school. England's deficiencies were not trying to save teeth. If you look at the teeth of people from England, Ireland, Scotland etc., you often don't see good teeth.

England is good, peaceful, civilized country with no guns but there is a lack of preventive medicine and dentistry. We were strong in making dentures. High percentage of population of England has partial or complete dentures, maybe greater than 30%. This is going back to the 1950s.

I needed orthodontal work. England did not do well at this. US emphasized gum health and preserving existing teeth for all your life. When I finished dental school in England, I wanted to come to the US to do my DDS degree. There are two different degrees based on different philosophies so there are two different undergraduate degrees which were complimentary.

Several of my colleagues went to US just for a couple months to train and came back with expertise to practice more sophisticated dentistry in England. This was in 50s, 60s, and 70s. Dentistry was most advanced in US in California, why you ask? Because of Hollywood. The stars' smile was their income! Every detail you could care about in teeth would be addressed because of Hollywood photos. Their teeth had to be perfect for those up-close movie shots. Everything was developed there and now we are all concerned with maintenance for tooth health, gums and even heart health attributed to teeth and gums.

Guys Hospital contribute $1,000 for me to come to US to learn. My parents also contributed. This was 1970. We are not considered doctors in UK. In 1972 I got my DDS in US and then I went back to England to teach at Guys Hospital.

I got very poor grades at USC in fillings and tooth repair, crowns and bridges etc. I didn't do well because of the English system. In US I didn't have to open a book. I did great on the academic side. I was getting 90-95%. Friends from France, Yugoslavia, Philippines, China, would say, about my grades, 'how did you do that Larry'?

We had very good instructors. It took me 18 months to pass my State of CA board. USC had designed this program for foreign students and you kept going as long as it took. It was the best dental school in US. I was so fortunate to specialize. I knew dentures. I learned restoration work and gum work. I learned root canal and became efficient at it. When I came back and taught, I also maintained a private practice emphasizing root canal. I was one of the few who could do the US style of root canal treatment from the 1970s in England. Basically, few could do or pay for root canal in England. Few people tried to save teeth in England. Due to the government system. There was a different emphasis and you just lost your teeth and had dentures made. You can see the difference when you see the peoples' teeth from England, Scotland and Ireland and can tell dentistry was not a priority for them or they just could not afford reconstructive work or did not know about it. If you could pay for it privately you could get root canal. Government did not pay for it.

Private patients would pay me which is different than the government system, which would offer to pay you for a partial denture. Many could not pay for the sophisticated work.

I admire the National Health Care system in England. My brother who is a doctor in the US has to work to get funding. It becomes very bureaucratic search for grants and funds in contrast to the British system. This was not an issue in England. My dad got paid well and worked hard and he paid to get me to study at Guys hospital.

USC drained my reserves. In 1972-1977 I stayed in England performing many root canals. People now wanted to save their teeth instead of losing them and having dentures. I then came back to US for endodontic studies. I entered a high-pressure program at UCLA. USC is a private University and has a customized DDS course for foreign dentists. You stay until you meet the standards. UCLA didn't have a customized dental program for foreign students. Thus, this program did not offer the freedom of a customized course to foreign students which gave credits for training they had received in their own country and could continue until they met required proficiencies.

A big turning point in my life was whether I would come back to the UK. My friends and patients told me they needed me and England's dentistry did as well. Few could perform the dentistry I could based on my US training. My parents wanted me to come home as well but ultimately, I decided to stay in the US. I have no regrets.

I recall driving through the tunnel from Santa Monica to Malibu where you can see the sand and the coastline and it reminded me of those vacation days near the Mediterranean Sea. The happiness we shared then. I remember it well and knew I had to live near the coast. My previous life influenced me to stay.

If I had gone back, I would have been a big fish in a little pond. I would have had a lot of business. We were located near an US Air Force base and all their medical and dental work was paid by the Air Force. I had people coming from this base and traveling from all over Europe including France, Spain and Italy just to come to an American trained dentist.

The 1980s was a great decade for me and my family. Though I had made the decision to stay in the States my family could travel here often. I lived in North Ridge and had beautiful home. My brother was in Lancaster so we had great family get together every year. That ended in 1989 when my dad had a heart attack visiting me and died here. It was a joyous time, my parents visiting their sons, all together but my mom had to take my dad back to England and plan a funeral. My dad had kept my mom pretty independent through her debilitating arthritis and she became more immobile. With him gone she eventually had to go into a nursing home which made the last two years very tough on her. Family there were very supportive but she was miserable without her husband.

I bought my home in 1981 for $139k in Northridge. It was 1600 square feet, 3 bed, two bath on a third of an acre with beautiful gardens, a swimming pool and orchard. America is the land of opportunity as I was only in my second year of employment in the US and had all this. I taught in Northridge at USC for both undergraduate and graduate studies, I loved teaching and the reason I got my green card. You could not get a green card for dentistry, US had enough dentist but teaching was my in. My citizenship came in 1995. I took my time and it felt more complete. The foreign student program at USC sponsored me and I continued to teach there.

I am kind of a mix as I am a lover of England and the US. I am not into private practice that many seem to be driven by. I have this idealism of not money involved in your career. I have a special respect for people who work when money is not involved. I still admire the National Health Care System. There is such sharp division with people who have a different view. I liked Trump's policies and what he was doing. I did not like his bedside manner.

America had a great reputation when John F. Kennedy was alive and President. Everyone in England loved JFK. All countries loved the US. On small TV screens in black and white we would watch adventures such as Hopalong Cassidy and other Hollywood films that we identified as America.

It has been an adventure and I feel very fortunate when I look back at my life.

Attitude is a little thing that makes a big difference.
—Winston Churchill

CHAPTER 13

> *To conquer a nation, first disarm its citizens.*
> —Adolf Hitler

> *If war is horrible, servitude is worse.*
> —Winston Churchill

SAIGON, VIETNAM
Interview with Mark Lai, October 15, 2021

Hi, Mark. Tell me where you're from and about your life growing up.
I am from Saigon Vietnam and I was born in 1964. Growing up in my country what I remember, it was 1972 it was the New Year in Vietnam. I remember vividly, my father, carrying me in his arms as we were running away from men who were shooting at us. They pointed guns and they fired at us. They were the communists; we were lucky we were not hit. I remember we were actually being fired at. My father cradled me in his arms and ran and got me inside a safe place where we could hide. The Vietnamese Communists did not know where we lived or where we were. They could not track us.

Tell me about your escape from Vietnam.
The Communists took advantage of the New Year where there was a lot of confusion. This is when they were trying to take over our government. America was there and stopped them. Our new year is in early February.

I have seven brothers and sisters. My sister came to the United States in 1969 and worked for the US government so that made it easy for her to get to the US. Before that time my father tried to escape from Vietnam with my second sister and brother. My sister got to Thailand and the rest of us were turned back. They could not make it.

Did you travel to other countries prior to coming to US?
No, but my other sister made it to Thailand.

What were your experiences in school, in the college educational system in your native country?
Going to school before 1975 was harder than school here **(in USA).** We had to work very, very hard. I finished high school in Saigon. Saigon was a big city so there were a lot of students in 1975. As I said my sister worked for the US government and she had papers so she could leave Vietnam. When my father was trying to escape in 1975, we came to the Embassy and we saw the helicopters taking people off the top of the roof top of the American Embassy. My father said he wanted us to get out but we were just too little and so it would not be safe to climb the ladders to the top of the tower to get us out. I came to the United States in 1982 and I became a citizen in 1987. Having my sister here was a great benefit and she sponsored us.

Mark, how do you perceive the USA today as compared to when you first came here?
We left in 1982. My sister sponsored us to leave Vietnam. We had to bribe many officials to get out even with my sister's connections. That was the only way to move the paperwork forward. You had to pay bribes to government officials. We had tried to get out earlier in the 70s. My dad and others planned on an escape in a fishing boat. This was the method a lot of Vietnamese used to escape Vietnam at this time. They were caught. The fishing boat was confiscated by the Vietnamese communists. They investigated the boat and found a great deal of food and supplies. The boat was designed to handle about five fishermen so they wondered what was going on. They knew we were trying to escape with all the supplies that was beyond the capacity of the boat. My brother did not make it out. The government found out we were trying to leave and they stopped us. We know

that someone tipped them off. It's the only way that they knew about the boat. We were not threatened but they did seize the boat and asked a lot of questions. For my father it was scary. Vietnam is a beautiful country, the life there was simple, not complicated. The government with the Communist takeover made it very hard to live. They wanted to control everything. They controlled the food, they controlled how many people were allowed into your home even to visit as a guest. They controlled how many people could live in your home. I know when my father escaped with me from the communists' firing rifles at us, he went into a safe place like a church. I am not sure; I was very young.

I was brought up Catholic in Vietnam and I'm a practicing Catholic in the US today. The Communists tried to limit our religious practices. It was not like that in Vietnam before the communists. Things were much freer, much less complicated. With the Communist party in power, you could not do anything. You could not say what you wanted to say. You had to be very careful if you said something against the government you would be put in prison. The police would come and charge you and put you in prison.

The US is a wonderful place with wonderful people. My wife and I are thankful to be here. I cannot explain, the difference between going through what my family and I experienced in Vietnam with the Communist takeover even as a young child and what is the US. The Communist knew everything about you. That is what scares me about what's going on here today. The Communists knew everything, they would talk to other people about you, they would pry into your private life. I think this is what is happening in the US today. It's just like Communism in Vietnam.

I asked about guns and if they were confiscated in Vietnam.

My observations are when we watched television, 'they' don't say anything bad about Biden but when Trump is mentioned all you hear is all this negative stuff. It makes no sense to me. The balance I use to see here, seems to be gone. Growing up I know people did have guns but they were taken away. The communists were very sneaky in their language to us. They twisted everything making things confusing. They told us we would be safe and they wanted us to collect all our gold and all our jewelry and all our wealth and put it in one place. My father, as well as others, knew this was just not right. Why would they want us to put all our wealth in one place? People were so fearful that they threw their jewelry and their money out into the street. I never understood. They were tricky about their language they said it was just to collect money so it would be safe.

I asked Mark about their health-care system.
It was horrible! It was just horrible. There was no real medicine. If you went to a clinic, you would get one pill. That 1 pill would be for cancer, for a stomach ache, for an earache. it would be that same one pill. That was the medical help you got. Herbals was the only thing available that most people practiced.

I asked about religious freedom in Vietnam.
Most of Vietnam, 80% is Buddhist and about 10% are Catholics. The communist tried to limit all religions. What I like most about the US is the freedom. You can actually enjoy listening to the kind of music you want. That surprises you right? You couldn't do that in Vietnam; you couldn't listen to the type of music you like to listen to. You had to listen to what they selected for you. I so enjoy listening to the kind of music I like; enjoying the kind of food I like. In Vietnam you cannot listen to American music.

I asked Mark what he misses about his country.
I guess I miss a lot, though I was very young. I don't want to go back there now. I don't want to go on tours because then you're just a tourist. There's a lot of homeless and vagrancy. I just don't want to experience that now. I would not be a Vietnamese in Vietnam. I would be a tourist!

I asked Mark what he likes most about the US.
I like the US a lot. You can enjoy life and have many opportunities, very unlike communist countries. in Vietnam if you were wealthy, if you were educated, if you wore glasses, if you are high military rank or high grade in the police, you would be arrested. You would be taken to prison and spend prison in the mountains where it was freezing. Or you would just disappear.

My father-in-law was in prison for 10 years. He was in a Mountain Prison. They took him because he had a high military rank. He worked from 6 a.m. to 7 p.m. and only got one rotted potato to eat every day. The prisoners starved. They only fed them potatoes, not rice that we are accustomed to. Most of the potato was rotten. Any living animal or creature that walked by was killed for food. It didn't make any difference what it was; it could be dogs, cats, rats or wild animal, it was eaten. They were starving. Even when the Communists did provide us food in the cities, it was things that we did not eat. They would give us oatmeal or flour. We in Vietnam don't eat oatmeal and flour. We didn't know what to do with it. We eat rice and that is our main source of food.

I asked Mark what similarities and differences he sees between other countries and the US.
You have to understand thousands of people tried to escape Vietnam to get to a better life, to get to freedom, to get an education in 1979. During that time frame, 99% of Vietnamese died in the ocean, they risked drowning in the ocean by escaping on small boats just to get away. Just to get away from the communists. I am a lab technician and I understand Medical and Public Health. Medical practice is very good here and it is a world apart from Vietnam. I look back and see people from Vietnam trying to escape communism the same as I saw the Afghanis trying to escape from Afghanistan holding onto an aircraft. That was just like we Vietnamese holding onto boats, most of us drowning. My father-in-law was in that Mountain Prison in Vietnam for over 10 years. All would risk death just to leave. I saw that again and again when I watched the Afghanistan photos. The communists would limit your food. You might get a 5 lb. bag of rice. That's all you would get most of the time. They would give you potatoes, no meat, oatmeal as I said things that we just don't eat. Here (in the US) you have everything. Your choice of food, supplies, opportunities, education, jobs. People born here just don't seem to get it! I see that changing now and it scares me.

I asked about Vietnam protecting its borders.
Mark laughs.

The only people wanting to get into Vietnam now are the Chinese. They're taking over and they come across the border without much problem. Many of the street names in Vietnam have been changed to Chinese names. I don't think the Chinese are just trying to take over southeast Asia, I think the Chinese are trying to take over the whole world. That is what I believe.

I asked about incidents or experiences that happened in the US that were different from Vietnam

I have to say seriously when I first moved to US, I moved to Kansas. It is a wonderful place with wonderful the people. Everybody treated us with respect. There was no racism. We felt no animosity towards us being Vietnamese. My wife is from Vietnam also and we are very glad to be in America. We enjoy the education system. I see it as a very good system. I am very good at math and I am challenged here. In Vietnam, they did not allow me to take math. When you went to school the government chose what you would study unless you were very good or exceptional, then they would let you take math. I was not allowed to even though I am good at math. In Vietnam everyone wants to study math. They know that will help them get ahead so it's very strict and limiting. It seemed very strange that they would not let me take math. The governemnt discouraged me and other students. Students were forced to take majors they didn't like or they didn't want. So, few studied.

I have not seen racism in the US. I did not see it when I came here. The people are friendly in the US. I must admit we wanted to go back to Kansas from California. We just found the people extremely nice. They're very cordial people. People are nice in California but it's not the same. It's not as close and family oriented. We always planned to move back to Kansas. My neighbor there would actually come out and help me cut the grass even when I didn't need him to. He would come every week to help me cut the grass. People are just friendlier in Kansas than they are in California. We wanted to go back for a long time but now my wife and I have family here in California. We definitely enjoy the warmer weather and it would probably be tough to go back now as I sold my house in Kansas. This is our home.

People in California are pretty aggressive and almost crazy, unlike the people in Kansas but as I said we find good people and this is our home.

CHAPTER 14

He alone who owns the youth, gains the future.
—Adolf Hitler

It's easier to fool people than to convince them
that they have been fooled.
—Mark Twain

If we lose the kids, we lose the country.
— Ann Coulter

PLAUEN, GERMANY
"Rudy" Heusuk Morton

Authors Note: The following appears a very similar perception to what Rolando Chinea (Chapter 8) reports occurred in Cuba and parallels his take on political use of Corona virus outbreak in US.

Taken from "Open Letter to All Young People under 25 Years of Age," by Rudolph "Rudy" Heusuk Morton. The content that follows is taken from the above-mentioned open letter in its entirety.

www.mortonplauenyouthexchange.com

Since the very beginning of the COVID-19 pandemic, confusion has been perpetuated with untamed ferocity by social, network, and printed media. From the beginning, we have not known who or what to believe about the pandemic's current status, possible treatments, if/when it might end, or how to protect ourselves and families. Contradictory information comes at us daily from both the government officials as well as the scientific community. All of the misinformation serves to keep people confused, scared, and likely to succumb to submission.

The solution for ending the pandemic rests with people living in the first third of their life – our **youth**. When the bubonic plague ravished medieval Europe, it was the younger generation that took the lead in restoring normalcy by facing it head on. Without their leadership humanity could have gone extinct. Throughout history, it has been the younger generation who sought to make the world a better place for their offspring and future generations. I believe that it is now your turn to take up the reins of leadership and guide humanity down the road to a better way of living.

Those on other end of the spectrum who entered the last 1/3 of their life expectance long for stability and preservation of their civilization which they had created and lived in.

Unfortunate are those in the middle, parents and grandparents. They are pulled in either direction desperately trying to maintain family peace to prevent further rifts between generations. The rift and suffering caused within families by this current pandemic, is incomprehensible.

Having said that I wish you hear me out.

Having taken up space on this Planet for over 80 years, I can honestly say that I have enjoyed opportunities and challenges due to one line from the United States Declaration of Independence: "*We hold these truths to be self-evident, that all men are created equal, that they are endowed by their Creator with certain unalienable rights, that among these are Life, Liberty and the Pursuit of Happiness.*" Going forward I will refer to this quote as *LLPoH* (*Life, Liberty and the Pursuit of Happiness*) and instead of lecturing you on what you ought to do, I am going to share my life experiences that were contrary to the concept of *LLPoH*.

I was born into Plauen, Germany, during a period when *national socialism* was in its hay day. The enthusiasm of the majority of people was unstoppable. It was amplified, in sports, entertainment, and the constant propaganda aimed at the German people were unstoppable suggesting achievement of greatness, to the point where young people joined in droves all sorts of government agencies from military to work camps building Autobahns.

Little did they expect that they were led down a path of self-destruction. It came in the form of WWII with its unbelievable sufferings bestowed on mankind across the globe. I lived through that period. It brought in ration cards issued to the people on how much bread, meat, flower, or sugar you were allowed to buy. Not only in Germany but also here in the USA. Hence the name victory garden. You may want to google that to find out what it really was. But, when you got to the store to buy food with your ration card, the shelves were empty the issuers of ration card were unable to provide and the ration card was mostly a distraction making people believe that help is on the way. Thus, leaving you hungry. Since the same rationing rules applied to fuel (coal) more often than not you froze sitting next to your stove.

The next political system I lived under briefly was the communist regime of East Germany imposed on Germany by allied victors of WWII. That regime lasted from 1945, when the Soviet Union took over the eastern part of Germany and lasted to 1989 when the so-called Iron Curtain wall fell. Again, googling that event can shed light on many subjects.

My home town of Plauen ended up 26 KM inside the Soviet Zone. I for one, was fortunate. I was at the tender age of nine years old, when my brother who had served in the German navy during WWII, came home illegally in 1947 for the first time since the war ended. He had stayed in the British Zone of West Germany that was occupied by the Western Allies, the USA, Brittan and France. My mother and he made a deal that he was to take me with him to West Germany, because she was too frail and sick to take care of me, and also, she wanted me to grow up under western rules governed by LLPoH. My father had died in 1941. We walked out of Plauen during a warm May night in 1947, toward the direction of Hof, Bavaria in West Germany. Had we been caught we most likely would have ended up like so many others in some Siberian Gulag. (Another interesting story to google).

My sisters and mother stayed behind. My mother passed away in 1952, shortly after we had come home legally to visit her. Here are a few excerpts from what life was like behind the Iron Curtain in the Democratic Republic of East Germany that was formed in 1948 out of the Soviet Zone as it was shared with me by my sisters.

First as an east German citizen you were prohibited from coming any closer than 5 Kilometers to the boarder. Citizen were locked in, not only in to East Germany but also in all other nations that were controlled by the Soviet Union under their leader Joseph Stalin.

Second, the East Germany manufactured auto mobile was called a Trabant, affectionally called a Trabi it had a two-cycle engine like most of our lawn mowers. Assuming you had enough money saved up to buy one of those you had to apply for one. Waiting time for your turn to get a Trabi, was ten (10) years.

Third. the food and all other consumer good supplies (whatever you find at a Wal Mart today) was regulated and distributed by government planners. Example, planners decided how many pounds of potatoes a store can have to sell. Here is a quote from my sister she worked as a sales clerk in a HO government store. She said when a shipment of potatoes came in to the store clerks and all those working in the store picked out the best potatoes for their families and then what ever was left was put on the floor for the public to buy. That was a rotten thing to do you say? Yes, it was but it was also driven by a basic human instinct, the desire to survive something embedded in us that will never change.

Fourth. When the wall (iron curtain) fell in 1989, the stream of Travis heading west to get a climb of freedom under the *LLPoH* system was hundreds of miles long going into Western Germany. Arrivers were astounded by the opulence in western stores with their unlimited supplies of merchandise. That too can be googled.

It was in 1990, after the wall fell that I helped 40 youngsters from my hometown of Plauen to come to the USA and perform in Morton, ll. Youngsters that were born into the former socialist squalor, exited to be allowed to visit the bastion of *LLPoH*, the USA.

www.mortonplauenyouthexchange.com

So why am I writing this story? Socialism, whatever kind makes no difference, is when a group of people under the slogan, **we must unite**, seek to control the population.

Under the LLPoH concept the individual human gets to choose his or her own destiny.

I for one, at age (83) was lucky to have lived most of my life under the *LLPoH* concept, but been made keenly aware of what lays on the other side if one submits.

Since 25 years old and younger folks have statistically the bigger part of their life is in front of them puts them at a cross road to choose life under the LLPoH concept or submit to having their destiny ruled by central planners.

Carefully filter information you hear from what seems like creditable sources on what you should do with it.

Will you be free to live in a *LLPoH* society? Or are you willing to bow to your masters to whom you surrender your liberty, who will throw you crumbs like Stalin throw to the maimed chicken and tell you what you can or not can do for the good of the masses?

That is the very thing that sets humanity apart from the animal world. It is our ability to choose while we can. Use it or lose it.

It starts with open uninhibited dialog between those believing and trusting the *LLPoH* system versus those promising undefined liberties by power seekers. Good day"

Death is the solution to all problems. No man, no problem.
—Joseph Stalin

CHAPTER 15

Attitude is a little thing that makes a big difference.
—**Winston Churchill**

BULACAN, PHILIPPINES
Interview with Marilyn Tolosa July 29, 2021
A Love Story

Marilyn, tell me a little bit about the Philippines and your life there.
I came from a large family with 8 children, very common in the Philippines.

My mom was a homemaker and she had a business on the side selling general merchandise. It was like a little convenient store located downstairs where we lived upstairs in the house. The eight kids would help in the convenience store and assigned daily chores. My dad was a self-employed liaison officer who assist government retiree applicants preparing their paper works and submitting it to designated government agencies that will process their applications. This is common in the Philippines as well. People who didn't track themselves for retirement or were not knowledgeable in the retirement process. My dad would help pull strings to get their retirement benefits fast tracked and processed half the time required. He really helped people collect their retirement benefits and shorten the process of legally doing it. People would actually pay my dad to get their retirement on a timely manner. He knew a lot of people who works from government agencies and was very well networked. He would do all the paperwork required for processing each of his retiree clients. Letting my dad do the preparation and submitting their paper works to government agencies that process retirement application shorten the time of retirees waiting. My dad's clients bypass the long process and waiting in line to government agencies that is in charge of approving retiree applicants. Standing and waiting in slow moving line in the Philippines is very common and you had to pay bribes at each level to get any paperwork done. My dad would help them cut through this paperwork and through all the bureaucracy so they would have to pay less and fewer bribes. If there were five levels of bribes, my dad might get it down to two levels. It's sad but it's common.

I am the youngest of eight children and the oldest is 16 years older. My grandparents on my dad's side lived in the same compound where we grew up. They provided care for the children while my parents were working.

Another experience growing up in the Philippines is going about daily lives routine. Public transportation is the only mode of travel. Only the rich people have private cars. You don't drive around in your car. I experienced everything in transportation from ferries to little b boats being paddled around where you would pay $0.01 or 1 peso. We used buses or what we called the jeepneys. An extended jeep where you would all line up and rows for seating. Taxis were also a luxury.

Tell me about your schooling and childhood.
All of us went to Public Schools from elementary through high school. Five of my older siblings graduated and got their college degree from public State University. The remaining 3 younger ones, including my self-attended and graduated from a private college in Manila. I attended the Centro Escolar University in Manila, located near the Presidential Palace that is called Malacañang Palace. I went to college for three and a half years and studied Mathematics and minored in Behavioral Science. I always wanted to use

my secondary degree as it interested me more. My minor it just seems more enjoyable to me.

What did you do for work while studying in school?

I worked part-time doing research as an intern for the International Rice Research Institute (IRRI) for about 2 and 1/2 years. I had to move to Los Banos in Laguna for work where I worked up to 4 years after I graduated from college. I had to move from my hometown which was in the province of Bulacan.

How did you meet your husband and when did you become a US citizen?

I was a maid of honor at one of my friend's weddings and the groom's first cousin knew Nick. I met Nick at this wedding just by accident. My husband to be, Nick said it was love at first sight and it was for both of us. Nick was in the US Navy. He originally came from the Philippines and left and joined the Navy in 1969. We dated for a while. We carried on a long-distance relationship for a couple years. You have to understand it took two to three weeks to get a letter from Rota Spain where Nick was stationed overseas, to the Philippines. It's truly a romantic story. We continued to share our letters every year on our anniversary. We would read our letters to each other ever since we married in June 1st 1985. My daughter Christina shares in our anniversaries and she reads our love letters now.

I arrived in the states in 1986 I was fast-tracked as a naturalized citizen as Nick was with the US Navy. I had studied English and didn't have any problems with the test. I also took American history in the Philippines and I studied everything so in the interview I passed easily. The interview was conducted in Hawaii and I was naturalized in Honolulu.

This is where my adventure living in the US started that I compared to day and night. The Healthcare System in the Philippines is very difficult. You have to pay cash and carry. There is no such thing as health care insurance. If you don't have the cash, you don't get the medical care. You have to give the money up front for a doctor's visit or in hospital emergency room. If you need to go to a hospital for emergency case, they will ask for a deposit before they admit you, but without that deposit you don't get the necessary medical care needed.

My adventure in the United States was pure culture shock. Americans have everything. I was studying about American culture but I grew up in a rural province in the Philippines where life is very simple and we don't have modern amenities to enjoy. Lifestyle in the Philippines is very different than the US. From Honolulu we traveled to Brunswick. Georgia. We were stationed at Brunswick, Georgia for two and a half years. I really enjoyed the Healthcare System offered by the Navy. We benefited greatly being with the Navy. It was very different than Healthcare in the Philippines. In addition to the culture shock from the benefits in the healthcare system was the luxuries offer in US. We had no luxuries growing up. You have everything here; flowing water from a tap, electricity, and sewer system. You don't have to wait for electricity. We had no flowing water. Fetching and collecting water is a daily task. Electricity was intermittent at times. We would actually collect rainwater and stored in water tank depot for drinking, cooking, bathing, everything. The power would be out often, it was intermittent and you would never know when power outage will occur. We often did our homework with candles. I didn't even use a calculator till I was in college.

My grandparents raised livestock and because of lack of refrigeration was very sparse. We actually salted the meat to maintain it for as long as we could. Thus, everything we had and ate really was organic. There were no pesticides. We ate mainly veggies and rice that we grew. I would collect the eggs from the chickens and then when the chickens were too old to lay the eggs, we would use as food.

When you're born in the US you get scheduled for immunization as required for medical care, not so in the Philippines. I wasn't vaccinated until I started grade school.

Religion in the Philippines
I'm a practicing Catholic and it's a little bit different in the Philippines. It is more Orthodox and they use all the old traditions. 80% of the Philippines is Catholic and the Muslims are not treated well in the Philippines. I don't like how Muslims are treated.

Did you see racism in the US? How does it compare to now?
Yes, I would say there was racism here when we went to Georgia especially. They would call us the yellow people. It was not bad on base where we assimilated, were well-liked and got along well with everyone. Going off base could be a bit of a challenge. We were looked at a lot but I would say there is more racism exist in the Philippines against the Muslims.

People did warn us when we came to the US, especially to the south what we would face. There was some racism, it was just the experience of the day and I think some prejudice is part of human nature. Things were much different when we moved to California but it still exists. My daughter and I still see racism a bit today. My daughter just got married and her husband is part white German, Native American and black and he calls himself 'half-breed'. That's something he calls and described himself. I don't think anybody calls him that but that is his terminology for himself.

I agree there has been some cultural shock and some prejudice but I have nothing but gratitude for my time in the US and for the chances given to me by being here. My husband Nick truly embraced the US Navy. He loved his life with the Navy, it was his life, it was his career. This life was not available to us in the Philippines or to him. Even if with my education, I had a career in the Philippines, I would not have the life that I have in the United States. As crazy as politics are in the US, I would not trade it at all for my earlier life experience living in the Philippines. You do not understand how very corrupt the Philippine government is and has always bee. It is ruled by nepotism, by two family dynasties passed down over generations. They rule everything and nothing has changed.

What kind of government exists in the Philippines?
The government in the Philippines is a republic with a presidential form of government. Wherein power is equally divided among its three branches: Executive, legislative, and judicial. We elect the president by popular vote. This actually is not as good as it sounds. It's popular vote and you can have a president from one party or believe one way and a vice president in an opposing party that is total opposite in political thinking. Obviously, you can see this would be very difficult to get anything done in your government. For example, you could have a Democrat president with the Republican vice president which is the current situation. This is why our government in the Philippines is so chaotic.

Currently, there is a dictator and brutal president. Our president term last for six years as compared to the US 4 years term. In his first year our President promised to control illegal drugs which is a serious problem in the Philippines. Illegal drugs use is very rampant and there are all kinds of drug dependents and users going on in the Philippines. The problem is he went after the low-hanging fruit, the people that were using drugs and not the Distributors or dealers. Those caught are not imprisoned or go through any justice system as one would in US, they're killed with no due process. They are just executed, tortured, shot whatever. It is scary. I worry about my family there. Once arrested the Philippines you don't return to your family unless you can pay people off.

What about pharmacies and access to medicines?
Yes, we have pharmacies and you can get medication. You have to be able to pay cash and you can get any meds you want except for habitual narcotics. You don't have to have a prescription. It's pretty amazing that you can buy medicines without a written prescription and you can get them when needed and its necessary.

How is shopping and access to merchandise?

It's funny but the malls in the Philippines are fancier than anything you have here in the US. It's amazing. We have the *Mall of Asia* which is just beautiful. I don't think you have anything like it here. It's like one huge Rodeo Drive of all the most expensive commodities in the world in one mall. Privately owned and run by the Chinese corporation and not by the government. Majority of businesses in the Philippines is totally run by Chinese business tycoons. They own the Mall of Asia, and other majority of shopping malls all throughout the Philippines. The Chinese own a lot of businesses in the Philippines. Originally when the Chinese came to the Philippines, they were not allowed to be citizens and run a business. Now majority of businesses really is run by the Chinese capitalists and investors. They actually help run our government business sectors and support anyone running for government office that will patronize and protect their business interest.

Tell me about eating out in the Philippines

Our restaurants and food ranges from street vendors two very high-end restaurants. You will find it all in the Philippines. Food is important. It's like an island community and the type of food you would find there, like in Hawaii or Thailand or somewhere like that where all types of food are available.

What are your perspectives coming from the Philippines to becoming a US citizen?

When I came to the US my perception changed. As I mentioned to you, I studied American history and I knew English quiet well. Opportunities given to legal immigrants and Americans are just amazing. You know where you're given talent is going. You can get an education; you can build on your skills and in doing so you know you're going to progress. You will succeed progress and succeed if you work hard using your areas of expertise. That's not the case in the Philippines. This is what Nick taught me; if you have skills and you have a very good work ethic you can get ahead in the US. I needed something to do when he was deployed. I was bored because I'm used to working. I got a job working at the Navy Exchange. I was in Customer

Service and I worked myself up to supervisor. I took online classes paid by the Navy to get my degree. I wanted to use my background in Behavioral Science and it has been very worthwhile. I never felt held back in any way. People would ask me if I was Chinese, Japanese, Thai whatever, they just didn't know. They would comment on how good my English was. I learned English and Japanese in the Philippines. I spoke it well and I didn't have a strong accent so they never actually asked me if I was Filipino. I took four years of English in college and I studied English all through High School. Most of the Filipinos know how to speak English. Often Thai, Korean, Japanese, Chinese are actually trying to catch up speaking English. I think the Philippines was way ahead when it comes to proficiency in English.

Our dream was to move to California and become homeowners. To work and live away from the base. We first lived in San Diego and bought some property in La Jolla in 1991. My daughter Christina had already been born. Then we moved from San Diego to Port Hueneme/Oxnard area where we live today. We fell in love with the area and with the weather. We bought a second home here the one we live in now. We both worked our tails off to be able to pay for the down payments and mortgages. We wanted to enjoy and work to share our American dream with each other. We truly feel like we are living the American dream and are so happy that we accomplished all this. In 1994 Nick retired and went back to school. With the Navy he was a chief financial petty officer and was in charge of the Navy's payroll so he had a lot of responsibility and a really great position. He used his GI Bill to go back to school and studied accountancy and then he worked for the local IRS. He received a second retirement in October 2010 and passed on, in December 15th 2014, one of the saddest days of my life.

The other very sad day in our lives was 9/11. I was getting ready for work in Oxnard. I could not believe it as it is happening and watching it on television. I could not believe anybody could attack the United States like that. An act of terror! Nick was already retired when this happened. It was the saddest moment in my life experience. I recall our daughter Christina asked us if we are watching a movie when she saw the plane hit the towers.

Nick and I lived our American dream. Christina, our daughter and I still read our love letters to each other on our anniversary. I feel blessed to be an American citizen and thankful for all this country has given to both me, Nick and our daughter Christina. I am still sad he is no longer with me.

The word "racism" is like ketchup. It can be put on practically anything—and demanding evidence makes you a "racist."
—Thomas Sowell

CHAPTER 16

Mostly is it the loss which teaches us about the worth of things.
—Arthur Schopenhauer

If you want to be successful, it's just this simple. Know what you are doing. Love what you are doing. And believe in what you are doing.
—Will Rogers

RIMMANAPUDI, INDIA
Interview with Rama Koganti October 14, 2021

Though most of the interviews conducted in Coming to America *have been local and in person, I have been contacted by others outside the area who felt their stories supported my intent and would be of interest. An acquaintance reading* Coming to America *in* Citizen's Journal *shared Rama's contact information believing it would benefit readers and present a possibly different perspective about India. The follow-*

ing interview was conducted via internet and phone.

Rama, where were you born? Country, town?
I was born in India, Rimmanapudi, a small village, in Southern India. The closest large metropolitan area would be Hyderabad, known as the Silicon Valley of India. **(Bangalore is also known as the Silicon**

Valley of India due to its promotion of the IT sector). I left India to continue my education at about 24 years of age.

Tell me about growing up in your country and any comparisons to US if applicable.

I grew up in a middle-class family in India. My father was a farmer, and my mother is a housewife. My mother raised 4 children. I was the 3rd child in my family

I went to a private school from 1st grade to 5th grade and public school from 6th grade to 10th grade (there was no kindergarten concept in public schools in India then). You will have to sit on uncomfortable wooden chairs whole day. Up to 5th grade, we had only one teacher and he teaches all subjects (for all 5 years)

From 6th grade to 10th grade, I attended a public school. It was a change for me to see different teachers for different subjects

In India, after 10th grade we had to decide math, or biology, commerce/economics, or history majors. I chose Math to purse my passion in Engineering.

(Author's note: The thread on education and making a specific choice early on appears similar to interviews with those from the UK and may tie back to their history.)

Did you travel to other countries prior to coming to US?

I never went to other countries prior to Canada. My first trip after graduation was to go Canadian University known as Concordia University. However, throughout my career I have traveled and experienced countries such as England, Sweden, Brazil, China throughout Europe and Central America.

What were your experiences in school, in the college educational system in your native country?

After 12th grade, I attended my undergraduate degree in Mechanical Engineering in India. It was a great experience. It was not a semester system as you have in the US. We had to remember 7 to 8 subjects and we had to take the tests at the end of the year. There was no cheat sheet concept in India.

(Author's note: I mentioned to Rama that that is a more recent concept in the US education system. When I attended school, there were no cheat sheets or calculators allowed in any class. I think Rama was a bit surprised by this. The US education systems depend on states and districts and have changed due to changing philosophies.)

Only for Design engineering course, are we are allowed to take in design formula book and only the formulas. All the tests were closed book tests. All the test papers were graded by different college professors to avoid any favoritism to students. For every subject, we had to pass the lab and theory subject. If we are not humble with the professor, you can forget about your lab test.

I worked as a site engineer after my under graduation at an industrial construction company. After one year of my work, I decided to pursue my graduate studies overseas.

When did you come to the US?
I applied to Universities in US and Canada. Concordia University in Montreal, Canada offered me scholarship for my graduate studies. I came to Canada in 1990. I worked as a Research Assistant at Concordia while I was studying my graduate studies in Mechanical Engineering. I received my first Master's degree in Mechanical Engineering. I really enjoyed my work at Concordia University as it gave me an opportunity to think about my interest in advance research and engineering which I pursue after my graduation from Concordia University

I decided to pursue my second master's in Industrial Technology at Eastern Michigan University in Michigan, US. I moved to the US in 1993 and I completed my requirements by 1994 to work in the industry. My first job was at an automotive supplier company in Michigan. After one year, I was hired at Ford Motor Company as a Research Engineer to work on Electric

Vehicle in 1995 to meet California mandate of zero emissions by 2000. My job was to develop an advance manufacturing process using lightweight composite materials to build a lighter vehicle. This was my dream job.

I asked Rama if he always had a passion to work in the automobile industry.

Yes, it was always my passion, even in India as I studied mechanical engineering. I loved to fix and repair things, mostly bicycles, Mopeds, and scooters very common in India. I knew from a very young age what I wanted to do.

Why did you want to come to the US? Have you become a US citizen?

The US is way ahead in advanced technologies. My dream job was to work in Automotive Engineering. That was my motivation to come to USA.

I got my Green Card in National Interest Program which is considered a fast pace program, based on my Research Work at Ford Research and Innovation Center, within a month and I became a US Citizen by 2006.

How do you perceive the US today as compared to when you first came here? (Especially during these times of change)?

My impression remains the same. It is a great country with great opportunities. Generally, you are recognized based on your talent. That is true for the company I worked at also: Ford Motor Company. You are recognized based on your talent and level of work.

Are your parents and family here or in your Country?

My both parents are in India. They visited me few times and it never interested them to remain here regarding the cultural and language aspect. My brother lives in San Diego so I do have family here.

How does your family/friends perceive the US?

They perceive US is a great country.

Do you see parallels of things happening in your country, compared to the US? Good and bad?

India is growing technologically. There are many opportunities now that did not exist when I graduated. Many young Indians work for multi-National companies and they were making decent salaries (generally $1500 to $10000 per month). These companies were not in India when I was growing up. When I worked in India, my salary was $100/month.

Opportunities are much more prevalent in US than anywhere in the world, especially India. I grew up in a caste system in India being Hindu. Yes, it still prevails. I was born in a higher caste/. That is how the government labelled my caste. It is a very complex subject whether jobs or educational admission should be based on reservations (caste system) or based on their economic conditions of the family. Though majority of the lower caste people are economically challenged, and hence the Government allocated the Government jobs based on the caste system (to bring lower caste people to the normal level). My chances were lower to get a job and private industries opportunities were also very limited, at that time, hence I had to move to North America for better opportunities. *(See Chapter 6 for varying perspective on India).*

Do people own guns in your country? Did they ever, and were they confiscated?

Only rich people can own guns in India. They have to apply and complete lots of documents to get a gun.

How does the education system work? How is it paid for?

I did my Graduate studies in Canada. It is a great country. I got a scholarship and the University paid my tuition fee and living expenses

See Rama's previous input on education.

How does the public health and medical system work?

The public health care system in India is terrible. Even today. You go to the public health care system only if you are desperate and many are. They have nothing to offer and their doctors are not great. All good doctors go into private care or to the bigger private hospitals. I have never gotten medical care in India and never visited a government operated hospital. In the US it is so much different. I worked in a County hospital in Texas in Tarrant County so I am familiar with medical care. The hospital provided excellent care and it was free to those who were economically challenged.

Explain what you mean by freedom and liberty.

In general, I believe most educated people coming from democratic countries can openly say what they want. You can speak your mind. You can criticize the government policy or ruling. However, if you make any personal allegations (rude comments) on the ruling party leaders, you can actually be arrested.

India is going through growing pains. Many of its leaders are not educated though I can't put a number to it, and become leaders only due to hierarchal structure. So, if one speaks out against them on social media they can be silenced and arrested.

India is trying to move away from the caste system. In my opinion jobs should go to those that are in financial need or economically challenged rather than to one in a higher caste but that is not how it works in India. In the US, I do not see any disparity among races or religions or beliefs. US does not care, all things considered. The opportunities are there and if you are willing to work for them you can achieve. At least this is what I experienced.

Author's note as of 2022 India ranks one of the most dangerous countries in the world for women (see Chapter 6) and India's current treatment of minorities including Muslims and Christians and other religious groups is eroding their recent successes (Foreign Policy.com Dec 30, 2021) and 'seriously backsliding' according to World Report 2022.

Describe the religions of your country. Is there religious freedom, or have you seen any persecution?

By birth I am a Hindu. I practice Hinduism today. India has religious freedom and they allow many religions to practice in India. People are free to choose their religion.

I did not see persecution. I think India allows all religious practices. There are many Muslims and Christians and many are friends. People are free to choose. There are pockets of prejudice. It is not perfect, but think much unrest is politically motivated.

What things do you like most about the US?
People are very kind and philanthropic in general. The Country offers opportunities to everybody. It is up to the individual person how they will receive it. America is the land of opportunity. I have traveled throughout Europe, Asia and Central America and seen firsthand. America is by far the best. Americans are philanthropic, more than most.

I have worked for Ford Motor Company and did work for the US Army for a couple years in White Sands, New Mexico. I was proud to work for them and understand the Army culture and the sacrifices soldiers and their families make to serve this Country.

What thing do you miss about your country?
After spending 32 years in North America. I miss my friends and families. I try to spend time with my friends and families whenever I visit India.

What do you dislike most about US?
Social Media, guns, and drugs. They are spoiling the younger generation. I am fine with social media to use to communicate, however, people are spending enormous time on social media and I think it is damaging especially to young people and many studies exist to prove that.

What similarities do you see between the two countries and/or other countries you have been to?
Cultures are different and yet democratic values are very similar. In India, children take care of their parents in general. This is an expectation from your parents in India. I would not say it is happening to every family.

In the US parents are given to nursing homes and they have a terrible experience with loneliness, depression, etc. at the nursing homes.

How does your country's market economy work? Largest industry, agriculture, imports, and exports?
India is generally doing well in technology, commerce, agriculture, manufacturing and IT.

Does your country secure its borders? Do you think that it is a sovereign right of a country to protect its citizens? Can someone just come in from some country and take up residence in your country?
I do not know of anybody who can do this in India. If somebody marries an Indian, they can become Indian Citizen. But I am not sure if India has a permanent residence or Green card equivalent. I am not aware of this.

Can you describe some incidents or person experiences that happened in US that would be different in your country or vice versa?
My supervisors Adrian Elliott and Matt Zaluzec at Ford Motor Company recommended me to lead many visible programs at Ford Motor Company. It would not happen in India, at least 30 years ago. Now things are getting better in India because of global exposure. For my surprise, they created the innovation bug in my mind and I do not see that innovative culture in India as much as we see here. They nominated me for many awards at Ford Motor Company. I was co-recipient of Henry Ford Technology Award in 2006 and 2007. This is the highest recognition that anybody can get. I have received two years in a row for my work on Ford GT (Supercar) and Ford 150/250 vehicles. I also received Society of Automotive Engineers Henry Ford II Award for Excellence in Automotive Engineering. The Indian system is very hierarchical, and you have to please the superiors to be recognized.

Are you glad to be in America? Why or why not?
I am very glad to be in America. My wife 'Madhuri Koganti, also from India is a successful Neurologist. My son Kireet Koganti is attending his final year medical program at Texas A&M University and my daughter, Avani Koganti, is applying for her undergraduate programs. This country gave me and my family so much and I am very glad to be in USA.

Rama, what is your take on things you see happening in the US now as compared to when you first came here?
My opinions are things in US are becoming more politically extreme. Moving to two extreme positions. Did I see this when I first came here? Maybe, or possibly I was just too involved in my work or too far down the 'food chain' to know. But I saw the Bush and Clinton and Obama presidencies and things appeared more diplomatic. This is just my opinion. Everything seems to be very polarizing now.

For example, the questioning of science and the COVID vaccine. I find if the science says the vaccine is required then people should be vaccinated. You can't choose which side of the science you are going to follow. If you follow or believe the science, then get the vaccine. I believe one should follow the rules based on the science and evidence. If you don't believe in science, then don't go to a hospital, don't drive a car, or don't take a flight. I respect people's choices, either religious or their personal choice.

I posed to Rama that many Americans may not oppose the vaccine, but based on our Constitution and freedom to choose, being mandated to get the vaccine puts a different perspective on the vaccine for some. It was no longer science, now it was politics.
I can see that.

Rama kindly provided a brief list of accomplishments of which he is very proud. Rama also mentioned that the Ford Motor Company does not give their Prestigious Awards lightly, and he is grateful to have received two.

- I have 5 US patents (and many in pending)

- Published over 100 publications

- Chairman for international Mechanical Engineering Congress in 2015

- Currently, active Vice-Chair for Society of Automotive Engineers

- Received two Henry Ford Technology Awards (from Ford)- Prestigious Award in Ford Motor Company

- Received Henry Ford Award from Society of Automotive Engineers (SAE)

- Received numerous Awards at Ford Motor Company

- Worked briefly at US Army/DoD and received a US Army Civilian Award

CHAPTER 17

Freedom is never more than one generation away from extinction. We didn't pass it to our children in the blood stream. It must be fought for, protected, and handed on for them to do the same, or one day we will spend our sunset years telling our children and our children's children what it was once like in the United States where men were free.
—Ronald Reagan

We don't let them have ideas. Why would we let them have guns?
—Joseph Stalin

It's easier to fool people than to convince them that they have been fooled.
—Mark Twain

TEHRAN, IRAN
Interview with Hengameh Kazemi
Oct 26, 2021

Where were you born? Country, town?
I was born and raised in Tehran, Iran. Tehran is the capital of Iran where I grew up and finished high school. Tehran is the largest city in Iran. My mother is from Tehran also but her parents lived in a city called Yazd. My dad was born in Qazvin and grew up in Rasht (**known as the "City of Rain"**) but moved to Tehran when he was seven or eight years old. My husband jokes that all Iranians are from Tehran.

I have two siblings, both of whom live in Sweden now but we all went to high school in Tehran. I moved to the US 43 years ago and have been back visiting Iran only one about 37 years ago.

I can tell you; times and customs have changed. During my grandparents and my parents time the custom of marriage is very different than here. You don't have a girlfriend. My father just saw my mother on a train and he fell in love. That is rare that you get to see the girl before you're married. My dad had to ask my grandmother if he could marry her. The girl's parents are the ones you need to get permission from. My mother never saw him until he asked her mother to marry him. The whole ceremony of marriage is complex.

Tell me about growing up in your country. Comparisons to US if applicable.
Before he got married, my dad was a columnist for a Russian owned newspaper in Iran. He wrote mainly in Farsi.

I asked if he was a journalist, and Hengameh said no. He was more of a columnist.
The columns he wrote were mainly on business and economics. The paper he wrote for was very International and they would attend many international get-togethers. When he got married to my mom many things changed. He went from being an international columnist to an accountant. He thought this was a better fit for a family.

My mom was a tailer first and later a beautician. **Photo removed due to copyright.** "A scene of a hair salon you would no longer expect to see in Iran - but even after the Islamic Revolution, hairdressers continued to exist," says Prof Afshar. "Nowadays you wouldn't see a man inside the hairdressers - and women would know to cover up their hair as soon as they walked out the door. Some people may also operate secret salons in their own homes where men and women can mix." (BBC News, Feb 2019) Tailoring was way too much for her. She once got her hair done by a beautician and paid a great deal of money for it. When she came home my father hated it and asked her to redo it her way. That incident got her thinking about becoming a hair stylist herself which she signed up for the following week. To clarify, being a beautician was not considered a prestigious position for our family. In my grandmother's view, you might as well be street girl. Education means everything in our circle of family and it always trumps money.

When I was going to school during Shah's regime, we could wear whatever we chose, study what we wanted, we had many successful female doctors, judges and scientists. We had freedom of religion and although in Islam a man could have up to 4 wives and many temporary wives, legally, men could only have one wife. I never knew anyone who had more than one wife until the regime changed. Since the regime change, that law was changed and now there are many men who have more than one wife.

When I was attending school, we had many fun activities similar to US. We had annual school talent shows where my aunt for instance did a Persian dance. We had parties where we gather at friends' houses and dance through the night. There were ski resorts, bowling allies, and skating rinks where girls and boys were able to attend together. There were several bars and discos where alcohol was served for those over 21 years of age. After the revolutions, slowly but surely, these were taken away by having male, female gathering separately. Women were no longer allowed to sing or dance if men were present. All of the movies, TV shows and music concerts where women were not properly (religiously) covered were forbitten. Alcohol of any sort was forbitten and discos with bars were closed down.

Did you travel to other countries prior to coming to the US?

My parents had traveled extensively. The year before I was supposed to go to Sweden to continue my education, my mother and sister traveled to Sweden. However, US was my first trip outside of Iran. I have since traveled to quite a few countries since then and on each trip, I find myself being grateful for living in US.

My dad went to Austria and Italy and traveled a great deal through Europe. This is after my mother and he had traveled a great deal in the past. My dad went to visit an aunt living in Austria. We have family and friends that live all over Europe so it was not unusual for them to travel to see these friends and family. We also had an aunt in Sweden. On his last trip my dad got very sick and he was hospitalized in Sweden. As an accountant he was extremely worried about the cost. He was always very cost-conscious man. When he got out of the hospital, it was a long stay he was very fearful of what the cost would be. He asked them what do I owe you they told him nothing! He was so happy. You understand Sweden is considered a socialist country and this was a socialist program.

Also, Sweden and Iran have a long-standing relationship. Sweden built many ships for Iran and Iran was always buying these ships. My dad felt that would be a great job for my brother but you had to be able to speak Swedish. So, my dad came home from Sweden, packed my brother up and shipped him off to Sweden to learn the language and go to school. Dad's thinking was even if he didn't finish school, he would still have the language and he would be able to have a successful career. My brother was about 17 or 18 years old. My brother fell in love with Sweden, never finished college but he did learn the language. He never worked in the shipbuilding business. My dad was upset that he never finished college.

What were your experiences in school, college educational system in your native country?

I happened to be ahead in school. Studying at Tehran University in 1977: While many women were already in higher education at the time of the revolution, the subsequent years saw a marked increase in the number attending university. This was in part because the authorities managed to convince conservative families living in rural areas to allow their daughters to study away from home."

"They tried to stop women from attending university, but there was such a backlash they had to allow them to return," says Baroness Haleh Afshar, a professor of women's studies at the University of York who grew up in Iran in the 1960s.

"Some educated people left Iran, and the authorities realized in order to run the country they needed to educate both men and women." (BBC News, 8 Feb. 2019)

I graduated high school at sixteen and was planning to go to Sweden also for school. In Iran you don't have your own passport when you're under

18. I was on my father's passport to travel. This is when we planned for me to go to Sweden for continuing education. Then my dad passed away and I was unable to go. I stayed in Iran and took the National Test where you have to choose a field of study and I flunked. In Iran the National Test, based on your scores decides the school that you would attend.

With my dad's passing, and failing the college entrance exam which was only offered once a year, I decided to leave Iran. I started researching other countries, I chose not to go to Sweden as I didn't want to learn Swedish. I also discarded Germany, as I didn't like the language. France was too expensive and England required two years of English before I could be accepted at any university. I also found US was more than welcoming as long as I could pay for out of state tuition and living costs. I went to Milton College for a year, and transferred to UWM (University of Wisconsin, Milwaukee) before I dropped out for a year and got married. I later finished my accounting degree in Seattle, Washington.

Why did you want to come to the US? Or did you want to come to the US?
You had to comprehend English before you would be accepted into most Countries' university systems. I looked at England, France and Germany also, however, they did not seem to have what I needed so I started looking at the US. US had less requirements as long as you could pay the high tuition. I started by contacting an agency in Tehran, where the appropriate paperwork was completed and I was accepted in Colorado and Texas. With that, I was able to apply for student visa. However, instead of Colorado or Texas, our family friend, suggested I go to Chicago where he picked me up and took me to a small private college in Wisconsin where I was able to sign up for classes immediately.

Although I had a student visa from two universities in US, the flights were limited as US had asked its citizens to leave Iran.

I came to US in 1978, while there were US hostages here in Iran, so there were already some tensions. However, compared to now, those were the good days. US was working with the new regime in Iran to work things out and get the hostages back which happened right after the US election of Ronald Ragan.

I left Tehran within the three-day period when the Shah had left and Khomeini had not come to Iran yet. I recall purchasing my ticket to Chicago, in a black market under a foreign name. Once on the plane, I was among mostly Americans who were fleeing Iran. Luckily, I sat next to a very nice middle age American. He was very familiar with Iran and its customs. He took me under his wings and gave me a great deal of advice about going to Chicago.

During this trip we got stranded in Holland for three days due to bad weather conditions in Chicago. The airlines put us up in a very nice hotel. Back then it was much nicer to fly. The planes were beautiful and how they treated you was great. The first night at the hotel, we were having dinner and I met another young American. He sat at our table where I was sitting with my friend from the airplane. I did not speak English very well and this new gentleman was asking me questions about where I was headed and going to school. Suddenly the man who took me under his wing said we have to leave right now. I was not sure what was going on but he was very insistent that we have to leave now so I somewhat trusted him and we left dinner. He told me I was naive and because I did not understand the language the man was asking me to stay with him when I got to Chicago. He shared that many American men can be really terrible but he said I had to grow up and if I don't understand the language I need to ask. I need to tell them I do not understand. He was teaching me all the way and when to play by Iran rules and when to play by American rules.

Our family friend in Chicago picked me up at the airport. Next day, we headed to the private college in Milton, Wisconsin where he knew the foreign advisor. I signed up right away and started college without knowing any English. The US currency at the time was 7 toman to $1.00. Today that rate is 30,000 Toman to $1.00. *(The toman is the super unit of the official Iranian currency, the rial. One Toman is equal to ten rial.)* Also, what I discovered when I got to this country, I realized my high-school level of training was much higher than most of the education here in the US. Since I already knew the material, I concentrated on taking math and chemistry in college to help me learn English. I even taught calculus in my second year of college as a tutor. The education level at college was so far below in the US, compared to what I had studied in Iran. I had no problem passing them even without speaking the language.

Have you become a US citizen?

My husband and I were married about 5 years when we had taken an overseas trip and were coming back. At the airport, my husband took only a few minutes to clear the boarder where as it took me well over 2 hours. Once through the line, I decided, to become a citizen where I would also be allowed to vote. I started the process of becoming a citizen through the naturalization by the US government.

I immediately married a guy from Chicago. He lived in Palm Springs and I lived in Wisconsin. I was about 19 years old. Within a short time of our marriage, he decided he wanted a divorce. He however, found he would be disinherited if he got a divorce so he wanted me to ask for the divorce. I did not have a green card and he had never applied for a green card for me. This was a problem. If I got divorced, I would be deported. I married some-one else only for the green card. He agreed, and that was 40 years ago. We went to a courthouse in Vancouver. At this time in the US, it was relatively easy to get a green card. It took about 6 months. The problem was finding my records. There was reciprocity with Oregon and Seattle. We were told to go to one place and then another. My mother-in-law actually contacted some US Senators so they could find my files. My records were found in with the illegal Mexicans papers in the basement or the courthouse. We were married a couple years and by then I finished school. My new husband and I decided to stay together.

When we decided to marry, we had to do it the Muslim way. This is what my mom insisted on. My new husband had to be Muslim. He wasn't Muslim but he didn't care so he changed and became a Muslim to marry me. I found a mosque in Seattle where we could get married. Again, this was something my mom insisted upon. My husband had already been mar-ried and he was paying child support. In between all this Muslim wedding business, I had also been in a very bad accident. I left school for a while. It seemed like my accident took about three months being hospitalized so it caused some delays.

Describe the religions of your country. Is there religious freedom? Do
you think that is important?

While growing up, we had freedom of religion where we had churches,
mosques, synagogues, and …. and no one was forced to pray. After the
revolution, however, everyone was forced to be Muslims, even if it meant
pretending to be one. Friday prayers became mandatory! A lot of people
who actually believed in God have now become atheists all due to the pressure from being forced to the religion. My husband was a presbyterian and
he changed to Muslim to satisfy my mother's wishes. In contacting the
mosque, it took a great deal of communication and back and forth calling
to get with somebody. I was told I could get married there and I would just
have to donate to the mosque and it was up to me to decide how much I
wanted to donate. We decided on $100. Also, we were told we needed wit-
nesses. I asked an American friend and her boyfriend to be my witnesses.
We traveled to the mullah's house, at his direction, as the mosque was being
used. This was to get all the approvals and be married. When the mullah
saw my blond, blue-eyed friends he said 'they cannot come into my house.
They are not Muslim.' It was never mentioned that the witnesses had to
be Muslim. I do not approve of this type of religiosity. So, the mullah of
the mosque, called his friends to be our witnesses. While at his home he
told me that my husband to-be had to go into the shower and speak special
words under the shower. He read to him what to say from the Quran. 'Now
you are Muslim. My husband did not understand and said I already took
a shower but they insisted that he go and take a shower and whisper these
words from the Quran while showering. All of a sudden multiple Muslims
showed up to witness our ceremony. They had been at some other ceremony.
When all the work was done and we were supposed to be allowed to get
married I asked him how much? He said to write a check for $200. I was
furious. I had already been told I could make the decision on how much I
would donate. We had chosen $100. When I left his home, I immediately
stopped payment on the check. My mom called me from Iran about 2 years
later and said that a mullah had contacted her and said I had an outstanding
bill to his mosque, that he needed to talk to me he said he would sue me in

the US. I had no proof of my marriage. I figured we didn't need anything. I was pretty young.

My husband is a retired Marine. He was in the Marine Corps for 20 years and used his military benefits to go back to school. That is how we met in college. At 32 I decided I wanted children. I had not wanted children before. Now I have a daughter and she is 26 years old. My husband already had daughters and we have a marvelous family.

I trained to be an accountant and I was going to sit for my CPA (certified practicing accountant) exam and was told I make more money than I would being a CPA. I continued to work as a controller and an accountant. My husband needed some medical help and I worked hard and then took a break. Now I volunteer and I do everything. I volunteer for The Villages Clark County which is a nonprofit organization directed to help seniors to stay in their homes and active in their own neighborhood.

The concept, I'm told came from an aging neighborhood in Boston where neighbors decided to help each other and it worked so well that it was registered as a nonprofit and now it's being suggested for everyone interested in various states. We provide assistance for the elderly to maintain their standard of living in their own homes. For instance, currently, I provide in home help and assistance in their day to day living. Currently, I'm volunteering to read the book that was authored by a gentleman who is now blind. This book was used for the PhD program at Portland State University. He is 84 years old and full of life.

I also volunteer for *The Garden* which is owned by Seventh-Day Adventist. We grow vegetables for the low income and the homeless. In addition, I also work for the Vancouver Lake Crew which is a nonprofit organization through University of Portland, getting juniors involved in water activities. It provides a great deal of camaraderie paddling around the lake.

Do you see parallels of things happening in your country compare to the US? Good and bad?

The most distinctive parallel I can think of is the civil unrest as the people of this country take sides. For instance, the political climate in US where the boarders go from no illegal immigrants allowed to everyone is welcome regardless of legal status. This is occurring although, the laws haven't changed. Also, in my opinion, people as a general rule were much more understanding and believed more in community and helping your neighbors than they do now.

The political unrest has been very apparent over the past 42 years since the revolution. As different groups come to certain power, the power pressure goes on. So far, the religious groups have been the strongest as they are in power by changing the laws as they feel gets them to what they want. Iraqi's whom we were in war with for eight years, are not welcome to the country with open arms. Same with Chinese as they're now investing millions in the country. When I was growing up in Iran, all of the neighbors knew each other and we as children play in the streets from sun up to sun down sometimes as it was safe. However, these days, everyone is afraid of being reported by their neighbor so the community style is disappearing.

My sisters and brother live in Sweden and they love it there. My sister and mom went through the unrest in Iran while Iran and Iraq had their eight-year war. Afterward, my sister and Mom traveled to Sweden for a visit when my brother helped my sister stay in Sweden. There was a time we didn't have to cover ourselves. Many of the religions in Iran are now impacted. Many religious groups have to pretend that they are Muslim. Christians and Jews all pretend to be Muslim. The mullahs are just stealing everyone's' money. I feel so sorry for young girls now in Iran. They sell their parts of their bodies; they sell their kidneys and many of them have become prostitutes just to get some money. ***(I have heard this same report from a local Iranian woman friend.)***

I went back to Iran around thirty-even years ago and everyone was unhappy and they're even more unhappy. There was happiness when I was growing up there. This unhappiness is even worse today. The Chinese and Arabs are all coming into Iran. They use the girls. In the very religious city, many Muslims come to visit from China and Arab countries. The Chinese government has moved into the southern part of Iran. The Chinese and Arabs take all the jobs.

Several in your family remain in Sweden and like it very much. Can you describe some of the similarities and differences with the US?
My preference to stay in US first and foremost is the language, considering English is the major language spoken in the world. I also appreciate knowing hard work is rewarded due to the capitalist nature of this country.

The medical services are more readily available in US than in Sweden. Due to Sweden's socialist status, there are too many red tapes to go through, to see a specialist for instance. Taxes are much lower here. The average tax rate in Sweden is around 45%. The one good thing in Sweden is that no one is left behind regardless of their status. However, for a hard-working person, I find US more rewarding.

Over the last 40 years, I've seen the changes Sweden has gone through as a socialist country where I see the country more of a socio-capitalist country. I believe in helping those who are willing to help themselves and only rely on the government assistance where needed.

Explain what you mean by freedom and liberty, or the pursuit of happiness.
While growing up in Iran, people and specially women had a freedom of choice in their religion, what they wore, to a large extent what they said, what they wanted to become when they grew up and a lot has now been lost. Women can no longer be judges for instance or hold a high office. They have to cover themselves as Muslims whether they are one or not. That means, even non-Muslims have to respect the Muslim religion and abide by their rules even though it's all pretenses. I was told Friday prayers have been made mandatory especially if the person wants to continue with schooling or get a job. When I was in Iran, most people, got their positions based on what they had learned in school, now it's which Mullah you know which as can be seen has hurt the country tremendously. For instance, there is a religious city called Ghom (***also spelled "Qom," "Ghom," "Ghum," or "Qum"***)

* where there is a lot of salt in the grounds and hills. A family friend was one of the engineers on that project and told me about the site. Due to the saltiness of the area, they have to pump the water into the city rather than diverting the water from elsewhere by building a dam. Unfortunately, the Mullahs who took over, decided "if God wants it, it will be ok"! So, the money was spent and the dam was built, limiting the water from going to the nearby city of Esfahan, through the hills. Shortly thereafter, not only was the water in Ghom* too salty, but Esfahan started having droughts, which to this day, has not come back to its original state.

I feel so sorry for many women now remaining in Iran. They have become more of a property than a person with feelings. In one embarrassing video I watched, one of the religious Mullahs in a mosque was comparing having a wife to having a camel and what to do to keep them subservient!

There are many unhappy married women who basically are at the mercy of their husbands. Divorce is very difficult as if there are any children in the family, the father gets the right to keep them. A lot of women either don't work or don't get paid as much as men due to the limitation of what they can and cannot do per the Mullah's rules. You really cannot get divorced because that means you're no longer a virgin and you should be a virgin to get married. Honestly, of everyone I've talked to, not a single person would have allowed Khomeini to come to Iran had they known what a corrupt regime it will be in the name of Islam. The Iranians would love to have a leader to follow and kick out the mullahs. The history has taught us over and over again, religion and politics simply do not mix well. The current mullah's have come to steal what they can financially, emotionally and spiritually with the rules they make up as they go along. That's something, I hope I never have to worry about living in US.

I am a female and I am an Iranian and I think Trump was on the right track. I may not have liked all the personal things he did or said but during the Obama years I was sickened about what was happening. I could not believe what he was doing when he sent all that money back to Iran. All Iranians knew what was going to happen to that money. It was not going to go to the Iranians. Now they are planning to extend their nuclear program. I like how Trump handled Iran. Iran needs a strong hand. I don't believe any of the American News anymore. Biden terrifies me! Trump was right on trade and on the sanctions and many of his programs.

People here need to travel to see what is going on in other countries. They need to see how other people have to survive. US citizens are so naïve to the rest of the world. I don't think the US military can even compete with Muslims who willingly strap bombs onto their bodies. How can the military compete with that? From what I've seen of the US military today, I'm afraid the standards have come down a lot when it comes to physical fitness and that in itself is a scary thought.

I've been very happy in this country knowing I can study what I want, be with who I want, work where I want, and can be myself and be as productive as I choose to regardless of my background.

CHAPTER 18

I feel that the American Dream can be achieved best in the Nordic countries, where every child no matter their background or the background of their families can become anything, because we have a very good education system. We have a good health-care and social welfare system that allows anybody to become anything. This is probably one of the reasons why Finland gets ranked the happiest country in the world.
—Sanna Marin, Finland's prime minister, to the *Washington Post*

The first lesson of economics is scarcity: there is never enough of anything to fully satisfy all those who want it. The first lesson of politics is to disregard the first lesson of economics.
—Thomas Sowell

HELSINKI, FINLAND
Interview with Milla Leino July 2021

Milla's interview was conducted via email, as she was leaving for Finland and would not return for several months. Verifications and corrections were made online. As of this writing Milla returned to Finland and now is located back in the US.

Where are you from, and when did you come to the US?
I was born in 1983 in Helsinki, Finland and came to US 2018.

Have you become a US citizen?
No.

Why did you want to come to the US? Or did you want to come to the US?
Me and my husband moved to US because of my husband's military orders. I had been living in Ethiopia since 2012 before moving to US. My husband and I met through common friends in Ethiopia in 2015, we were both working there at the time.

Above photo of me hiking in Simien Mountains national park in Ethiopia (7 months pregnant). I have been lucky to be able to visit some of the most beautiful places on this planet. Life in African cities can be very chaotic but when you leave the city, nature is just incredible.

How do you perceive the US today as compared to when you first came here (especially during these times of change)?
Since I've been here only for 3 years, I haven't seen a big change.

Ae your parents and family here or in Finland? How do they perceive the US?
My parents live in Finland. I'm sure my parents find US a fairly good place to live (keeping in mind I was living in Africa before moving here). They get their information mostly from news and sometimes we discuss some things together what is happening in this country. They have also visited me here.

Do you see parallels of things happening in your country compared to the US? Good and bad?

Like it is happening everywhere in the western world, also in Finland's far right political movement has unfortunately become stronger with racist undertones. On the other hand, there has been a strong countermovement too. At the moment, women lead all the five parties in the coalition government and the Prime Minister is 34-year-old woman, a mother of a 2-year-old girl.

Do people own guns in your country? Did they ever and were they confiscated?

Gun ownership in Finland is among the highest in the world, although crime rates remain among the worlds' lowest. According to some sources I researched online, the levels of gun ownership are very similar in Finland and US, about 35 percent of households having a firearm in both countries. But in Finland, the firearms tend to be hunting rifles and in US handguns. Moreover, in Finland guns tend to be located in hunting cabins or vacation homes, which are plentiful in Finland and Scandinavia.

You mentioned that you have free medical and education in Finland. That sounds great. How is it paid for?

Public healthcare in Finland is not free (unlike for example in UK), though charges are very reasonable. Public healthcare is the responsibility of municipalities (local government) and is primarily funded by taxation but also by patient fees.

In 2020-2021 the maximum out-of-pocket fee for treatment in primary health care ex. seeing a doctor at a health center, is €20.60 (around $24.50) this may be charged a maximum of three times per year. Fees for public healthcare have an upper limit per calendar year, beyond which clients are no longer required to pay. In addition, there is an upper limit on annual medicine expenses. In 2020 the threshold was €577.66 (around $686).

How does the education system work?

Education from pre-primary to higher education is free of charge in Finland. Schools up to the university level are almost exclusively funded and administered by the municipalities by taxation.

The education system in Finland consists of daycare programs (for babies and toddlers), a one-year "pre-school" (age six), a nine-year compulsory basic comprehensive school (age seven to age sixteen), post-compulsory secondary general academic and vocational education, higher education and adult education.

Finland has consistently ranked high in the PISA study, which compares national educational systems internationally. One of reason for the success is that the teachers are highly educated. Both primary and secondary teachers must have a master's degree to qualify. Teaching is a respected profession and entrance to university programs is highly competitive. A prospective teacher must have very good grades and must combat fierce opposition in order to become a teacher.

Municipalities are responsible for providing early childhood education and care for children under school age. The early childhood education and care is high quality and inexpensive. The fee is determined on the basis of the family's income and size and the time that the child spends. What I personally like about the Finnish early childhood education and cere system is that it focuses on teaching the kids to "learn how to learn". Instead of formal instruction in reading and math there are lessons on nature, animals, and the "circle of life" and a focus on materials-based learning. It is strongly believed that when children develop learning to learn as a life skill and see the real-life applications of the knowledge they gather, they will become lifelong learners. In other words, the children are given the opportunity to learn by playing and having fun and the teachers' job is to feed their natural curiosity for exploring new things.

The comprehensive school starts at the age of 7 and consists of 9 grades. At the end of the comprehensive school, each young person must apply for post-comprehensive school education. Compulsory education ends when the person reaches the age of 18 or when they complete an upper secondary qualification (high school or a vocational school). Graduates are eligible to apply for further studies at universities or universities of applied sciences. They are all tuition-free for students coming from EU/EEA countries and Switzerland. Non-EU/EEA students enrolling in English-taught degrees are required to pay tuition fees.

There are only few private schools, but I happened to go to one of them. When I was 8 years old my best friend was applying to German School, so I told my parents that I want to do the same. Hence, I took the test too and got in, and went to German School from 3rd to 9th grade.

How does the public health and medical system work?

The aim of Finnish health policy is to lengthen the active and healthy lifespan of citizens, to improve quality of life, and to diminish differences in health between population groups. The child mortality rate in Finland is one of the lowest in the world; the infant mortality rate is below 4%. The life expectancy for women is 81 years, for a man, 73 years.

Primary healthcare in Finland is described as follows: Finland is divided into some 450 municipalities. Each municipality is responsible for arranging healthcare for its inhabitants. Primary healthcare is provided by health centers established by a single municipality or jointly by neighboring municipalities. Municipalities have the right to buy services from other municipalities or from the private sector. Health center services include medical consultations and provision of dental care, preventive care and environmental healthcare. Health centers run maternity and child health clinics, and arrange school and occupational health services.

Finnish municipalities have switched from a primary healthcare system to a family doctor system. Each family doctor is responsible for about 2,000 patients. The aim is for a patient to be able to contact her or his doctor and have needs for treatment assessed within three working days. This system has proved very successful.

Benefits of long-term treatment relationships include a reduced need for hospital exams and reduced healthcare costs. Outpatient care is also provided by occupational and private healthcare units. Employers are under an obligation to arrange occupational healthcare for employees which can be arranged through municipal health centers or private practitioners.

About 4% of Finnish doctors work in occupational healthcare, offering both preventive services and primary healthcare.

Finland is divided into 20 hospital districts, each providing specialist consultation and care for its population. Local municipal authorities are responsible for funding specialist treatment for inhabitants of their areas. Each hospital district has a central hospital with departments for main specialties. Finland has five university hospitals. These provide the most advanced medical care, including highly specialized surgery and treatment for rare diseases. The university hospitals are also mainly responsible for the clinical training of medical students, and for medical research. In comparison with the situation in other countries, the number of hospital beds in Finland is fairly high.

Health services are available to all in Finland, regardless of their financial situation. Public health services are mainly financed from tax revenues; partly municipal, partly state tax. Central government's contribution to municipal healthcare is determined by population numbers, age structures and morbidity statistics. A number of other factors also affect its computation. Finland spends less than 7% of its gross national product on healthcare, one of the lowest among EU member states. The public sector finances 76% of total healthcare expenditure, users of services 20% and others 4%. Other contributors include employers, private insurance and benefit societies.

Private medical treatment is provided by municipalities and the state. Particularly in cities, many doctors, dentists, and physiotherapists offer private care. There are also a few small private hospitals. Only about 8% of Finnish doctors earn their living solely as private practitioners. However, about one third of doctors run a private practice in addition to working in a hospital or health center. Most private practitioners now work in group practices.

Everyone in Finland is covered by obligatory sickness insurance, funded through taxes by the state, municipalities, employers and the insured population. The sickness insurance scheme reimburses fees paid by patients to private doctors, costs of medicines prescribed, and transportation costs arising from treatment of illness. By far the greatest expenditure in relation to health insurance is compensation for sick leave and parental leave. All licensed Finnish doctors are covered by the reimbursement system, which is administered by the social insurance institution. (Source: https://healthman-agement.org/c/it/issuearticle/overview-of-the-healthcare-system-in-finland)

You mentioned that we in America don't have all the "crazy freedom" we think we do. Can you explain in what ways?

I guess the question of freedom depends on how you define it. I understand that for many, freedom means to be free FROM something, for example from government control. On the other hand, you can think freedom as being free TO something, for example everybody should have the chance to pursue better life for themselves. I think one of the problems in today's US is that the latter is not true anymore. According to statistics, US is not any more socially mobile. If you are born poor, there is higher and higher probability that you will stay poor. Here I would like to quote Finland's Prime Minister Sanna Marin. She told to The Washington Post: "I feel that the American Dream can be achieved best in the Nordic countries, where every child no matter their background or the background of their families can become anything, because we have a very good education system," Marin said. "We have a good health-care and social welfare system that allows anybody to become anything. This is probably one of the reasons why Finland gets ranked the happiest country in the world."

What things do you like most about the US?

My favorite thing in US is the amazing nature. There are so many different landscapes and natural habitats, everything from deserts to mountains to beaches. I like the multiculturalism too.

What thing do you miss most about your country?

I miss the most the ability to walk or bike anywhere (because of the sidewalks and designated biking routes in the cities), the public transportation system, and much cheaper and better mobile and Wi-Fi network services anywhere (in very remote areas too). In addition, I miss the security, no need to lock your house doors or fear to walk alone in the night.

What do you dislike most about US?
I don't like the gun violence and structural racism. In addition, I'm concerned of the growing socioeconomic polarization and income inequality. The women right's situation in some states makes me angry and very sad.

What similarities do you see between the two countries and or other countries you have been to?
In the end I find Finland and US very similar, life is more or less the same in these countries (compared to Ethiopia, where the real difference lies. Unlike Finland, Ethiopia has been under communist/socialist regime and only recently started to open up a little bit, though now the ongoing civil war has probably ended up any progress, sadly).

How does the Finnish market work? Largest industry, agriculture, imports and exports (if you know)?
Finland has a highly industrialized, largely free-market economy with per capita GDP almost as high as that of Austria and the Netherlands and slightly above that of Germany and Belgium. Trade is important, with exports accounting for over one-third of GDP in recent years. Finland is historically competitive in manufacturing, particularly in the wood, metals, engineering, telecommunications, and electronics industries. Finland excels in export of technology as well as promotion of startups in the information and communications technology, gaming, cleantech, and biotechnology sectors. Except for timber and several minerals, Finland depends on imports of raw materials, energy, and some components for manufactured goods. Because of the cold climate, agricultural development is limited to maintaining self-sufficiency in basic products. (Source: https://www.cia.gov/the-world-factbook/countries/finland/#economy)

Does Finland secure its borders? Can someone just come in from some country and take up residence in Finland?
If you want to move to Finland, you have to apply a resident permit based on work, studying or family ties, or if you are an asylum seeker, you have to apply asylum. If you're application is approved, you can stay.

Can you describe some incidents or personal experiences that happened in US that would be different in Finland or vice versa (to make story personal)?

When I had my baby, I was lucky to be working for the Finnish government at the time (in Ethiopia), because I had 10 months of employee paid parental leave. I could have returned to my job after my leave, but we had already moved to US before my son was born. Also, if we were living in Finland and having a baby there, my husband could share the parental leave with me. The new gender-neutral policy grants nearly seven months of paid leave to each parent, for a total of 14 months of paid leave.

Are you glad to be in America? Why or why not?

I am very happy to have the chance to live in America. I see the life as an opportunity to explore the world and get as many experiences as possible. I have had the chance to live in very different kind of places and meet people from all cultures and backgrounds. Every one of these experiences has taught me so much that I'm forever grateful for them. I don't know where we end up later in our lives but I'm looking forward to all the adventures that are waiting for us!

CHAPTER 19

The problem with socialism is that you eventually run out of other people's money.
—Margaret Thatcher

If you want to be successful, it's just this simple. Know what you are doing. Love what you are doing. And believe in what you are doing.
—Will Rogers

GREAT URSWICK, ENGLAND (UK)
Interview with Adrian Elliott, Oct 15, 2021

Where were you born? Country, town?
I was born in a farming community in Northwest England, an area called the Lake District. It is very rural. I lived in Great Urswick, a village with a population of about 1,000 people. As a child, I helped on the farms almost every day.

I was born in the 50's. My parents, with the aftereffects of the Second World War, worked long, hard hours to save for a home and the family, and were very frugal. They both worked for the pharmaceutical company (Glaxo), but also operated their own business selling milk and eggs, from the hens they reared. They worked both jobs so that they could afford to buy their home without taking a mortgage. These were the days when you didn't buy anything unless you could afford it.

My father lost three brothers and his father during WWII. He, himself, left school at the age of 14, working in a butcher's shop, before being conscripted into the Navy as a teenager. Whenever I asked him about the war, he would always say "war is futile". I remember that quote to this day. My parents were quiet and very practical. All clothes were repaired - not bought new. I loved the outdoors, whether it was helping the farmers or hiking, birdwatching, fishing and camping. I am the oldest of 4 boys. We would take annual vacations to different parts of the UK, not at all extravagant – staying in guest houses – and spending the time looking at historical and geographical sites. I remember that if it was raining it was pretty miserable. I appreciated my parents taking us away. I loved camping in my teens, and I have extended it into my adult life. During the COVID (corona virus disease 2019) pandemic, I have taken the opportunity to camp in many of the US National Parks.

During WWII, my father lived in the heart of London, which experienced significant bombing. For much of the war, he was in the Navy on a cruiser. The sister cruiser, operating with them in the Pacific, was sunk. My mother lived in a shipbuilding town in the North, which was a target for the bombing. She was moved, like many other children, to other towns as a safety precaution. There was a great deal of bitterness.

I recall that the need for steel was so great during the war that they had taken out the railings at my high school. There were many examples where they had taken metal to support the war effort. The railings were never replaced, and you can still see the metal stubs. I also remember my mother talking about the fact that sugar, butter, milk, and other products like this, were all very limited or rationed. Our diet during my childhood years was limited, and rather plain, with a great reliance on potatoes.

During my time in Secondary School, called Middle School in the UK, in the town of Ulverston, I did the bare minimum to get by. I was not particularly prepared and ashamed of my performance. However, I studied hard in university.

Tell me about growing up in your country. Use comparisons to US if applicable.

My teachers in Britain were generally good, but the ones I remember the best were the biology teachers. They gave us a very good, broad education, and challenged us to think. I enjoyed the passion of these teachers. I think this benefited me years later. It gave me an interest in biological sciences and biochemistry, which I pursued at university, but there wasn't a lot of work available in this field. I subsequently received my Master's at the University of Manchester, in polymer and fiber science. The adhesives, plastics and composites later helped me in the automotive industry with Rover Group and Ford Motor Company.

Did you travel to other countries prior to coming to the US?
Growing up, I didn't really travel anywhere outside of England and the annual vacations as a family were always within England. I don't have a lot of fun memories about these vacations, it was just good to get home and be able to hike and fish with friends, and work on the farms. After graduation from high school, I started to travel far more with friends from school and college. Other European countries, particularly France, Spain and Portugal were the primary destinations, but the aquamarine waters and expansive sandy beaches of the Greek Isles drew me and many other baby boomers, who enjoyed the opportunity to go 'au naturelle'; something that seems particularly alien in American culture.

What were your experiences in school, in the college educational system in your native country?
I went to a small elementary school in an adjacent village, there were only six students in the class: two boys and four girls. Academic achievements were not my priority. The teachers were the 'Old Guard', very strict and sticklers for the rules, employing corporal punishment for minor transgressions. You could get hit by a cane or measurement ruler just for holding a knife or fork incorrectly. School did not really challenge me, and I didn't work hard, but I was fortunate that due to natural intelligence I was awarded the book prize every year.

My lackadaisical attitude to education continued through secondary school, where a modicum of intelligence was not really enough to guarantee a place at university.

Tell me about your job/profession here as compared to your native country. When did you come to the US? Have you become a US citizen?
I came to the US in 1993 and became a citizen in 2001. It seemed like a long process, first obtaining a green card. The whole process took 7 to 8 years. There was massive amount of documentation and written work to become a citizen.

Why did you want to come to the US? Or did you want to come to the US?
It was never my intention to come to the US permanently. I worked in the US (Virginia Beach) in 1983 for several months, and thoroughly enjoyed my time as a footloose and fancy-free guy in my 20's. A couple of years later, I moved from the UK to Switzerland to work for Dow Chemical. On return to the UK, in 1993, I was asked by Ford Motor Company to come to work for them in the US. Having got married and had a child in Switzerland it was my intention to stay in Europe. I would have stayed, except the offer from Ford Motor Company was hard to decline.

How do you perceive the US today as compared to when you first came here (especially during these times of change)?
When I first arrived to the US I lived in Dearborn, just outside of Detroit, and I soon integrated into the society. I was hired for materials development and application at Ford, but there were so many other opportunities. I would have been comfortable to stay in Europe and I have to admit the crumbling concrete infrastructure of Metro Detroit was a bit intimidating and off-putting. Although it was a major move for me, with significant differences between the UK and the US, the R&D facilities at Ford were impressive and it was a major opportunity. I was effectively told 'here's your budget (a significant amount), this is what we want you to do, go ahead and do it. Just a wonderful challenge and it gave me so much flexibility. I had access to all the equipment I could possibly need, and I was allowed to hire my own team. I initially developed composite materials and the joining processes for vehicle body structures, but in time encompassed lightweight metals, such as aluminum, and high strength steels. It was state-of-the-art work, and I was respected and rewarded. I hired great people. The work

was published in technical journals, many of the applications and designs were patented, and I felt honored to be here.

Prior to Ford, I worked in an engineering process company called Furmanite International. I worked there for approximately 6 years, during which time (1986) I went to the US, as previously mentioned, and did a brief stint in Virginia Beach where I worked on sealants for the nuclear industry.

Are your parents and family here or in your country? How do your family and friends perceive the US?
My parents remained in England, and they would come to visit maybe once a year until about the year 2000. As they aged it became more difficult for them to travel. My friends like the United States a great deal and looked forward to annual visits.

Do you see parallels of things happening in your country compared to the US, good and bad?
Yes, a lack of tolerance for mass immigration, and in particular refugees from war-torn countries. The issues at the US-Mexico border are a topic of great debate, but a major influencing factor for the UK and Brexit was the free flow of immigrants into the country and the immediate access to benefits.

Do people own guns in your country? Did they ever and/or were they confiscated?
You can own a gun in England if you are a landowner or you belong to a gun club. To own a gun, you must go through a strict vetting process and keep the weapon under lock & key. There's very little hunting now – just on private land. I do not see the need to own a gun and feel that strict laws relating to ownership are essential.

How does the education system work?
You pay for your university education in the UK. I find the educational system there much better than in the US. On entering university, you to pick a subject (major) and pursue it for 3 to 4 years. I pursued a science degree. You can potentially change the major, but not as easily as you can

in the US. I think the UK has a good value system and recognizes good work. Even if the subject you choose is not ideal for you in England you are still able to accomplish something. It is to better yourself, so you still have an opportunity in that field.

I currently tutor high school chemistry students in my spare time, because of a shortage of experienced teachers locally. I find that the teachers in the US don't help the students to flourish. In university you can change subjects almost indefinitely, and so your education can drag on with no fixed time for graduation. There is the opportunity here to go at a slower pace, but I don't think that necessarily helps the students. They don't let you slow the pace down in England. I don't think the schooling system recognizes how imperative and serious education is for the future of their children

How does the public health and medical system work?

I would say the medical system (National Health System) is okay, but not ideal, in England. Some of the population now supplements the public health offering with private insurance. Many good doctors are leaning towards private practice If you have general medical ailments, Britain's public health system is fine but if you have something like cancer or broken legs or need a heart or kidney transplant or anything serious, it is not the greatest. It can take up to a year for some diagnoses and treatments and sometimes people don't have it a year.

Explain what you mean by freedom and liberty or the pursuit of happiness?

I have always felt that I was free in Europe, so I find it surprising when US citizens claim that they have more freedom. In the UK, I believed in free enterprise and was a strong supporter of Margaret Thatcher and felt of myself as a Conservative. I struggle in the US regarding the two (polarized) parties. Although a proponent of the corporate world and enterprise in general, I feel healthcare should be available to all, I am pro-choice, I am for sustainability of the environment and especially cannot condone drilling in Alaska. By default, I lean more towards the Democrats here. I feel free. I see freedom and I recognize that many, for instance in Afghanistan and Iraq do not have the luxury of freedom. Populations of most countries in the developed world have freedom, but there are always exceptions, such as much of the Chinese population, and especially the Uighurs. I don't see 'freedom' justifying the Capital Hill riot. As regards other significant movements, such as BLM, then they have a strong case, although I don't condone violence.

Describe the religions of your country. Is there religious freedom? Do you think that is important?

In Britain and most of northern Europe, there is religious freedom, but it is not really practiced anymore. Very few people go to church – probably equating to less than 10% in England. Of course, in southern areas of Europe, such as Italy and Spain, there's much more religious practice, but not so much in the European Union as a whole. Religion doesn't figure into daily life, and I feel most are agnostic and don't feel the need for religion. The difference between here and the US I see people talk about religious practices here and I find a lot of hypocrisy. They may not be the nicest people, but they regularly attend church. I was brought up to be very practical, with no reference to religion, and could never mention things like fate. I was told, for instance, that accidents had nothing to do with fate, just an error on the part of an individual or group.

My father was born a Methodist, but he really didn't practice it religiously. In later life, he would go to Easter socials but that's about it. I'm an agnostic. I was surprised at people that go to church in the US. I find them hypocrites. I think church becomes a habit and they are not the kind and generous people they proclaim themselves to be. I don't think we need religion to be fair or just. I think sometimes it's used just as a crutch.

What things do you like most about the US?

My career and being given so many opportunities. I was funded well, and I had a great deal of freedom to figure out what I needed to do. There was a great deal of recognition and the surroundings I had in my company were all supportive. There was very strong emphasis on technology. The freedom to do what you want, when you want. More significant opportunities here than most other places.

I love the beautiful scenic areas, particularly within the National Parks.

What do you miss about your country?

When I return to England, I hate the immediate smell, noise and congestion in and around the airport, and the difficulty of commuting anywhere near the big cities., but when I get out into the country and visit little pubs and cafes, I miss that camaraderie. I love the greenery and the little cottages, the atmosphere and little cafes. Everyone is out walking around villages. The openness is just welcoming. I feel content when visiting my brother. The atmosphere ingratiates the community feeling. In the US. land is so available and vast. You just can't take a bus somewhere or go downtown. I am in Florida near Cape Canaveral. When I moved here it was a new development, now it is sprawling humanity.

What do you dislike most about US?

The residential sprawl that develops without thought to community centers, pedestrian ways or public transport. I dislike the materialistic attitude, without a great deal of thought for sustainability.

I dislike the attitude and actions of the police in general. They no longer seem to be here to serve the community – I blame the qualification standards for entry and inadequate training thereafter.

What similarities do you see between the two countries and/or other countries you have been to?

I see many similarities between the UK and the US. The UK seems to parallel and follow what's trending in the US. Some of the differences relate to health care services. The UK has a National Health Service, and although a good standard, the wait for tests or vital procedures such as heart or cancer treatments can be excessive. Many friends are finding it necessary to get private health insurance to supplement the National Health System.

I find the US a more materialistic society. In England we only spent if we could afford it. When I came to US. I was astonished by how much people spend on things I don't consider essential, and things they replace frequently. I remained frugal for a long time, but now I seem to be falling into that same materialistic way. I have just retired and when I go to the UK now, I'm willing to buy more and eat out more.

It's so sad that in the US. so many are below the poverty line and yet the rest can just splurge and not save. The poverty line is less evident in the UK. In the fast-food industry, you're able to pay below minimum wage, while in the UK you are paid a more acceptable wage- although lower than many service jobs. Many of the lower paid roles have been taken by immigrants from Eastern Europe.

How does your country's market economy work? Largest industry, agriculture, imports and exports (if you know).
The economy in the UK is mainly a service industry with little heavy industry anymore, and relatively little in the way of manufacturing. We have OEMs (original equipment manufacturers) in the rail and aerospace industry, but we're primarily a service industry. Post Brexit, British manufacturers and producers are finding it far more difficult to sell to the EU (European Union). Britain is no longer the heart of the financial world, but still has major financial services, with companies such as Lloyd's of London, Barclays and HSBC (Hongkong and Shanghai Banking Corporation). Pharmaceuticals are still of significance with companies such as Glaxo Welcome and AstraZeneca. Tourism is still important to the country

Does your country secure its borders? Do you think that it is a sovereign right of a country to protect its citizens? Why or why not?
Yes, the UK has tightened up the border post Brexit. Although, there is a steady flow of refugees attempting to enter the country by sailing across the English Channel from France. Many are still being allowed entry, although more are being dispatched back to France.

A country has a sovereign right to secure its borders, but all countries have a responsibility to help refugees fleeing war or persecution. The difficulty is striking a balance that is fair and equitable. The different cultures existing in different countries is one of the most amazing and cherished things, and the thought of losing that rapidly due to mass influx of other nationalities would be sad. However, it has to be recognized that the world has always and will perpetually change as different races migrate from one region to another.

Can someone just come in from some country and take up residence in your country?
As part of the European Union, then Britain allowed this. Now, post Brexit, more restrictions are in place.

Can you describe some instances or personal experiences that happened in US that would be different in your country or vice versa (to make your story personal)?
Being escorted back from Detroit to Canada at gun point by the TSA (Transportation Security Administration), after it became apparent that my wife's Swiss passport had lapsed by a few days, after we had spent a few hours visiting the neighboring Canadian province. We were not yet citizens, but all other documentation was valid – US driving license, green card, etc. The heavy handedness of border guards is renowned, and this action was despicable, and would never have happened in Britain.

Zero tolerance in school for minor transgressions, results in detention or suspension without thought to how it impairs the education, or without trying to inform the individual how their actions were inappropriate. My boys, who were well educated, but lively individuals, fell afoul of the system at school on numerous occasions, and detention always resulted without the teachers trying to educate them as to why they were punished. This would not happen in Europe to the same extent. I believe that many teachers in the US are not in the career because they want to educate the young.

Are you glad to be in America? Why or why not?
I enjoy my life in America. I am happy and driven by the challenges. I am glad to be here. I would consider going back to the UK, but my wife is Swiss and there would be an equal chance of us going back there. There is no perfect place. The US is an appropriate place, and our family is here. We

have kids and grandkids, and it makes it difficult to move. For many of the reason already captured, the US could be so much more appealing. If the polarized views could be discussed and debated and compromise achieved, if education could be improved, and if sustainability was taken more seriously.

We must reject the idea that every time a law is broken, society is guilty rather than the law breaker. It is time to restore the American precept that each individual is accountable for his actions.
—Ronald Reagan

If you have always believed that everyone should play by the same rules and be judged by the same standards, that would have gotten you labeled a radical 60 years ago, a liberal 30 years ago and a racist today.
—Thomas Sowell

CHAPTER 20

It is enough that the people know there was an election. The people who cast the votes decide nothing. The people who count the votes decide everything.
—Joseph Stalin

Education is a weapon whose effects depend on who holds it in their hands and at whom it is aimed.
—Joseph Stalin

The great strength of the totalitarian state is that it forces those who fear it to imitate it.
—Adolf Hitler

PYONGYANG, NORTH KOREA
Interview conducted with "Kay" Kookhwa, November 7, 2021

When and where were you born? Tell me some of your family background.
I was born in Pyongyang, North Korea. It is important for you to understand our background. From 1910 to 1945, Korea was under Japanese rule for almost 36 years. Before 1910 we were one Korea. In 1945 the US bombed Hiroshima and told the Japanese to let Korea be free.

My family lived in North Korea for many generations. All Korea was totally controlled by the Japanese until the US finally defeated Japan. There were struggling factions and the 38th parallel was determined dividing North from South Korea.

Because Japan invaded Korea for 36 years, Korea had become a very poor country. It's easy to control people when they have nothing or are uneducated. Most of the people realize how much control and how much pain is cost by the Japanese.

In Korea I come from a rich family. We were too rich and too well-known to be bothered by the regimes.

How does the education system work?

There were no schools available to most in Korea. You just didn't go to school unless you were very rich. Then Japan would decide who would go to school and who would not. My father always went to the best schools. My mother was home schooled by her parents who were professors. There was a law school in Japan. School or even what you studied was not by choice. Japan selects who goes to school and what you will study. Since my dad was so smart and wealthy, he was chosen with his two older brothers to go to Japan and study law.

My grandparents and his brothers were operating a silk factory in North Korea. They employed hundreds of people. My Grandparents owned a silk factory and farm land for over 100 years. They were the only lawyers (my dad and my two uncles) in all of Korea. My two uncles came home to North Korea and my dad stayed in Japan. Do not misunderstand, even going to law school as a Korean and to represent Koreans you were still under the Japanese Emperors rule.

Thus, for all Koreans Living in Japan, my father is the only lawyer to handle all the legalities and businesses.

My dad was very powerful in Japan and he was allowed to judge Koreans in Japan. Whenever there was a problem, it was given to my dad to decide. My dad was very much against communism and socialism movements from some of the Korean people. So, he would have people put to death for doing something illegal if they were pushing communism. He could decide who would die and who would be allowed to live. This was the way it was during this time. That was the power and job he was given. Communists were trying to influence everyone in Korea at this time.

The Japanese provided my father 24-hour security (round-the-clock), and for the family. He had a lot of enemies, and a lot of friends due to this power. Because of his position and this power, he was given this needed protection. Then the Japanese sent my dad to Mongolia in 1942 to govern Koreans and the Chinese in that region. Japan was trying to capture Mongolia and put China under their regime. The Japanese provided homes and security for us. He met a lot of individuals in Mongolia and Russia as friends. In 1945 the US tried to free Korea from the Japanese.

The Japanese plan was to control Mongolia and put them under their rule. Let the Koreans be under Japan's rule but the United States did not want that nor did my dad. My dad knew what was going on. My father decided to sell everything he owned in Mongolia and returned to North Korea. He had heard rumors about the bombing of Hiroshima and he wanted to get home to his family.

The Russian Communist Party were backing North Korea while the UN and the US supported South Korea. It was a continuous push-pull situation for Korea. In the beginning there was an attempt to have one Korea. That is what all Koreans wanted. It didn't happen and the 38th parallel divided us forever. During this time, my dad was home and I was born several years later in North Korea.

The Communists loving Koreans wanted my dad and uncle to join them to govern North Korea with them. He came from a super-rich and powerful family, he didn't need money, he turned them down. My dad was always against communism and the Soviet Union. He had already lived under Japanese rule and he wanted to raise his family in freedom. He wanted to be free and in hopes of a changing North Korea, we spent two more years in North Korea.

In our 1948 family meeting it was decided to escape to S. Korea and who was to go and who was to stay. We didn't want to go all together for fear of what would happen if we were all captured together. The family decided to have my dad escape from North Korea to South Korea first. He went first and hired what you call a 'coyote' and they know the way to escape through razer wires and mines and to locate a 'rabbit hole' to escape to the South. The coyote showed the way. My parents walked all night through a steep mountain range. I was 2 years old and they were very concerned that I would make noise. I didn't know any better and would cry and carry-on and laugh. They prayed that I would be quiet going across the border. The family held hands and they told me I had to be very, very quiet. Somehow, I sensed something was going on. I was very quiet and my mom carried me on her back. My dad brought a lot of gold with him to sell for cash, so we would have money to survive until he could provide for us. We carried no pictures or any other belongings that could identify who we were.

When we got to South Korea we saw UN, US and South Korean soldiers on the other side. They took us to a room for questioning. In this interview room my dad was asked his name and he said *Lee dong gun*. The interviewers immediately knew who my dad was they told him you will all need new identities. There are spies everywhere so you will be given a new name. My dad knew there were spies and knew he could be captured so his name and his age and his birthplace were all changed. My mom and my two sisters were all provided new identities as well. They did not change my name. I was just too young and I would be unknown to the North Koreans and the communists.

With my dad's law degree and all his knowledge, he was offered a high up government job right away. My mom was against this. She said if his face was published, he would be hunted and killed. My mom wanted a life and so did my dad so he refused the government job. Then he was offered a job where he would not be exposed or have to deal with the public. His photograph and face would not be made public. We had everything we needed to start a new life. We were comfortable and we were provided everything. Other people were escaping every day and most of these people were peasants and they had a hard time settling down and getting a job. But, living in South Korea made them happy, it was easier for them because they could not be recognized.

My dad had a lot of information and he was given a lot of information also. As soon as North Korea realized my dad and family were gone, they took it out on his family back in North Korea. My uncle's family was supposed to come later. This was based on that 1948 family meeting. My uncles and our entire family were erased. They were all killed. We called it 'disappeared' back then. First, they harassed my grandparents for a while but then all were killed. The entire family was wiped out; all my aunts, my uncles, all my cousins and children. I have no one left outside of my immediate family who came across with my mom and dad. All the people we knew in North Korea and some of the well-known employees of my dad's and uncles' company were killed too. The communists do not like rich or educated people. They wanted you to be unemployed and then they could control you. My grandparents and his children were considered a big threat.

June 25, 1950 through to July 22, the Soviets pushed north and we were pushed. It was an ongoing back and forth push- pull for control of Korea. South Koreans were okay and we felt we were camping out here. You know we didn't have established homes. My dad kept saying we are going to go back to North Korea. We are going to claim our land and our homes that were in our family for hundred years and Americans are going to help Korea to push the Communist back. I remember having my crayons and my toys all packed and ready to go back home to North Korea! That was our home. We played like we were camping out in South Korea. None of us really felt we lived here.

We lived in a palace, it's like (white house in Korean standard). Korean custom is for all families to live together. There were many living quarters for all of the families. and servants' families: cooks, house keepers, and gardeners etc. There were many kitchens.

My older sisters remembered how wonderful it was to have a lot of playmates and many people around them. We also had many guests from Japan, China and Russia visit my dad. We were not like many other people; we had a car and a driver. My mother was very pretty and dressed in western clothes and came in the car with the driver to shop. She was famous (well known) as a rich princess. In all of North Korea no one ever had leather shoes or western style clothing. North Koreans only had rubber shoes and handmade cotton clothes. My sisters played in their silk shoes and often some of the servants would go around and pick up my sister so she would not get her silk shoes wet in the muddy ground.

The war ended in 1953. My sister was born in 1949, another sister in early 50s. Do you know the Korean War has not ended? It never ended.

There is a ceasefire and that has existed for 70 years. For those 70 years my family always thought we would go back to our home in North Korea. My parents decided to get us out to Hawaii and they were waiting for a visa. During this time my dad developed kidney problems. He was getting sick. He never really wanted to leave North Korea. He felt forever guilty that since he left, he was responsible for his family being killed. He felt that if he remained in North Korea, they would all still be alive. We believe that this is what made him ill.

My parents love freedom, money can't buy it. It's okay to trade wealth and fame for freedom in their heart. Dad passed away in South Korea. He was a train engineer and that was the job the government gave him instead of the much more public position. After he died, my mom took on all the responsibilities of raising the family. You have to understand, my mother never worked, she never cooked and now she had to raise five daughters on her own.

Most women in Korea were not educated at that time. My mother's side was very educated and they ensured that she would have an education even though there were no public schools for girls. My mother was home-schooled by her parents being professors. My parents were fluent in Chinese, Japanese and Korean and my dad spoke Russian also.

My two older sisters could now work and I was in high school. Mom took a job as a cook and we moved into public housing. I know this is hard for you to imagine but my mother had always been very wealthy and I can't imagine what she was going through having to go into public housing. She was so sorry for us that she had to raise us in public housing as compared to the life we had had. We all cried then and mom kept blaming herself. Said it was her fault that she wanted to be free and that's why we were in public housing now for our freedom.

My older sisters worked for a drug company and I worked for a restaurant part time as I was still going to school and wanted to help out my mom. During this time there were many US and UN soldiers around. One soldier in particular seemed to be very fond of me and he kept coming by to eat and saying I want to take you to America. I kept telling him I don't live here we're waiting to go back to North Korea. He was persistent and I said I will go with you under one condition, that you take my sister who is 5 years older with us. That is the only way I will go to America with you. This man introduced my sister to his best friend and they fell in love and got married and then we all came to America in 1966. It was a wonderful experience. My sister and I have always lived very close to each other.

Those two soldiers were the nicest, kindest, most generous people I have ever met. The soldiers were good people and were excellent providers for me and my sister. Everyone we met in the US was good to us. We were never exposed to bad people and we never saw any prejudice or racism that is so frequently spoken of today.

I entered City College in Pasadena to further my education. After many years we got divorced as I found he was cheating on me. He told me he knew it was wrong but he said 'she chased me' but I divorced him anyway. We had been married 16 years.

I then went on and got my real estate license and became very successful. I was a real estate agent for 33 years and I kept coming back to it even though I retired several times. I had two girls, one is in San Francisco and the other is in Orange County. They're wonderful daughters. My one daughter in San Francisco became very liberal and my other daughter is very conservative. We don't talk politics too much in the house. My daughter in San Francisco does not see or understand our background and what my family went through to come to the US.

My mom came to the US 2 years after I came. I brought her here. My oldest sister came down with a mental illness and died in Korea. My mom continued to apologize to us and how she raised us in public housing and having to leave North Korea. We told her how much we love the United States and we have accomplished so much here that she would be very proud of us. She wanted us and our families to be free. We shared with her that the US is our adopted home and this is our adopted country. A country that made us feel safe. We are safe, we are successful. We can choose to go to school, to church if we want and work hard and do the things we want which we did not have nor ever would in North Korea. My mother hid her true identity for more than 30 years.

Never in my mind would I consider that my beautiful adopted home country would push socialism. I can't believe it. We always thought we were camping out in South Korea; it wasn't our home. We were very happy once we came to the US. We were accepted, we were accomplished. I became very successful in real estate and my sisters are both accomplished. We are comfortable and safe here and we are free and that is what my mother and father both wanted. They wanted us to be free to do whatever we wish for. We can talk about anything we choose to talk about and we can disagree but we are not silenced or killed for it. In North Korea you would be killed for just speaking out. These were very real threats and all that fear was gone when we landed in the USA.

I see things changing here now and it seems like North Korea now. What my parents described. When it happened there, they started changing things. The government said one family cannot own all the land and that the government would control who owns different things. Even if a family had owned the property for thousands of years, the government could take it. They would decide who went to school and what they would be taught. They would decide who got married and when the Soviets and communism came and we started hearing that everything was going to be free.

You didn't have to work, it was just going to be given to you, and you would be taking care of. You will be given one to two meals a day. This is the beginning of socialism when they start offering you things for free. That everything will be taken care of by the government. People started growing opium in North Korean and they smoke it. It damages the brain and that's all they do all day; it keeps the people very compliant; everything is given to them. They have no jobs, no rights, they just get handouts, they have no water, no medicine and the medicine they are given is fake. My dad always told us this is not a life they wanted for us. Dad and mom wanted America as they knew America was a free country. This freedom is what my dad wanted for North Korea but after 70 years I know now that that will never happen for North Korea.

I pray that in this country young people will see by comparison what socialism can do to people. They want to sell their soul for free stuff, instead of creating their own ideas and making their dreams come true, and that life that you lived once is wasted.

I was never a believer in religion or practiced any faith in Korea. I practiced no religion but I became Christian when I saw the freedoms we had in the United States. I became very active in the Christian faith and now I have been doing missionary work for 12 years.

I minister on USC campus to Chinese scholars that the Chinese government sent their top scholars to the US for one year. I think they are undermining the students and I believe they are stealing intellectual property and our schools' technology. I was able to have a classroom and set up just like we did in church every Sunday. I am not a formal pastor but I went to theology school for a couple years to learn. I did this with a friend from China who came to study to be a pastor, and we worked together for 2 and ½ years. and opened 8 underground churches through 8 Schuler. All of the scholars I talk to do not like their government in China.

Some of the South Korean churches are set up on the Chinese border as a hideout place for the North Koreans to stay after they defect from the North. They welcome them and help take them into South Korea. These peasants often have an easier time to escape because they are not well-known. There is a river between North Korea and China that is the route of escape (you need to be a good swimmer to make it). North Korea is accepting US dollars. If you have a Chinese passport, you can travel to North Korea. Due to accepting these dollars my friend travels several times a year to bring food to poor villages.

There is a group in South Korea that sends a balloon filled with medicine, dollar bills, and actual news from South Korea. The North Koreans only hear fake news saying that South Koreans are starving and that America is responsible for keeping South and North Korea apart and maintaining the 38 parallel across the land to North Korea. I continue to hope and pray for all land on where the poor people live.

I am scared to death that what happened in North Korea is happening in this country, true socialism. Once we go to socialism, if it does happen here, it will never go back. Look no further than North Korea: 70 years later we are still divided.

I didn't know why I came to Ventura and now I do. I am providing meals for between 200 to 300 homeless people. God seems to always find a way for me. I work with the Ventura Family to Family program. It has been going on for 39 years and was established by a group of Catholic women. Most of them have since died but one in her 80s is still alive and has helped train me. I took over her position 6 years ago.

There are many US veterans who come and get food and it my heart breaks to see how these veterans are treated in this country. They fought and provided freedom for everyone that lives in this country and they are left being homeless. I have met young vets and older veterans, some very damaged and some hanging on but have no resources to succeed. Again, it breaks my heart to be in the US and see all that people have and they treat their vets like this! I am trying to give back for all that we have been through and the freedom to be here in the US. I buy whatever I can and I cook. I buy all the food and I have many wonderful volunteers to cook with me and to feed the many homeless. It is a rewarding thing to do to enjoy this freedom and give thanks to be here.

CHAPTER 21

Education is a weapon whose effects depend on who holds it in their hands and at whom it is aimed.
—Joseph Stalin

Nothing would be more fatal than for government of the states to get into the hands of the experts. Expert knowledge is limited knowledge: and the unlimited ignorance of the plain man who knows only what hurts is a safer guide, than any vigorous direction of a specialized character. Why should you assume that all expert doctors, engineers, etc. are drones or worse?
—Young Churchill writing to H. G. Wells

RIGA, LATVIA
Interview conducted with Edmunds Sondors, November 10, 2021

Some background

In Latvia, pre-WWII, the president was Karlis Ulmanis, well known as a member of the Latvian Farmer's Union (1917-1934) made the Latvian fishing industry famous by naming the famous canned sardines Sprotes. The fishing industry caught many sardines. Latvians would smoke and then can them in oil and called them "Sprotes" or Spratzs. Spratzs is a delicacy even today and became very famous Latvian gourmet food. The currency at this time was in Lats. Lats was a very strong currency. We had 5, 2 and 1 Lats silver coins, similar to the US silver dollars. Due to our very strong economy at the time, Latvians wanted to stay away from Russia and communism.

Where are you from, and what was it like growing up there?

I was born in Riga, the capital of Latvia. It's about twenty kilometers from Salaspils, Latvia, the small town where I grew up. Latvia was under Russian occupation since 1945. Thus, I was born and grew up under Russian occupied Latvia. I was raised by a single mom with no brothers or sisters. Prior to Russian occupation, Latvia was a very strong capitalist country and was very successful being near sea ports. Latvians were very agricultural people. They were primarily farmers, raising sheep, cows for milk, wheat and there was a huge fishing industry.

My mom was a single girl and she worked in the Salispils Peat Factory in Kudra. Peat is an energy resource used to burn for heating. She stayed in one tiny room with three other girls in the early 1960s ended up in an apartment known as the Barracks. While working on the peat production farm in the forest, she decided to get an education, and studied food production and chemistry. After graduating from the school, she went to work at the liquor factory, as a laboratory chemist. Although she had an education, the wages did not reflect that, as workers on the assembly line made more money. So, she gave up the laboratory work and went to work on assembly line to earn a bigger pay check. She worked in the factory on the assembly line all her life to support the family in our native country until retirement. My mom met my father in the town of Kudra, outside of Salaspils, Latvia. Kudra was even smaller than Salaspils.

My mom in Kudra, Salispils peat factory 1956.

I grew up in this small village with 16 buildings called Barracks, each housing between 4 to 12 families. The town had single dirt road going through it. Buildings were built after second world war (WW II) as temporary housing, called Barracks. They were poorly built with no insulation. The first building I lived in with my mom was a single room, about 6 feet wide and about 8 feet long. In our first small room, mom stayed there with me until I was about 1 to 2 years old and then she moved down the hallway to a larger room which was maybe 6 X 12'.

We had a brick stove, that mom used only in winter time for heat and cooking. Also, we had small kitchen table, small desk, closet, foldable twin bed and single foldable chair /sleeper. When both were un-folded for sleeping, there was very little floor space left. The bathroom was basically an outhouse in the building without water and heat in winter time. The common bathroom, meaning shared by multiple families, was just a hole in the floor just like an outhouse within the building. The running water was in the community kitchen down the hallway, next to community bathrooms. There was no running water in the bathroom. I stayed in this other room with mom till I was about 7 to 8 years old. We used the brick stove for heat and a hot plate for cooking or heating the kettle.

When I was 11, we had an opportunity to move to a larger place in the building across the road. This was a two-room apartment with separate kitchen. Although we upgraded to separate bedrooms, to get water we had go outside to a manual pump, and carry water by buckets. Also, the bathroom was outside, across the road. It was an out-house for 3 people, male or female separated by a wooden partition, with no lights or running water. Because the common bathroom was so far away, we usually would end up peeing in a bucket and then emptying it the next morning. In the second place we lived which was bigger, there still was no running water and we went out and pumped water from a well.

Here we used an outdoor outhouse. In Latvia the temperatures can get very cold and you had to be fully dressed go out to the communal bathroom which consisted of three holes under a bench. That bench was nasty and no one wanted to touch it, let alone sit on it. There was no light in the bathroom to locate the hole and no lights to get there. When it was all iced over you really had a tough time staying on a toilet. (*Edmunds laughs.*) Nobody wanted to touch those toilets. There's no toilet paper, we used newspaper. It was very cold and would ice up and you had to balance yourself up on this bench to be able to go while slipping all over and not wanting to put your hands down.

By the 1970s these Barracks were considered emergency buildings and new development in Riga was under construction. This is all state construction. This newly constructed area was more spread out, what you would call maybe suburbia.

SIGULDAS INTERNĀTSKOLA

In first grade I walked to school about 2 miles. Boys and girls were together in the same schools. There were actually two schools; there was a Russian School and Latvian School. The Russian school was a two-story building and bigger than the Latvian School. My mom would walk to the train station at about 6 in the morning, she would work all day then take the train home to find me coming home late, dirty with no homework done. I caused a lot of problems for my mom as I was a young kid and I was always getting into trouble so she sent me off to boarding school. I would steal bread when I was hungry. I just kept slipping and my mom was concerned about this so the boarding school was probably a good thing.

To attend boarding school, I had to leave my house Sunday afternoon, walk 1 mile to the train station to get to capital city Riga, which is about half hour on the train, then get on to a different train, ride about an hour and half, and if lucky, get on the bus for about half hour ride to school. If I missed the bus, I had to walk about 5 miles. I would get there on Sunday afternoon for the 8 am class the next morning. We had to be in school until

Saturday afternoon and then make the same trip back home. We only had free time from 3 pm until 4.45 pm. In this boarding school I was about 8 years old and had to wear uniform.

I went from 2nd second grade to 8th grade in the same school with about 25 kids in a class. There we were boarded in dorms with 8 to 20 kids to a bedroom.

We would stay in the dorms and be monitored all the time. We would have dinner together and then monitored to do the homework and at 10 p.m. then it was lights out.

Me at my indoctrination class. These classes were taught just as though they were math or science.

I finished school in 1982 completing eighth grade. After finishing 8th grade, I enrolled in a trade/high school, a three-year trade program. Half of the day was spent studying curriculum, the other half you studied your trade. After 3 years I earned a 4th degree carpenter certificate (6th degree being a master), and went to work at a large construction company.

What did you enjoy growing up?

We enjoyed swimming, playing in the forest, and this was a real forest! We enjoyed climbing in the trees, making bows and arrows and pretending to be Indian warriors, building and riding bicycles and mopeds, making bonfires, fishing and much more. During this time of Russian occupation, Latvia, Lithuania and Estonia were admired by the Russians compared to the other republics in Russia. Latvia had very successful manufacturing of automobiles, trains, electronics, textile and a lot of other industries, and was very popular throughout the former USSR. And being close to the Baltic Sea, had very nice beaches and resorts.

In Latvia there are three major shipping ports, which made Latvia huge in fisheries. Russia used Latvia as a window to the world just like Peter the Great. The Russians always knew that Latvia was very beautiful area, very bountiful and economically successful.

Why did you want to come to the US? How do you perceive the US in your young life as compared to when you first came here?
My mom told me about my uncle, who immigrated to the USA after WW II, and was living in Ventura, California. She rarely talked about him as it was not acceptable to speak positively of the USA, especially having a relative move there. My uncle had joined the Latvian Legion. The Latvian Legions were made up of Latvians who joined the German Army to fight the Communist Russians. This is why he had to leave and not come back to Latvia after the war. He had his leg blown off during the war. The Germans returned him to Germany to heal, and was provided a prosthetic leg. He could never return to Latvia or he would be killed, or sent to Siberia labor camps, since he had fought against them. My uncle somehow ended up staying in west side of Germany after the war. He was fortunate that he did not end up in East Germany and he stayed there until 1952. This also made it easier for him to come to the USA. Had he been in the east I am not sure he would have been able to come to the US. I have to say this about the Germans, that they take care of their soldiers. They never turned their back on their soldiers after the war was over, including my uncle. They paid for his prosthetic even when he came to America and they paid for his new prosthetic leg whenever it was replaced until he died.

In middle school, I was thinking about America. We had always been taught that America was a rotten, capitalist country. That America was decadent. At this time Latvia was under communist rule. In our country at that time, you would go to prison for years for speaking against the Communist regime. You could actually disappear if you spoke your mind. You could not talk or even state that Latvia was 'Russian occupied'! Just saying that would send you to a political prison, or labor camps to 'die naturally' (due to heavy work, harsh Siberian environment or exposure to nuclear wastes). You could not say anything about Latvia being once being a capitalist country in the past.

You could not show or fly the old Latvian flag. Russia re-made the Latvian flag to suit their agenda. Can you imagine your country's flag being changed to meet another country's agenda? It still makes me angry.

My first taste of America was in the late 70's, when I saw a photo of the music band *KISS* at the flea market/swap-meet. In Russian occupied countries there was no experiencing music or bands like this. The government-controlled media did not play any American or British music, or any shows at all. Russian music performers would all be dressed in suits and ties, and behavior was very restrictive of how one could react at a concert. You could not whistle or stand up and scream, only clap. You had to be all very politically correct. But we kids started seeing those pictures of *KISS* and other music groups. Kids would buy these pictures. You can't imagine a restricted young person seeing the faces of the *KISS* group and maybe hearing their music, or watching the action movies of Chuck Norris, Sylvester Stallone or Arnold Schwarzenegger! It really made an impression on the young people under Communist rule. It was all very underground in the early 1980s and was called the black-market media.

Once I got a hold of a Marlboro plastic shopping bag. This was a big deal in grade school. I put all my school books in that bag and I was very popular when the kids saw this Marlboro bag. At some point the blue jeans: Levi's, Wranglers, Montana and Lees became very popular in the black market. People paid hundreds of dollars for them. Jeans came in dark blue, but we wanted them faded to the light blue to be cool and look American. So, we rubbed them with bricks or stones to get them to fade faster, rather natural fading after many wash cycles. We were wearing those Mohawk style haircuts.

I was drafted into the Russian Army at 19 and was sent to Georgia for 2 years. After discharge I went back to work for the same construction company I worked for after graduating from my trade school.

During my military service, after you served six months you were given a half day pass. You had to wear your uniform and we went to the town of Orjonikidze. There were basement stores that you had to walk down to. It was all very underground kind of stuff and all were in rebellion and not  asking permission from the government. Here you could watch videos. They had VHS tapes playing. This is where I saw a Chuck Norris and Sylvester Stallone, all these kind of action movies. You would pay about a dollar (rubles equivalent) to watch them. This reinforced my whole concept of America. Wild west cowboys with guns, big and fast cars, all kind of fire arms, ladies in bikinis, it was the Wild West and everything goes. It was so different than anything we were taught about America. It showed freedom! You could listen to the music you wanted, you could dress the way you wanted and you could practice any religion. We saw all this freedom in these movies and even though now I know much was just Hollywood it was very real for us.

My mom was Catholic but she never got to practice her Catholicism in the Soviet Union. If you wanted to succeed you had to become a member of 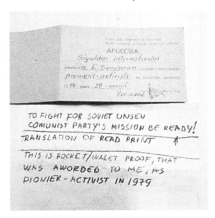 the Communist party and she did. This was the only way you could get ahead was to become a member of the party so she had to give up her Catholic faith. It wasn't so much that they destroyed churches in Latvia, but they discouraged faith by people having to join the Communist Party to get ahead for better living. Practicing any religion was detrimental to just getting by. In Russia they actually took down the churches just like in the US, now where they're taking down statues. I find this very troublesome.

When I made my decision to come to America, I only told my wife. I told no one else as it was dangerous. I didn't tell my mom or anyone else. I knew if I came to America, I would stay in America. My wife did not believe me. It was like I was telling her I was going to go to the Moon. I spoke no English. In 1992 I came to America. I was 25 years old. My uncle was here.

When my uncle got to the States through Ellis Island in 1952, he worked for avocados and lemon growing farmers in Oxnard. It was a group put together by the Catholic Church and they would take in displaced people. The program entailed, if you gave them two years of labor, they would provide food and shelter for you. My mom had told me that my uncle lived in America but she would not talk about this. She mentioned it once and then she would never talk about it again. It was dangerous to speak about America.

Also, the Germans I speak of earlier when my uncle joined the Latvian Legions denounced Hitler and the SS (abbreviation of Schutzstaffel or Protective Echelon). The Legions were not his Hitler's soldiers. These Latvians were drafted by the German Army to fight Communism. I emphasize this because what I see happening in the US and the current situation in Afghanistan. The action taken by the US government in Afghanistan recently with the American troops is appalling. The Germans, I believe during my uncle's time, never would have done that. They backed up their soldiers which is something I always thought America would do.

We eventually could speak openly about anything in government during the Reagan/Gorbachev era called "Glasnost". I was still in the Russian military and was watching the TV news. In Riga, Latvia in 1987 I saw people walking with our pre-Russian occupation Latvian flag on TV.

This was a serious charge to carry the Latvian flag. This was very risky during this time but you could see things changing. I knew if I stayed in Latvia even with my high degree in carpentry, I would make maybe $250 a month. You can't move up. You will never succeed or get promoted to being the boss. People have to steal or be born into those jobs. This is just the way socialism and communism work.

Communists and socialists know the workers will steal food and materials, that was purposeful to keep their pay low. I had only hand tools and I put all my effort into my work. I invented specific carpentry tools, methods and jigs. Even when I told some about the inventions that I made you would not get any credit or acknowledgement. Inventions or anything creative would never be acknowledged under socialism and communism. They know that some people will not work hard. It was almost like the majority had blinders on for any creativity.

In capitalist countries if you work hard, you get ahead and can be creative and inventive. Under socialism there is no incentive to get ahead or try to be more or even be inventive. When I mentioned some of the things I had invented and so showed off my jigs and tools, another carpenter said 'Well, if it worked or was meant to be invented it would have been already done'. These were my coworkers, possibly others would have been more open minded but we were almost limited to even thinking about going above these people. They seemed to stifle any creativity. That was just the attitude and then I realized I really wasn't going to get anywhere even being inventive and creative. This man was wrong. I actually developed a stronger, more stable carbon steel blade earlier than the one that is in use today. Then power tools became popular and hand tools were no longer as much in demand. This was in 1988 and 1989 I knew in my heart I was in a box and I was never going to escape unless I went to America.

In America I established my own business and have worked hard to be a successful businessman and support my family. This would have been so much harder in Latvia, if at all. I just felt more drive once I came to America. It was just in my heart to make it here. It may have happened in Latvia after many years, but I did not feel I could get anywhere there. I was exposed to the black-market ways to make money, and could have gone that route, but that was not my upbringing and not my choice.

Though I still love my heritage and language, I am a proud American!

Do you see parallels of things happening in your country compare to the US, good and bad?

Of all the countries in the world, we came to America because I believed that America is the greatest country, and the land of opportunity and freedom! We could have immigrated to many countries but came to America because, America is the best! When we first arrived in America, we had to learn the language, get driver's license, and deal with immigration. This was all difficult for us but we got through it. Making friends and fitting into American culture was difficult at first. I think most younger generation Americans are very spoiled, and do not realize what it is like in the rest of the world. They have been brought up having everything and many did not have to work hard or even try to achieve anything let alone fight for their freedom. They take so much for granted.

I have been in America for almost 30 years and I have not seen racism in America. This new accusation that America is racist is absurd. Never heard it the last 30 years, why suddenly now? I find Russia much more racist than anything I have seen in America. The racism I experienced in my native country was from Russians. Although Russia occupied Latvia in 1945, and stayed there for decades, many of them called people of Latvia fascists or Nazis, and other very offensive names in regards to being Latvian. They occupied us and they are calling us fascists! This is what I find racist. The Russians occupied our country and called us names. When I experienced racism in my native country, it made me very angry. In America no matter who you are, your color, your religion whatever, you can do what you want and if you work hard, you can make something of yourself. You are free.

Living in America makes me feel proud, free, and happy! A tactic of the Communists used in Latvia and other republics was their illegal voting practices. The Russians created an illegal voting event by sending in trains loads of military people dressed as civilians and then they voted for the Russian communists. This reminds me of much of the voting manipulations going on in this country today.

I am fighting for America to be what it was when I got here. I even considered going back to Latvia and attempt to make changes there after I observed what is happening in the US. But I see it clearly now what is

163

happening. This is what happened to me growing up in Latvia and to all Latvian people. Now I see the same is happening here. I get frustrated that many Americans don't seem to see or even care what is happening to their own Country.

It is a way to take people's wealth from them without having to openly raise taxes. Inflation is the most universal tax of all.
—**Thomas Sowell**

Capitalism: the worst economic system, except for all the others. Capitalism is no different than anything else in this world. It is imperfect because imperfect men created it. Humans are not perfect, nor are they capable of perfection. Avarice and greed are not unique to capitalism. They were present in the USSR, and they will present themselves in any man-made system
—**Matt Barnes,** *The Pitt News,* **2014**

CHAPTER 22

Freedom is never more than one generation away from extinction.
We didn't pass it to our children in the blood stream. It must be
fought for, protected, and handed on for them to do the same, or
one day we will spend our sunset years telling our children and our
children's children what it was once like in the United States
where men were free.
—Ronald Reagan

BOGOTA, COLUMBIA
Interview with Luis Chaves-Pardo, Dec 15, 2021

Where were you born? Country, town?
I was born in Bogota, Colombia

Tell me about growing up in your country. Comparisons to US if applicable.
My early memories of growing up in Bogota were filled with love and support from beloved ants and uncle, who were our main source of financial and emotional support. My ants Rosita and Lucrecia and her husband Climaco, were our benefactors and providers of whatever we needed for school tuition, uniforms and housing for my sister during most of her teens. They were present at our birth, baptism, first communion, wedding and main holidays.

My father left us early to fend for ourselves and with a tiny pension from his service with the government. My beloved mother Berthica was ill prepared to handle the finances and we struggled to make ends meet.

Thanks to the family welfare system, common in our culture, we managed to go to school and have a simple life.

Because of our precarious and limited financial condition, I realized early in my teens, that I needed to make it on my own and relieve the burden to my family of paying for school and living expenses.

Did you travel to other countries prior to coming to the US?
We had no financial means of traveling much further than small towns, where we had relatives that were always happy to see us and spend quality time.

During my last two years of high-school, I attended night classes at the German Consulate near my school. A close school friend and I were planning to go to Germany and study at the Free University of Berlin.

As fate would have it, I was not too serious about German class and spent more time organizing weekend parties with friends of school. Of course, when it came time to pass the German proficiency test, my teacher recommended I take one more semester to ensure better score that would allow me admission to the University in Berlin with a scholarship.

Frustrated with the outcome of my plans to go to Germany, I contacted fellow students from my school who had migrated to the US to work and go to school.

They were most encouraging and offered to house me, as I arrived in New York. I firmly believe that, we all reach certain critical paths in life, when a simple decision changes the course of our lives completely.

What were your experiences in school, in the college educational system in your native country?
Growing up with limited financial conditions, I had to attend neighborhood private elementary schools that were very limited in facility and teaching personnel.

In high school, I always felt that we were not getting the best education because of limited financial resources for the schools to provide adequate facilities and equipment. For me, everything looked poor and I wanted more and better. Despite the lack of resources at school, teachers were very motivated to teach and support us.

I left my country midway into my last year of high school. Shortly after, I began to work in New York, I applied to Bay Ridge High School for after-hours school. I was surprised how easy and simple the standards were at the time. I could not believe in "Open book test?" What? What was wrong with studying and memorizing for the tests? I recall taking my finals on chemistry and very candidly asking the teacher "are you leaving the Table of Elements open? And he replied "of course"! I then said "all the answers are practically there" his reply was "good for you".

Tell me about your job/profession here as compared to your native country.

Well, since I migrated to this country as an 18-year-old, I do not have any reference to actual personal work experience in my country; however, from my observations and knowledge of how things used to work in Colombia, it was not what you know or how well prepared you were for the job, but "Who you know or recommends you for the job".

In the US, when interviewing for a job, I was never asked such questions as to who sent you. Instead, I was asked to talk about my knowledge and experience in the field and interests on the job I was applying for.

When did you come to the US, and have you become a US citizen?

I arrived in New York City on June 13, 1963.

Yes, I received my US Citizenship on August 14, 1968, while serving in the US Air Force, at my last tour of duty at Hill Air Force Base in Ogden, Utah.

Why did you want to come to the US? Or did you want to come to the US?

As I mentioned early, my first choice of country to go to school and work was Germany; but my destiny was to come to America.

How do you perceive the US today as compared to when you first came here (especially during these times of change)?

From the time I first came to this country, I was extremely busy trying to balance school, family and work. My schedule was quite occupied with work and carrying a full-time academic load and attending to a growing family. By the time I was graduating on June, 1973, with an Electrical Engineering degree from Cal Poly, Pomona. My Colombian wife and I already had three children. My time during those years of having kids, going to school was totally dedicated to supporting all of their activities and keeping busy in sports like soccer and tennis. I was a soccer coach for my children during all of their high school years.

In reality, there was not much time for other outside interests like politics and civic duties. Since my retirement from St. Jude Medical, ten years ago, my wife and I have spent much of our time traveling the world.

The political arena during this decade has deteriorated and reached a sad and destructive path since Trump became president. I was not a politically involved person before and much less now. All I can do is pray that someday we may regain the dignity and integrity of a democratic country like ours should be.

Are your parents and family here or in your Country and how do they perceive the US?

None of my family members ever lived here. They all reside in Colombia.

I do not really know how they perceive the US since they have never been here. I have two nieces who live in Europe, one in Austria and another in Germany. They are both professionals with great jobs and married to German citizens.

Do you see parallels of things happening in your country compared to the US, good and bad?

I believe people, regardless of national origin, race, religion, profession and political affiliation, behave in their environment motivated by basic economic and social drivers in fulfilling their personal needs. For instance, unethical behavior that is driven by financial gains such as bribes and under-the-table money exchange is common everywhere to some degree. In Colombia, un-ethical practices are common in all aspects of personal or business relation-ships. The difference between Colombia and the US is readily obvious in Colombia, whereas in the US is most common at the upper corporate economic levels and not readily visible to the average person.

Do people own guns in your country? Did they ever and/or were they confiscated?

I never knew that any one member of my extensive family, who owned fire arms, except for my uncle Jose, who was an officer in the Colombian Army.

Carrying arms has a negative connotation in our society and assumed the vandals are the ones who carry weapons.

Tell me about medical and public health options in your native country versus the US if you have experienced them. Is medical care free in your country?

Since I left my country early in my teens, all I can judge is based on my emergency trips to Colombia, when close relatives were sick and hospital-ized. The Medical field in Colombia is well established and I observed very humane and loving treatment by medical and nursing stall to their patients.

By contrast, the American health system is primarily driven by economic incentives, that make treatment and medications extremely expensive to the average person.

How does the education system work?

Because I left my country in my teens, all I can judge is my family. In par-ticular my two nieces, living in Europe, went to college in Colombia and are currently extremely well established in their jobs. One niece is a dental surgeon and has commented that their clinical procedures in Colombia are more detailed, as compared to her observations of coworkers in Germany.

Explain what you mean by freedom and religious freedom.

The pursuit of happiness is a universal human driver, that is impacted by the ability to realize our dreams within a society that respects universal human rights.

Colombia, like most Latin American countries, is predominantly a Catholic Country; however, other religions are free to function without any restrictions.

What things do you like most about the US?

My best impression, from the time arrived in this country, is that everyone gets a chance to make their own choices on their lives and work toward achieving their goals.

I can honestly and humbly say, that I have fulfilled and, in some areas, exceeded my dreams of having a career that would reward my efforts and give me a happy and secure life, so that I can be of support to my children and grandchildren.

I also like the fact that "If you work hard and apply yourself to whatever endeavor, there are tangible rewards from people around you who recognize and reward you for your efforts. I made my grade not only for my personal efforts but for the total support of people around me, who opened doors and gave me a chance to demonstrate my abilities."

What do you miss about your country?

Of course, the loss of the family love and care for each other is hard to realize once we left our ancestral home. But, in life nothing comes free and some sacrifices are made to fulfill our goals and dreams for a better life.

What do you dislike most about US?

I was so very busy raising a family, going to school and working that little time was left to do other things like getting involved in church or civic activities.

As more leisure time came after the kids grew up, I began to pay more attention about the political arena. The more I learned about politics, the less I wanted to be involved; however, I did my civic duty of voting at every election. Unfortunately, with the disastrous entry of Trump into the political arena, I became totally disillusioned with the political system, and withdrew from all related to politics.

What similarities do you see between the two countries?

In America, we are heavily dependent in our jobs and work hard to maintain a standard of living that meets our requirements. Too much time is dedicated to meeting or exceeding financial goals, while time marches by and we are getting older and sometimes fatter.

In Colombia, people seem to spend more time having quality time with family and friends. Family and friends are important to maintain a happy social life.

In Europe, people seem to work at a slower pace and spend more leisure time with friend and family. One only needs to walk around the city and observe family and friend departing in the outdoors and gathering at public places.

How does your country's market economy work?

Colombia is a country with many natural resources and agriculture is by far one of the largest industries. Coffee is a precious commodity and flowers are another mayor source of exports to the rest of the world. The textile industry has a long history of quality fabrics that compete well with the international markets.

Does your country secure its borders? Do you think that it is a sovereign right of a country to protect its citizens? Why or why not?

I can only comment based on the news from Colombian newspapers like *El Tiempo,* that I follow in the internet. Recently, there has been a significant influx of Venezuelan refugees. The high number of refugees crossing our borders has totally overwhelmed our ability to provide adequate Human Services. The lack on employment for these refugees forces them to resort to illicit activities and crime.

To maintain order and serve its citizens, countries need to maintain control of their territory integrity and secure their borders. However, in case where there is a humanitarian need to provide asylum to people in need, government needs to provide humanitarian aid and try to resolve the conflict at the source. The droughts prevent them from growing their own food and are left with no other alternative but just migrate to greener pastures.

Can someone just come in from some country and take up residence in your country?
Yes, as I indicated above, Venezuelan migrants are given entry to the country with no restrictions.

Can you describe some incidents or personal experiences that happened in US that would be different in your country or vice versa (to make the story personal)?
Upon my arrival in the US, I had changed travel days and did not have time to inform my fellow Colombian friends in New York, of my late arrival. Therefore, as I walked around the airport terminal trying to figure out how to call their apartment, a gentleman approached me and asked me something that I could not understand. He pointed his finger to the public phone and I showed him a paper with a phone number. He then proceeded to dial the number of my friend's place. After he talked to the person on the other end, he handed over the phone to me and put a hand full of small change in my hand. Wow, the first time I needed help, there he was, a kind man ready to help me. The person at the phone was the landlord of my friend's apartment and she spoke Spanish, telling me exactly what to do to get to their place.

Are you glad to be in America? Why or why not?
I am absolutely, positively and totally glad to be in the US and have benefited of many opportunities to work with very talented people in the Aerospace industry, who were my tutors and mentors during my years of being a college student.

Many doors were opened for me and many opportunities given to allow me to work, go to school full time and support my growing family. I wish I could just reach out to those who helped and supported my efforts and say "look this is the result of all of the good things you did for me."

CHAPTER 23

We must reject the idea that every time a law is broken, society is guilty rather than the law breaker. It is time to restore the American precept that each individual is accountable for his actions.
—Ronald Reagan

Because someone repeats something over and over and louder and louder, still does not make it true.
—Kathleen S. Roos, PhD

Why do our enemies see us as Americans and we Americans see each other as the enemy?
—Kathleen Roos, PhD

If a government is big enough to give you all the stuff you need, then the government is big enough to take it all away.
—Mark Brnovich, Arizona attorney general

CONNECTICUT, UNITED STATES OF AMERICA
Kathleen S Roos, PhD

My story of experiencing communism, socialism, dictatorships, monarchies, and combat zones where who knows what will happen

My story follows and is multipurposed. First, from my experiences and following common threads through these interviews, I think describing my upbringing in the US is important. There are many preconceived ideas of privilege or a cushy lifestyle about Americans that may not be accurate.

Secondly, I thought it important to address the common thread of education, which I felt extremely eye opening. The observation that America's educational systems fall short of the those in the countries my interviewees came from truly surprised me. I was surprised, yet as I have discussed with family and friends, our educational system has degraded over the last decades. Possibly some history may be helpful to the reader. Thirdly, following another common thread, in this country one has a choice, and there is opportunity for growth and to be creative. Actually, this is the very reason many of these people wanted to come to America. If you are willing to work hard, are motivated, seek out opportunities, and not fall to a victimhood or just "gimme" role, America truly is the land of opportunity. However, it is not going to be just given to you. And finally, I identify a more recent challenge for women, especially in sports. For young women to be required to compete against transgender athletes takes us back to the time when there were few competitive sports for women. I think many may remember the outrage expressed by many countries when the Soviet Union and Germany sent women to the Olympic Games who were enhanced by drugs, making the competition totally unfair. Saying that drugs can alter transgender male athletes to female athletes is not science. The chromosomes remain the same no matter what drug is used. What someone chooses to be for themselves is fine. When they impose that choice on others it becomes problematic. And when drugs are used to enhance performance, it develops an unfair playing field that most athletes have held sacrosanct. I could even mention the entire Lance Armstrong ordeal—all nations were put through an emotional merry-go-round by an athlete who took steroids and denied it. When Greg Lemond, a past Tour de France winner, stated Lance was taking drugs, Greg was denigrated as a poor loser. Yet Greg was right all along. Muscle mass, larger lung capacity, and so on all benefit a male athlete. Finally, I close with why I think America matters with a couple of short stories on the goodness of Americans and the significance of our founding documents and what it means to "we the people."

I was born in a small town, Norwalk, Connecticut (not small now). My parents were relatively poor. Saying one is from a poor family appears to be

a current badge of victimhood so I will clarify. Mom qualified for welfare and food stamps and refused them, saying she had earning power and would work just like a man. Later, when trying to buy a home, she was refused by the bank. She was told she needed a husband to sign for her. My mother refused to accept this rejection. She always said she had earning power and would purchase what we needed through hard work, be it buying a home in her own name or anything else. She fought the system. She was way ahead of Gloria Steinem (*spokesperson for the American feminist movement of the sixties and seventies*). Later, when she was a single mom raising two girls, finally did ask for help through Catholic charities and was denied.

Mom and Dad held blue-collar jobs most of their lives; Mom a telephone operator or waitress, Dad a night watchman at a trucking company. They were both talented, Dad a great golfer and mom a great singer, both had high aspirations, but nothing ever came of those dreams. Mom was a highly talented singer and was selected for two Broadway tryouts: *Two Faces* and *Finnian's Rainbow*. Then she had a mental breakdown. It was much later I learned about straitjackets and electric shock treatments. I had only two occasions to bond with my dad, Ralph, whom I adored. In the winter he took me to the driving range and I spent hours ice-skating at a pond the range had built while he hit golf balls. We did this twice, and I hung on his promise to take me snake hunting, but we never got to. Ralph used to catch snakes, especially copperheads, at Shorehaven Golf Course, where he caddied and would toss them into the trunk in a paper bag to relocate from the golf course and scare mom. I am sure I loved snakes and nature because of Ralph.

Ralph was an Army Air Corps World War II Veteran Staff Sergeant with the 332 Troop Carrier Squadron serving in the China-Burma-India Theater. His weapon of choice in Burma (now Myanmar) was a machete, moving through the jungle. Ralph was laid up with malaria and could not go with his crew on their last mission. Flying over the "Hump" (a term used by pilots who flew this dangerous section of the Yangtze River), his entire crew went down and was never found. My mother told me he never got over that loss. I knew of Burma very early on and the fight against communism in this part of the world.

During the early years, when I was about two, Mom had a mental break-down, and Mary and I were separated from each other and Dad. We were farmed out to relatives to care for us while she recovered and Ralph worked. Ralph had a breakdown also, I am told. I was fortunate to be cared for by my Aunt Beth, and Mary went to the Valerie family, where they would say prayers before each meal on bent knees on a hard floor next to their chairs. They were a very strict religious family, and though we were Catholic, our parents practiced nothing like this.

A vivid recollection in preschool: I was about three, and we were required to take naps and not allowed to get up to use the bathroom during nap time. I don't understand this rule to this day. I had a Band-Aid on my eyebrow from an injury, and it was pulling on my eye, so I got up to remove it. I was caught and summarily brought to the front of the class after nap time. In front of all the kids, my pants and underwear were pulled down, and I was paddled with a wooden paddle by the female director. Yes, I was very young, but this was horrifying—not only the pain, but the embarrassment. Mary and I were brought up to respect anyone in authority and to never think hate or even use the word. It was considered worse than swearing. I hated this woman and did so for a very long time. I also questioned God and became a bed-wetter early on. Thankfully, I told my parents, and to their credit, as there were few options those days, they took me out of that facility immediately. I think many events like this impacted my faith and belief in adults and God at the time.

After Mom's breakdown, she was hospitalized for less than a year, and Dad took us to visit her a single time. I really don't remember much. Years later, Dad got really sick. He was in terrible pain in his legs. I remember him downing large bottles of aspirin, without water, every day. He died a horrific and painful death from a blood-necrotizing bacterial disease at the Veterans hospital at Rocky Hill. He was forty-three.

I was eight and asked my mom and uncle Bob, with a group of adults hanging around the house, "When are we going to see daddy again?" I got this look and was handed a missal (*a Catholic liturgical book that describes texts and masses throughout a year*). A passage was pointed to, and I was told to read it and sent upstairs. I did not understand. I didn't know what paragraph to read, and a darkness seemed to come over me, and I started to cry. I was in hopes the tears would land on the paragraph I was supposed to read. But in that darkness, I knew my dad was gone. I was angry at God and angry at all the adults in my life. This was when I turned to an imaginary world of wild horses to protect me from adults. It was a survival mechanism; I was told later on.

Mom raised my sister and me as a single parent. With her work schedule it really came down to Mary, my sister, raising me. Mom married Jack, Ralph's best friend, within a year. Jack was a marine serving in the First Marine Battalion on Guadalcanal. He told me harrowing stores of survival. When I knew Jack, he was a firefighter and worked during the time when protective equipment such a breathing apparatus was rarely used. A primary reason for his death from lung cancer. He later became a fire inspector and was responsible for the 'No Smoking' signs posted at gas stations throughout the country. I truly loved and honored Jack. He sexually abused me, though we had been very close. I did not understand. I came to avoid going out on the boat with him or even being around home at all. It was a very hard time, as I had trusted, accepted, and loved him as though he were my own dad. As though he were Ralph. I think the secrecy and lies that surround sexual assault and abuse, especially when carried into adulthood cause the most damage. When a child is told they should be enjoying something they absolutely hate and despise and told not to tell for fear of hurting other loved ones, it is so destructive. And those lies and secrets, I think, are more damaging than the act itself. Mary and I suffered verbal abuse from both our parents and it can be as destructive.

In a short span—less than five years—Jack and I again became a close father-daughter team. I am not sure how, but we did. Youth can be very forgiving. He always referred to me as his "little Harold," as I would do all sorts of menial jobs helping him with plumbing, carpentry, electrical work, and jobs around the house. I learned a lot. My mother would only buy me trucks, horses, and soldier and cowboy toys. I never got a doll, and this was the era of the Barbie doll. I never told my mom about the abuse and didn't tell my sister or even my best friend until years later. I felt it would be a betrayal and that it would hurt my mom too much. In my later years, I see much of this sexual abuse as a disease of secrecy. My stepdad told me not to tell. He told me it would hurt my mom. I would never tell my mom, as I didn't want her to hate or turn against Jack. And I didn't tell my sister, as she already had relationship problems with Jack, and I wanted her to love him as I did. What a tangled web we weave through lies and secrets. I thought I was protecting my late dad's image of Jack being his best friend. That is a pretty weighty responsibility for a young child.

When I finally did tell my sister, I didn't think she believed me. When I asked her about doubting me years later, she told me it wasn't doubting me; it was feeling such guilt that she had left me in that situation. What an immense tear jerker that was. Jack died less than five years after Ralph's death, and I was with him at the end, making him Jell-O, the only thing he could swallow. Though Mom tried to keep me away, she told me later he asked that I not see him "like this." We all have our stories, but I never felt like a victim. Somehow, I knew I had the strength to weather almost anything. Mary always called us the original latch-key kids (kids home alone as they had working parents and never home during the day) and survivors. Both Ralph and Jack were baptized Catholic prior to death. Our Priest, Father Henchy, told Mary and me that desire of my Mom was something many priests attempt to attain.

A common perception these days with all the victimhood celebrants is that those of us who have achieved professionally or academically are either privileged or entitled in some way. I have been told by colleagues and some of my students that my career and life must have been easy by making assumptions that my parents paid for everything. I paid for my education and everything else including my car and my home, eventually. I worked to get scholarships, both academic and athletic. I had a paper route very early on. I was a lifeguard, waitress, hostess, bartender, exotic dancer, perfume shop greeter, school and transit bus driver, and aerobics, fitness, and yoga teacher as side jobs throughout my career. Many of these jobs were difficult to obtain. One had to work at it to get in the door, so to speak. I did not enjoy waitressing and wanted something that was more challenging and more me. I saw an ad for bus drivers. I applied in person. I was rejected, as I was twenty-one, and you had to be twenty-two. Nothing was said about me being female,

Bartender at Miramar on Long Island while attending graduate school circa 1975

but I felt it and would not succumb. I returned when I was twenty-two and said I was ready. Well, not so fast. You have to drive a stick and have a class II license. OK, I am willing; how do I do that? I was told as a young woman; I could not be a bus driver. I would be hassled by the students and other drivers, I wouldn't be able to handle a break down, the parents wouldn't like it. I was not buying it. I waited till I was of age, went on to get all the licenses, and came back and handed the bus company owner all my documentation. He stood amazed and impressed and said, "Well, we start now." I was trained by Harold, a great guy, and the rest is history. He was black and we got along great. No one cared about your color! During my first lesson driving stick in a forty-four-foot bus, I applied the brake a bit too hard and sent Harold flying into the rear-view mirror. He came out with a bloodied head but was smiling. He was a very patient man. He high-fived me when I passed all the driving tests and we got a good laugh out of the actual driving test. I was so nervous. I performed all the required checks in my brain; mirrors, windows, brakes, safety checks, ready for take-off. I looked at my road tester and he calmly stated, you might want to turn on the engine. I drove all through graduate school, and that was how I paid my tuition and room and board.

I worked those jobs both part- and full-time throughout college and graduate school to be able to afford my tuition and board. When I still could not afford my tuition or room and board, I walked to the bank, took out a loan in my name only, and paid it back as soon as I was employed. My mother could not afford to pay and, refused to co-sign any loan for anything related to college and didn't. She was proud of my efforts to seek out scholarships and loans and pay them off with hard work.

I started my career job in 1973 as assistant director of biological sciences at Environmental Analysts with a master's in marine biology at twenty-two. That was a big title with big responsibilities that I learned to grow into. I had only men working for me. I was head of a sampling crew that performed major field investigations of the Great Lakes, Niagara and the Hudson Rivers and the first field investigation of Love Canal. The captain of the Canadian boat and the US crew answered to me, and there was total respect for how I performed. I was fortunate to work for companies that provided academic reimbursement. This was how I went on to complete my masters and earn my doctorate in environmental engineering. All came with having to maintain high grades, or no reimbursement. This was while working full-time and part-time jobs and attending school at night.

I can't really remember ever not working. I started at twelve years old helping Mom and Jack in their furniture-cleaning business, and I recall my mom and one of the head workers saying I worked harder than any of the men they hired. I loved it though. And in anticipation of becoming work age, I already got employed to waitress at Howard Johnsons, the day I turned 16. I cried when I could not start. I had the measles!

I was one of four women early in my career who attended major environmental, water pollution, engineering, and oil spill conferences. One became my mentor for years, Dr. Geraldine Cox, with Raytheon and then a vice president of the Chemical Manufacturers Association (CMA). I was guest speaker at major national and international environmental conferences, published over twenty articles in major environmental and scientific journals, and went on to design environmental programs for the US Navy and other military services. One such publication was with Mahidol University in Bangkok, Thailand, which I was very proud of. I was fortunate and had opportunities, but most often I sought those opportunities out.

Over my career I spent seventeen years working with private industry, state and local environmental protection agencies, and the US EPA and had many accomplishments. In 1989 I was provided the opportunity to establish an entire environmental protection program at a military base, Naval Air Station Miramar, known then as Top Gun. I jumped at the chance, though it was a major reduction in salary, and there developed the first and only Environmental Protection Symposium at a military installation, bringing in federal, state, and local environmental regulatory agencies, private environmental protection groups, industry, the surrounding community, animal rescue groups and the public in an effort to communicate mutual protection goals. This effort put an emphasis on 'we working together' to achieve goals, met with rave reviews but was never again funded.

I had done the reduction in salary several times in my career. It was never about the money. It was what I would truly enjoy doing, working hard and best achieving my goal of protecting the environment in concert with industry and military operations. I was never naïve enough to think one could just ignore industry and economics.

Today many young and older people forget or do not know the battles women have been through, not only to vote but to be considered equals in employment and in sports. My mother's house buying experience is a perfect example of women being denied privileges afforded to men in the not-so-long-ago past. Yes, "we have come a long way baby," and I don't mean the ability to smoke a cigarette, which is where the saying comes from. Many don' t realize how far. In my first career job as assistant director of biological sciences, I was paid $9,600. Within that first year, several other scientists were hired, all men, and their starting salaries were $12,500. I fought back and that was hard for me. I was told I had to understand they had families, and I was single. For one thing, this was not even true except for one guy. Eventually, my salary was adjusted as appropriate, but not without leaving that bad taste about equality in salary.

Women being treated the same as men in business has been an evolution. My childhood dream since I was seven was to become a veterinarian. I even sketched what my clinic would look like in Colorado. My goal was Cornell University. At the time, Cornell was known as the best veterinary school in the country. That was where I wanted to go. When the time came, I discovered Cornell did not allow women in their veterinary school! I attended a meeting where the dean was talking about opening three hundred slots for women. He added that "we do not want you, and we will make it very tough!" Did I hear that right? Yes, I was there. I went online to verify this info, and there Cornell boasts it was the first university to have both men and women attend. May be true of their college, this is not true of their veterinary school. By the time they would open, it was too late for me, as I was already applying to college.

I had always been very athletic and played in almost every sport available to women in high school and college. Most team sports were available only to men during this time—soccer, swimming, golf, track and field, and so on. The exception was field hockey. When I was a varsity player in team sports, our women's teams (field hockey, lacrosse, basketball) never had the budget for uniforms or travel and scheduling with competing schools in other states often scheduling 10-12 games a season that cost money and available to the men's teams. That was a battle of the times, and women in sports have progressed a long way. Many competing today are totally unaware of those battles. They just think it was always like it is today. It wasn't. I had a relative tell me it was easier for me competing when I went to school as there wasn't as much competition. There probably would be no women team sports if it weren't for my generation and those before and after me creating them. This comment is illustrative of how many now judge history by what they currently experience. It destroys our ability to learn from our past.

Men's and women's team sports play in leagues of comparable skill level and size of school. Occasionally we were scheduled to play Pennsylvania State or Cornell, and these schools, known as jock schools, were well beyond our league and capability. It was an honor and a challenge to play them though the women stood heads taller, majored in athletics, and were close, to pros and we undoubtedly would get creamed. My point is that women's teams played other women's teams that were comparable in skill level. A fair playing field, we called it. Same with the mens' teams. Our men's soccer team was highly skilled, and they did play tier-one schools. The current situation in the women's sport of swimming, where a male turned female is competing with other females, is appalling to anyone who has gone through all the progression and development in women's sports. Women in sports have achieved so much to be on equal footing with men's teams and not to be competing with males.

I ran marathons long before they became popular, especially with women, and completed fifty-two. When Ironman distance came about in 1980, I completed four and then onto ultra-events, including a rim-to-rim-to-rim run across the Grand Canyon (about fifty miles with major elevation changes) and then a bicycle ride from the north rim back to California, totaling 460 miles, mostly along Route 66. Temperatures ranged from 39 degrees on the north rim of the Grand Canyon to 111 degrees in Needles, California, and we completed the event in 3.5 days. Only a single rider, Brian Rapp, continued on with me, and we had no support vehicle. The other eight individuals dropped out at the start of the bike ride. They were too tired and too cold to continue, and they were the intended support vehicles.

Yet another remembrance that escapes many was that the marathon as an Olympic event for women was denied until 1980. It was actually published in news articles that women weren't considered strong enough—we would faint, would develop muscle mass like men, grow mustaches, and other ghastly statements about vomiting at the finish line and having our periods interrupted. Kathrine Switzer was physically pulled out of the Boston Marathon in 1967, and she completed it unofficially. The race manager assaulted her while she ran, trying to pull her from the race. Many young women in sports today do not know how difficult it was to compete for years for women. When I completed my first New York City Marathon in 1975, there were less than 30 women in the race. Within a few years, there were hundreds, then thousands. We have come so far, and now women are being made to compete against men who have decided to be women. This is going backward in time, people. Where is the #Metoo movement and all the feminists now? Remember when 279 mostly Christian young girls were captured from Nigeria by the Boko Haram Islamist terrorist group in 2014? All the Hollywood types were all over social media with a hash tag "save our girls" slogan. Didn't last long. Most of the kidnapped girls weren't released until seven years later, and Boko Haram remains active and dangerous!

Another common thread noted throughout this compilation is that America's educational system is seriously deficient in comparison to the countries these people came from. This saddens me. My family and I attended one of the best educational programs in the country, the Norwalk City school system in Norwalk, Connecticut. My mother, sister, and I attended the same high school. Though my mother attended Catholic school early on, she was adamant about us attending public school at that time, as the system was well known as excellent. The same is true of my colleges: Hartwick in Oneonta, New York, Long Island University, and New York University (NYU) I had outstanding teachers and professors, and to this day I remember and thank each and every one of them.

We had no cheat sheets, no calculators were allowed, you could use a slide rule in advanced math and physics classes. Many of our grade school through high school educational systems and funding in US are dependent on location, whether that be states or districts, and probably the time frame one attended. Thus, I can see that many immigrants might have attended schools in other states, and in more recent times, requirements were being lessened with the idea that all should succeed, no one should fail or be held back, and everyone should get a trophy. These ideals just work against education, not toward making young students think or want what works best for them. The idea that was much touted during Obama's time that I felt definitely impacted our educational system for the worse was his idea that everyone should go through four years of liberal arts college and get a bachelor's. I thought about all the trade schools, ranchers, agricultural farms, kids who are working in trades, and skills that benefit all and don't need or want four-year liberal arts college. It was such a limiting, short-sighted policy that I felt did more to damage education than almost anything until maybe now. I had a close friend who attended my aerobics classes who started up a trades and technical school and developed it into one of the most renowned technical schools. All his students went on to great jobs in IT and trades when they graduated. With Obama's policies, his trade schools went bankrupt. A disservice to us all.

In school, we did have to memorize (which I am told by a current California high school teacher is considered old school and not as much required these days), take other languages, give oral presentations, and use critical thinking skills. We took math, physics, chemistry, English grammar, languages, history from ancient to medieval to more current, civics, geography, geology, music, art, theology, and so on. One could choose to go trade school or liberal arts routes. We were fortunate to go through school at a time when music, art, and athletics were also valued and funded. Again, this depended on state and funding. Where I was, one had to take home economics if female or shop if male. I did not want to take home economics. I was not interested at all. I wanted more science or shop, and when I requested taking shop, my request was denied as "Girls take home economics; only boys take shop." And that was then. Though I was not a scholastic marvel, I worked hard and loved school, and though I did not get 800s on my SATs, I made up for it by taking many science classes and participating in extracurricular activities in music and sports. I think my love of learning is demonstrated by my college record, where the requirement was to graduate with 132 (required) credits. I graduated with 168, and they were mainly science courses.

I sang in choir and played the violin and continue to this day. My sister and I rented a violin for fifteen dollars a month. I played in the Norwalk Youth Symphony and Norwalk Symphony orchestras. In the youth symphony, an excellent orchestra under the direction of Mr. John Master, we accompanied Pablo Casals, the world-renowned cellist (to many today, he would be your Yo-Yo Ma). He was so gracious, he actually stood at the end of our performance and turned to the orchestra, bowed, and thanked us, telling us we were a joy to play with. I so wanted a copy of this recording but knew my mother could not afford the $15.00 for the record, so I never even asked. A regret to this day. I also got to play in our Connecticut All State orchestras and played and sang at the World's Fair.

The 1950s were the beginning of the Cold War, an era in the US when we were taught to duck and cover under our desks at school in case of nuclear attack from the Soviet Union (like a desk is going to help!). Ultimately, there was a major call for people to build bomb shelters. Since my family was relatively poor and did not own property, there would be no building of a bomb shelter. I recall vividly going to the movie theater and seeing films of what a nuclear detonation looked like, its destructive power illustrated by a simulation of a detonation and what would happen to an everyday neighborhood. Later in life I worked for Dr. Merril Eisenbud, a nuclear physicist and consultant for the US Navy. He was involved in the nuclear testing at Eniwetok and other Pacific islands. Dr. Eisenbud had advised against testing on these islands, as he knew his science, and with wind drift what would happen to the inhabited islands, though the testing islands were uninhabited. Years later I attended graduate school for my doctorate at NYU, where Dr. Eisenbud was the first health and safety chief of the United States Atomic Energy Commission and the first head of the New York City Environmental Protection Agency. He helped establish the NYU Environmental Medical Center at Stirling Forest. He was also the owner and director of Environmental Analysts Inc., where I started my environmental career.

As I look back at the 1950s and on, I see now the sacrifices made by our parents and grandparents, most serving in World War II. Others served in Korea, and far more classmates and friends were in Vietnam, the Gulf War,

Iraq, and Afghanistan. I served as a civilian in Iraq as the chief environmental engineer for the Multinational Forces–Iraq (MNF-I). My grandparents were all immigrants from Ireland, France, England, Holland. My stepdad's heritage is Danish, and my brother-in-law's family came from Italy. I listened and learned from their stories as well as my own experiences.

I remember Nikita Khrushchev of the Soviet Union taking offense at a United Nations General Assembly meeting in 1960 to a comment by a delegate from the Philippines who claimed that Eastern Europe had been "deprived of political and civil rights" and had been effectively swallowed up by the Soviet Union. Khrushchev continuously pounded the table with his fists, then took off his shoe and pounded more forcefully, stating, "We will bury you!" Now there is a lot of history here regarding Gary Powers and the U2 spy plane, but leave it to say it was scary to a young child and an exacerbation of the Cold War.

As I mentioned, I loved school and learning, whether from parents or teachers. We had an old dictionary that I would read due to the Latin derivations of words and how expressions came about. This fascinated me. Jack had a medical encyclopedia, a book on tropical fish, a veterinarian medical text, and a horrific one from World War II authored by Otto Adolph Eichmann (*one of Hitler's henchmen and organizer of the "Final Solution to the Jewish Question"*) with actual photographs that were beyond horrific. But I devoured these texts. A reminder of that book was meeting an older runner in our running club who had been with the 101st Airborne Division, which was responsible for freeing the prisoners at Auschwitz and the like. It was tough asking him anything about it, and he said he did not want to discuss it, but he did tell me that whatever I could conjure, imagine, or had seen, it was much worse.

When I was in junior high school, my mom bought me a Remington typewriter for my birthday. So I started a club, the Interested Club, with a couple of my friends, and we were, well, interested in the world. I was voted president and secretary, as I had the typewriter. The two others were the vice president and a member. There was no treasurer, as we had no money. I began preparing letters to different countries asking about life and what was so special about their country. How I found all these various addresses

I am not sure, but I did. After mailing out numerous letters to countries we were curious about due to either history or geography class, I started receiving boxes of information from the USSR, the only country that we heard back from. Our club lasted through the summer months while we were out of school. Then it was back to school, and we disbanded, though I continued to receive books and pamphlets from the Soviet Union. I was amazed.

In grade school we were provided hardcover textbooks for the courses we would be taking. We treated those hardcover books like gold. They were handed down from one class to the next, and you protected your book by making book covers out of brown paper grocery bags. Many, like me, really worked hard to protect these books, somehow realizing that they were valuable. This must have been passed down from Mom, as she taught me how to break a book's binding (the spine—so the book would not lose its pages) and other such memorable book-loving details. I say this because I was in awe of the hard cover, full glossy paper, and photographic quality of these texts sent by the Soviet Union. The

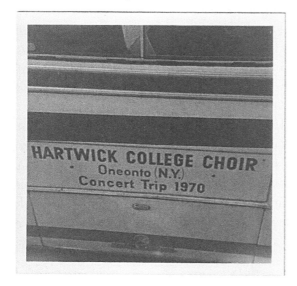

Photos of bus taking choir to airport and Dr. Dox (right) meeting with hosts throughout Europe. 1970

books were gorgeous and all brand new. None were multiple copies of the same book, but each a different book on how great life was in the USSR, from farming, land availability, and food production to military might, to the commitments of all to work to create the food basket of the world. The pamphlets were just as beautifully done as the books. I recall hearing about

Pravda, the famous Communist newspaper and propaganda machine. This was that machine in action in a new vein, getting to school kids.

I never responded to anything and stopped receiving correspondence, which was probably a good thing. I had started getting a bit worried. Later

on, I discarded all this information, thinking that it could come back to haunt me. But it was my first taste of the reality of propaganda and how the Soviet Union wanted to portray itself to the world. I was about twelve.

In 1970, I was extremely fortunate to be selected for my college choir, the Hartwick College Choir, to tour Europe under the direction of Dr. Thurston Dox. We toured five countries in a month, performing primarily in churches, cathedrals, and other venues. What is absolutely amazing about this time is that the Berlin Wall still stood, and we performed in East and West Germany and even in a

very old church in East Berlin. Our hotel was almost right up against the Berlin Wall. We could look out our window and see the top of the wall, the razor wire, and the gun turrets. I was horsing around like any freshman college student and told my classmates I would jump across over to the wall and walk on it, it was so close. I made like I was going to do just that. I am quite sure I would not have done this.

But friends grabbed me and pointed to the armed soldiers in the turrets, all with machine guns pointed in my direction. They had taken notice. "Surely, you're joking, Mr. Feynman." No, they were not joking, and it was a scary, eye-opening experience for me not to be a crazy-ass kid.

Traveling by bus from West Germany into East Germany was memorable. It was like going from civilization into a ghostly world. It was snowing and cold. West Germany looked developed and pleasant; East Germany was otherworldly: bleak and dark. No trees grew, and the ones that did exist were black. It was like they all had died and never came back.

The dreariness was disconcerting to all. When you have a bunch of teenagers go dead silent, you know they are taking something in. Obviously, we had East Germans escorting us who did not appreciate a gaggle of teenagers and treated us rather brusquely. We were provided bagged lunches and were told we could not eat on the bus. We had to get off and eat on the ground outside. There was nothing there—no park benches, no city, no streets, no lights. Just dead black trees and snow almost out of *Grimms' Fairy Tales* and the story of *Vasilisa*. It was cold, and we ate in the wet snow. We either sat on the frozen ground or stood trying to eat. The "Coke" they provided tasted like pepper. When we returned to the bus, the driver scolded us to not touch the seats with our hands, or we would be put off the bus!

West Germany (previous page)
East Germany Berlin Wall (above)

Finally, we arrived at the ancient little church where we were to perform. It was depressing. It was frigid out and just as cold inside the church. The church was beautiful and very, very old. We had to rehearse as soon as we arrived and perform later that evening. It was a grueling schedule. We figured no one would attend this performance. For one thing, we were college-age Americans, and who wants to sit in an ice-cold church and listen to these college kids for a couple of hours?

The church was packed with East Berliners, and all were very silent. We did not feel any warmth from these people at all. But we were a very good choir with some unbelievable talent and a great conductor. When we finished singing and pouring our hearts out with this beautiful church music, much of it in Latin, we met deathly silence. All was still until this tiny, stern-looking elderly woman in a babushka stood. I thought she was going to walk out. We all did. Then she started a very slow, loud clap, one, two, three, and then the entire church stood and clapped with more and more speed and energy. It brought tears to my eyes as it does now just to tell this story. I don't think these people had ever clapped in this church before. It is not custom. I saw her smile. I look back at this wonderful, fulfilling, and enlightening experience. These East Berliners would not stop their applause. The energy did not subside. The goodness and the strength of the people showed through the bleakness of their environment and being separated from the rest of Germany due to communism. They held our hands and just smiled at us, shaking our hands with so much love it was unbelievable. It took years before that wall came down, but it did on November 9, 1989. And I can say I met the people on the other side who did not deserve the life they suffered under that regime. (*It was the St. Nicholas Church, built between 1220 and 1230, replacing the 520 AD Christian Church where St. Nicholas served as a bishop. St. Nicholas Church became famous again in 1989 with Monday demonstrations and the peaceful revolt against communist rule*).

In 1984 again I was fortunate to be selected out of a group of eight scientists across the US to work for the Royal Government of Thailand as an environmental adviser. Thailand was run by a monarch and still is but also has a parliament. The Thai are a wonderful, friendly, and beautiful people, as mentioned by a previous interviewee, Dr. Leroy Carson, in this writeup. The Thai really liked Americans. My contract, once I saw it in Thailand, read like I was an American superhero who would single-handedly address and heal all Thailand's environmental woes. Well, that was not the case, but I achieved a lot and met some wonderful people that to this day wish I had maintained friendships with. It was like, OK, back to work, and I let that go. A regret.

Though I remember Thailand as an experience of a lifetime, it did have its challenges. For one thing, the selection process took almost a year, and there was a long time when I did not think it would happen. It was also difficult to know what decisions I should make concerning my existing job and ca-

reer. On my way to Thailand, I had no signed contract in hand, I was not part of a US group sponsored by USAID (United States Agency for International Development) or anything similar, and I would be working directly for the Thai government and paid in baht! I did not know much of this prior to getting there. Talk about a wing and a prayer. But I wanted the adventure. Many friends and colleagues told me not to go. One counselor said to me the Asians did not respect women as professionals and that I would not be respected. She also told me I would not be selected for the same reasons. Another friend that I really trusted said I should never go without a signed contract. Well, I went. Something was just in my heart to explore and trust.

Having to go through China to get there was eventful. The 1980s was a time of cameras, film, and no cell phones. Film was a big deal, especially while traveling, as your film could easily be damaged by security x-rays at the airports, and China was known to use very powerful x-ray technology.

I was told to protect my film, and with a yearlong endeavor like this, I had a lot of film. While passing through security, I was asked many questions, and I was the only white person on this flight of hundreds. I could not understand the heavy Chinese accent and was a bit intimidated. "Yes, I have film." I was immediately surrounded with security and escorted away from the other passengers and put in a small room. Now I was terrified. They were questioning me, searching me. Thankfully a KLM agent was notified as to what was happening, and two of them came after me. They translated, and I admitted that I had film. There was much back and forth, then laughter. They had asked me if I had firearms, not film! I was escorted back to the plane by the KLM crew and boarded my flight, a bit shaken and a bit embarrassed, as who could I possibly explain this to? Film, not firearms. They don't use *r*'s too well.

Arriving in Bangkok, I was just happy to be somewhere that I might feel a bit safe. It had been a grueling trip. I was met by my boss and colleagues, Dr. Jarapong, Mses. Sukanya, Cattleya, and Mr. Anat. A wonderful, smiling group—well, maybe except Dr. Jarupong. This is all for another story, but suffice to say that all those details that were never documented while in the States came through loud and clear, and me with only a one-way ticket paid by the Thai government. There was no getting on a plane and heading back home.

First thing was to get me medically examined. I had taken numerous

inoculations (vaccines) prior to coming. I thought all the required medical procedures were done. But since I was a *forang* (*Thai term for foreigners*) working for the Thai, I would have to be medically examined by the Thai for their contract. The exam was extremely intrusive and invasive. I do not recall a medical exam taken in the US that was this "detailed." Were they looking for drugs in cavities? That must have been part of it. I was horrified but survived. They attempted to sooth me afterward, but it wasn't working. I was humiliated and angry.

When I developed typhoid in Thailand and eventually had to experience their medical hospitality again, it was very different. Though I did have an American doctor, all others were Thai. When I came to, I thought they were angels, as I truly thought I might die. I survived the disease, was cleared, and went on to complete my work after losing almost 20 pounds in two weeks. My disease that disabled me for quite a time in Thailand resulted from a rather humorous incident. I was a runner and wanted to continue to do that while working in Thailand. The Thai were not accustomed to women running in shorts (not polite), and it is very hot and humid during the day, so I ran around 5:00 a.m. Obviously, visibility was bad, as were the roads. I ran at Kasetsart University, which was close to where I was living, so I could run there and feel a bit safe and away from traffic. Many *klongs*, or canals, run through most areas, and many are seriously contaminated with sewage. I would run with my huge gate key in my hand from the compound where I stayed.

I decided to run a grassy route one morning, and as I ran across this seemingly solid grass area, I dropped straight down into a klong. It was beyond shocking, and as I swam to get to the surface, I lost my gate key. My mouth had opened as I laughed, and I am sure I took in what I now know to have been sewage water. I was covered with mud and lily pads and must have been a sight.

It was getting light, and people were coming onto campus, and now I could be seen. I ran back to my secure compound with looks and stares like I was out of a monster movie. I knew getting in was going to be a problem. The Thai family I stayed with, who were wonderful, had about thirteen dogs for guarding. I rang the bell, and all hell broke loose with the dogs. One of the maids finally came to the gate and didn't recognize me through all the mud and algae. I tried to explain, but she did not understand English, and I was a shocking sight, especially for the Thai. When I finally did get to explain, laughter was abundant. Losing the key was, however, not good. I got deathly sick within a week of that event.

The Thai are very leery of the North Vietnamese, and there were still battles going on along the border. When we traveled near the border, you could occasionally hear arms firing. I traveled throughout Thailand for my job, and there were communist insurgents holed up in several locations, especially in the boot area headed down to Phuket and in the Northern Triangle with Cambodia and Laos, as well as along the eastern border, where Vanchatt and his family escaped from Cambodia *(see Chapter 1)*, where we could hear shots being fired.

Some of these travels were disconcerting. On one trip, we were traveling south through Thailand to visit some oil and mining companies and farmers using a variety of pesticides, possibly unsafe formulations, with incorrect usage guidance or no protective equipment. I was warned there were communist insurgents in this area and to be careful. I believe that is why our driver was doing about a hundred miles per hour on very bad roads. The drive was absolutely terrifying. There appeared to be no rules of the road in Thailand.

My Thai team conducting mining inspections: Thailand 1984

I was hunkered down in the back seat pleading that he slow down, being very polite so he would not lose face. No way! My safety was his concern, I was told. Not if I am dead. Then the shots rang out. Our windshield was shattered. I was pushed down onto the floor. (*You'll hear this song again*).

And he sped up! With no windshield, mind you. We were now being pelted by flying debris and rocks.

Me with Anat, a member of my environmental team, and my driver, who kept me safe in many precarious situations.

Putting many miles between us and the mountain range, we made it to safe territory. No cell phones, no pay phones, no radios, no nothing in the country. No way to call for help, so no need to ask why we didn't. The Thai would say "Mia pen rai" and just laugh! *(No big deal, never mind, or no problem).* I can personally tell you that living in many countries where communists want to take hold, they make life miserable for those trying to just get by.

I was told I had to take the train back by myself, and my entourage would return in the damaged car. I am not sure why that decision was made, but

there's just so much you should question when you are a guest in another country and don't want them or you to lose face. I needed the translators, and they became good friends. *(Another reason why what recently happened in Afghanistan sickens me. I was dependent on my Thai translators and Iraqi contractors in Iraq years later).*

Taking the train from Phuket to Bangkok was another event of a lifetime. I felt like I was on the *Orient Express*. It was truly exciting and a bit scary.

And Phuket is one of the most beautiful places on the planet. It will never be as I remember it, as there was only a single hotel under construction where I stayed on the water at this time. Nothing else. All the rest was untouched beach. It was out of the James Bond movie *Moonraker*.

My trip to Burma and back while in Thailand was another learning experience. Then on a trip to the north, another world from southern Thailand to visit ranches, a pig farm, and orchards of the Northern Triangle (to convince the locals it was better to grow peaches than opium—yeah, that went over with many giggles). My Thai friends decided we should take a side trip into Burma (now Myanmar). Burma is a hot place and has borders with China, Laos, Thailand, Bangladesh, Rangoon and India for terrorism, drug and human trafficking as well as rebel groups. Burma itself has over a hundred ethnic groups. I was informed by USAID (Agency for International Development), which was partially responsible for my contract with the Thai government, to not ever leave Thailand, especially into Burma. "You go there, you may not be heard from again, and there is nothing the US government can do for you." (The Burma Communist Party is the oldest existing political party in Myanmar. It was founded in 1939. The Union Revolutionary Council established Burma as a one-party socialist state under BSPP and adopted the Burmese Way to Socialism in 1962 to bringing almost all of Burma's political, social and economic life under strict military control. Burma then ran as an independent republic until 2008. On February 1,

2021, Myanmar's military took over in a military coup. Protests have been going on *since February 24, 2021.)*

My Thai colleagues say, *"No problem (Mei pen rai). We go from Chang Rai into Burma all the time."* Well, yes, but you are not an American, and I had been told the Burmese hate Americans. *"No, no they like us. They like you."* With great hesitancy I walked across the northern Thai border with Sukanya, Cattleya, and Anat, my environmental team, into communist

Burma. Again, it was like walking into another world. From the Thai border with the single white bar across the road, like you see in many developing countries, we went from no people around on the smiling Thai side to unsmiling Burmese sitting on

Northern Hilltribes people of Thailand. Children are often born to very young girls. Roos photos 1984

the ground along both sides of the road. It was eerie, as they were all just sitting cross legged or in a deep-knee crouch (Asian style), with blackened teeth, smoking and chewing and passing some Kun-yar or betel nuts back and forth.

Their teeth were black, and the look was either just intolerant or hate. I got a very bad vibe right away. Once they noticed me, they started waving their hands at me and becoming more aggressive. When some started standing up, I knew we were in trouble. Anat gently spoke to them. I had experienced Anat's time in Thailand becoming a monk. It is common practice for all young Thai men to experience being a monk. Not all remain. He was always very gentle and made a perfect monk in my eyes. I am not sure

he spoke their language, but they were communicating. They told him that they could come across, but they shoved their arms, pointing at me—but not with me. I had to go back across the border. So we turned tail, and not too soon from my perspective. My friends were very apologetic. Thai are not rude, and they considered this very rude behavior. (Rude? I could have been dead, and they were talking how rude! I just love the Thai for understatement). I was just glad to be back on the Thai side. When I relayed this information

Anat training to become a monk with me and Cattleya. Ritual for all young Thai men. 1984

back at the USAID office, I was giving an earful, and that was when I got that lecture about disappearing and never being found again. Another lesson learned. And I learned about human trafficking, which we heard little to nothing about during those years.

From Thailand I was allowed to take a little time off, but not enough to get back to the States. My USAID friends recommended I go to Nepal. I really wanted to go there after all my AID colleagues had told me about Nepal, its breathtaking scenery, and its people. I also wanted to get into Tibet and purchase a Tibetan carpet, a longtime desire. This was the time when it was forbidden to enter Tibet. The monks still maintained their faith and the place of

Interviews with farmers on pesticide use.

the Dalia Lama's once winter home, Potala Palace, in Lhasa. *Tibet is known as the Rooftop of the World (and it is). It has been part of China for around eight hundred years. In Tibet today there is no freedom of speech, religion, or press. The Dalai Lama fled in 1959 to India and lives among one hundred thousand other Tibetan refugees in government exile and will probably never see Tibet again. The Chinese killed over 1.2 million Tibetans, according to the fourteenth Dalai Lama.*

In 1955 Nepal restored diplomatic relations with China (PRC), and in a treaty signed in 1956, Nepal recognized Tibet as part of China. While I was in Nepal, Nepal was a Hindu kingdom under King Birendi, who made Nepal a constitutional monarchy, and was a member of the Shah dynasty. The dynasty was ended in 2008 after a 240-year-old monarchy. Today Nepal is a federal democratic republic with a constitution. It has a president as head of state and a prime minister who heads the government. The prime minister is chief executive of a 601-member assembly responsible for drafting a new constitution in 2020. While trekking in Nepal with my young thirteen-year-old Sherpa, I experienced much more of what life was like in

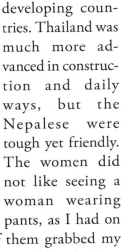

developing countries. Thailand was much more advanced in construction and daily ways, but the Nepalese were tough yet friendly. The women did not like seeing a woman wearing pants, as I had on hiking pants. Several of them grabbed my breast to ensure I was a woman. Disconcerting, to say the least. My Sherpa took me to his home, which was a mud hut along the trail from Pokhara to the base camp of Everest. The hut was made of water buffalo dung and sand similar to ones I saw later in Africa. However, these huts were smooth and rounded and not like the brick ones of Africa in Botswana. What they needed was money to survive. This is 1984, and things have changed drastically in Nepal. The trail and mud huts I saw have been replaced with high rises and businesses. The horrific 2015 8.1M earthquake destroyed much of this construction, as codes are not exactly followed in places like

Trekking in Nepal with my thirteen-year-old Sherpa. 1984

Nepal. Most significantly, the earthquake killed some nine thousand people and injured twenty-two thousand. Horrific numbers of loss.

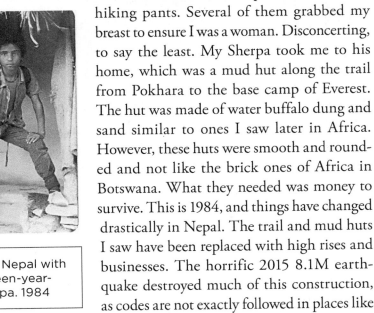

A magnifient recollection from the Nepali and Tibetan border was relayed to me by my USAID friend. He said he was on the steppes looking off at the Himalayas when a single horseman appeared and came charging at him at full bore. He stood terrified, as the horseman did not stop or seem to be holding any reins on the horse and just kept charging. He was holding something in his arms. He was turbaned, scarfed across the face, and magnificient as he sat upright, tall and bareback! In his arms was an infant. He had wanted to show off his infant to the forang. He said it was a picture ingrained in his mind forever. The story was ingrained in me. They smiled at each other, and for a Tibetan horseman, to smile is rare.

As we continued on our trek alone, I kept asking my young sherpa friend, "Are those mountains in the distance the Himalayas?" He kept shaking his head no, but I thought they must be. They were grand but looked a lot like  the Rockies or parts of the Alps to me. Finally, as we moved along, the clouds moved off, and this awe-inspiring sight took my breath away, literally! There were these towering, gigantic, six-mile-high mountains that overshadowed what I had thought were the awesome Rockies. The Himalayas lay before me, they were immense and they blotted out the sky. I can never forget that sight. It is difficult to describe. The sight was so startling and overwhelming I felt myself backing up for fear of falling backward. As soon as they appeared, they were quickly swallowed by clouds.

My young Sherpa friend knew nothing about the government but did know about the trail to Everest and how far I could go without a permit. He left me when we got to the part of the road that required me to have a permit. I knew nothing about having a permit. I was then on my own in a place where one really needs a guide, not only for trekking but for communication even to get food or sleep. I ended up sleeping in a cave with a bat and eating dahl bat with my left hand with chickens feeding off my metal plate. When I came out of my cave I was bleeding and covered with leeches.

In 1991 it was back to the Soviet Union, but not through boxes of propaganda material and books. It was now the Soviet Union, the USSR for real. It was August 1991. The time was Glasnost. I tell you; opportunity does knock. You just have to see it for what it is. I took these opportunities not knowing at the time how much they would impact me and my future development nor the impact it would have in writing this book.

Meeting of our Ambassador scientific
envoy team to Soviet Union.
Roos photo 1991

At my first offer even to go to Thailand, I said no. I had a great job, and I didn't even know where Thailand was! Then the potential to go to the Soviet Union was met by lots of fears and obstacles. This was a scientific envoy to the Soviet Union in 1991 sponsored by the US Ambassador Program jointly with the State Department, the National Science Foundation, and Soviet Ministries. This was part of US-Soviet time of glasnost in USSR, with Mikael Gorbachev and later Boris Yeltsin as its leader. It was still very much a communist regime. We were to meet with various ministries and industries and provide guidance and technologies to our various counterparts on what worked in the US, access, and funding. My working for the US Navy at the time led to some difficulties as to whether I would even be allowed to go, funded, or allowed in by the Soviets.

This experience forced me to reflect on my days with Rockwell International at the Science Center and Technology Group, where groups of Chinese and Japanese scientists were invited in to take notes and photograph our new developments and technology. I was very young and probably naïve, but I still had to sign security agreements and so on to be employed by Rockwell as a scientist. I am thinking back then on what we (the US) were doing. This is crazy. I am not even supposed to talk about this stuff outside of work, and directors have Asians photographing and picking our brains? That was early 1980s. That is another story, but it fits to what is happening (and has been for years) now in this country. The stealing of our intellectual property and here—in this case, we were pretty much giving it away, especially to a communist country like China.

During the Soviet Union's tough beginning to open up, it was not the friendliest place on earth. There were some terrifying times, and I am sure more so for the Russians during this time of unrest. Our envoy was accompanied by KGB (Komitet Gosudarstvennoy Bezopasnoti) types wherever we went, including our hotels and all site visits.

Waiting on lines for food and essentials. Daily practice in socialist and communist countries as delineated in common threads throughout these interviews. Our Soviet hosts provided us food that they themselves could not have access to. It was government provided. Roos photo 1991.

We visited all ministries and met with their directors and scientists. Our counterparts were very open and willing to talk, which surprised me. The KGB (the name was changing during Gorbachev's and Yeltsin's time) agents were not invited into their homes as we were. They discussed the long lines waiting for foodstuffs and clothing and shoes, if it was even available. They reported that possibly four pairs of shoes would be available, and people would wait on line all day until one showed up, and one of the pairs actually fit someone. I asked why don't they just tell people the sizes available. He just smiled at me. We visited the famous Gump Department store, and it was totally empty, it looked like a ghost store. One could imagine it had once been glorious, as I am sure it is today. All curved ceiling glass that reached to the skies, as though a magnificent greenhouse, but supposedly its purpose was to sell goods, not plants. That has all since changed.

Our colleagues would sometimes invite us to dinner, which was a major imposition on them, as no one had access to food. They had to wait in lines like all others. As government employees they probably had some standing, but not much, we were told. They were taking food from their own stores. That provided a great deal of insight into what had occurred through communism. They would tell us that there were no competitors for jobs like we have US. No one was left alive. All educated people had been eliminated, and only a few survived. They were disappeared into Gulags or outright killed if they were from an educated class, first by Stalin and then by Lenin. These two dictators killed more people than any wars of our times. *I was told, "you (in the US) have many scientists and engineers competing for positions in academia, industry, government, and so on. We have none. When you ask about environmental laws and regulations, we laugh—not to be rude, but to tell you reality, as we have probably more rules and regulations than the US. However, there is no enforcement of them, and if there were, someone would just pay them off with a bribe, and nothing would change." Bribes and graft have escalated with glasnost, not decreased.*

Death is the solution to all problems. No man, no problem.
—Joseph Stalin

Our stays at hotels were at moderate ones, not the fancy or most expensive ones. It was odd to note the construction, as many of us had engineering backgrounds. No two stairs would ever be the exact dimensions. One would be taller, another shorter, an eight-inch stair depth the next ten or twelve! Toilets were all different makes and installed differently. There appeared to be no construction standards or codes. There weren't any. *This is also a learning experience for many not educated in Western culture and development. The codes and standards developed in Western countries as the US's ASTM (American Standards for Testing Materials) and other construction codes, monetary codes, and standards took years, patents, and government oversight to develop. Sir Isaac Newton was prouder of his government patent job than he was of his laws of motion or calculus. The US is one of the best, especially in nuclear technology and safety. Our energy companies have spent billions researching and developing technologies to locate and utilize resources for the benefit of all society. Many just don't understand how much we will lose if this current socialist agenda is allowed to take hold. You may not have heat in winter, nor any cooling in summer, let alone be allowed to purchase just about anything you want. Let that sink in. Evolving new technologies for the betterment of mankind and the environment is one thing. Dictating the elimination of something that has decades of proven benefits before a new technology is proven is just demonstrating ignorance. The answer is planned transition. One of our colleagues worked in plumbing and design, and he was an avid photographer of every type of toilet we came across, including Asian ones in some locations. Electricity was iffy, to say the least. Construction codes and any type of enforcement to ensure codes and ordinances were followed was nonexistent. (This takes me to Iraq)*

Eating out or in hotels was always interesting. The waitstaff never smiled. I mean almost never. We took it as a contest to see if we could even make someone smile. Not in a negative sense, but just to make them know we were not their enemy. I don't think in many cases it worked—unless they were selling all the black-market goods on the street. Then everybody was your friend. They were selling parents and grandparents medals from World War II, a war that they particularly honor. Instead of parks or national parks, the Russians have monuments to the millions lost in World War II. An eternal flame was always lit at these sites, and they were beautiful and moving. Many weddings were observed at these memorial sites. Millions more were lost with Stalin and Lenin, but that was not observed, and those statues remained at the time.

I was challenged once when a Russian told me that they honor their history more than we in the US and that their historical monuments and museums demonstrated their devotion to their country and history. I acknowledged Russia's history and that museums like the Hermitage in Leningrad (now Saint Petersburg) are incomparable. The Hermitage is truly an amazing museum. However, I told him we are a new nation compared to Russia, and our national parks system belongs to all Americans and honors our lands, resources, the environment, and its native peoples (at least many of us do). We Americans cherish our national parks probably more than any museum. *America's National Parks: America's Best Idea* is a noted quote from Ken Burns on our national parks. It was a good shared talk.

I was invited to give a presentation to several ministries on how our US military actually complies with US environmental law and regulations. This was my occupation at the time. For one thing, I was greeted with almost hostile regard. This was a time (Glasnost) when Russians were turning against their military and had always been taught that America was a decadent and frivolous country. Though a civilian, I represented the US military and was not thought of highly. Not so much that it was the US military, but during these years, the Russians did not trust any military, especially their own.

Part of my presentation that was especially nerve racking was the incompatibility of technology: slide projectors. No internet or PowerPoints existed in 1991. I had slides presented in a Kodak carousel. The ministry only had single-tray slide projectors, not carousels, that were very old. Young people will not even know what I am talking about. I came prepared with backup trays. Always have a plan B. I learned long ago, especially in the military. The trays jammed, and I practically had to pick up the projector and force each slide in one at a time. The electricity went out a couple of times. The presentation hall was one similar to a large college campus where seats rose up level upon level.

I was so nervous forcing the slides and with my not-so-friendly audience that I was sweating bullets, which made my hands slip, and the projector almost dropped to the floor with loose slides. I got a couple of chuckles but not encouraging ones. No one helped. If I was to be made a fool, I was totally on my own. If this were not so serious, it would have been hilarious. I got the presentation done, with time for translation, though most spoke

some English. Half the audience was in disbelief that the US military "cared" about environmental issues, and the other half said I was lying and no military would perform compliance, cleanups, and the investigations I described, let alone set aside the funding to do so. I showed photos to back up everything. When I asked for questions, all hands went up, and I certainly was challenged in every way. I actually think I made some friends that day. I hope so. I always took my job very seriously and was very thorough, so I rarely got stumped.

Pripyat, Soviet Union, in August 1991, in Soviet-style protective gear. Emotional sight to see children's toys and day-to-day implements still in place in entire city abandoned forever. Roos in front of leaking Chernobyl Sarcophagus (above)

Visiting the Chernobyl site in Kiev (now spelled Kyiv) in 1991 was nerve racking. We were informed the sarcophagus was leaking by the US, but the Soviets said everything was fine. On our visit to Chernobyl, we were told we could choose not to go, similar to our visit to a Nazi Concentration Camp (Auschwitz-Birkenau, a World Heritage Site established in 1979). Only one of our envoy members was told not to go by his employer, and he represented our US nuclear energy sector. He informed all of us that his company advised him and our group not to go due to safety concerns even if we were to be put in personal protective gear (see photo above of the Soviet version of PPE [personnel protective equipment]) and wear dosimeters. At the site, we toured the sarcophagus, the surrounding areas, the burial of the dead forests, the town of Pripyat, and several experimental stations examining contamination to human consumption, feed crops, and wildlife. The wildlife they were concerned with were the minks and sable populations used in the fur-making industry. At the crops site, several tomatoes and other vegetables were plucked and cut up for us to eat. We were told they were safe as our Soviet guide popped tomato wedges into his mouth. Not one of us ate anything from the experimental zone. We had definitely entered the hot zone! Upon leaving the site, we were to decon (decontaminate), which entailed primarily changing back to our street clothes (no showers) and removing our hair coverings. Hair coverings were handled carefully, and we turned in our dosimeters. We got back on the bus in the hot zone, exited the area, and were driven to lunch, which required us to drive back through the hot zone! When we pointed this out, we were pretty much ignored, even though our US guides were a bit concerned. But nothing could be done. The Chernobyl sarcophagus was leaking and was finally replaced in a magnificent feat of engineering by a new sarcophagus placement in November 2017. Readers can find the video of the new sarcophagus being placed on YouTube, and is worth viewing.

The night prior to our departure from the Soviet Union, we were taken to a "special place" for our last supper. It was a very ornate restaurant, and the vodka and champagned flowed freely. The champagne, which we had to pay for, was twenty-five cents (US) a bottle! And it was fabulous champagne. We were very thoughtful of our waitstaff on all occasions, and though told explicitly not to tip, even by the KGB guys, many did anyway, proving our American version of friendship. Even so, getting a second cup of coffee was like pulling teeth. They did not operate by US standards of customer service.

We were to pack and be prepared for an early-morning trip to the airport. Our passports were always in hotel hands, then our guides, never us individually. This was very disconcerting, but I have experienced it often in my travels. That night I became deathly sick, with severe cramping, diarrhea and vomiting. My bed was drenched with sweat. By morning I was so cramped up, and fluid loss was so intense, that I could not stand. My roommate informed our guides that there was no way I could get on a plane. That very moment the news started reporting on a coup d'état in Moscow. Soviet army tanks were moving down the streets of Moscow. (Author's note: This is such a sense of Deja Vu with what is happening in Ukraine at the time of this writing.) They called me an ambulance. I had been told previously by the US State Department, in no uncertain terms, never to take any injections in Russia. The AIDS epidemic was out of control, and even medical people were reusing needles. My team had to leave to get to the airport on time. I was left alone at hotel with one of the translators with the ambulance coming. We were on the phone to the US embassy regarding my not being fit to leave. The embassy insisted my translator put me on the phone and told me I had to get on that plane in no uncertain terms. "We do not know what is going to happen here. Some of the embassy staff are already being evacuated. You have to get out of there. If you stay you may get home in several months, or they can imprison you for life. We have no idea how this is going to turn out!" Does this sound like recent days in Afghanistan or now Ukraine? It should. I was definitely scared this time.

The ambulance arrived, and a doctor came upstairs. And sure enough, out of a black bag, he was readying a huge needle from meds in a glass tube. I was in bed yelling ***Nyet, Nyet, No, nyet!*** My translator didn't have to translate. I didn't want a shot, and this time it wasn't fear of needles. I did not want to insult anyone either. Especially about AIDS or what the US guidance was, but I just keep saying no, that I had some type of phobia to needles. In frustration, the doctor broke open the glass tube and made me drink the fluid. OK, I will drink it, but you are not injecting me with anything. It was awful. The cramping didn't stop, nor did the vomiting or diarrhea, but they got me into a vehicle and to the airport. I thought my team was already gone. The security at the airport would not let me in.

My translator became my absolute hero. She got right in the security guy's face and yelled at him, telling him that I had to leave right now. "She is with a team of scientists at Premiere Gorbachev's request." Security tried to take my passport, which had been left with the translator to deal with embassy. She and the security guard were screaming at each other. I was praying. She refused to give it up until I was either joined with my group or at least provided some means to get back to the States. I am not sure if she was given my tickets also, but it appeared she must have been.

The fighting outside the airport continued. I was useless and totally felt

I was going to die or be imprisoned there. I was in so much pain, I almost didn't care at the time. You know, like the stages of being seasick. You will choose dying.

Finally, a security supervisor came out and talked to

My team at MNF-I working in Iraq 2009–2010. Rich Pribyl, second from left, back row.

the translator. I was escorted into the airport, finally, to connect with my group. If I could possibly have acted happy to see them, I swear I would have. They certainly were to see me, but I was so cramped over and worried I would mess myself or vomit, I could not respond to them. Prior to my translator leaving, I gave her all my blue jeans (a black-market commodity worth its weight in gold at that time), all my jewelry, and any cash I had that I could afford to give her and still have enough to get home. We flew on Lufthansa, a joy from the Aeroflot flights we had endured while in the Soviet Union. I did not even partially recover until we got to Germany. Besides our translator, several in our group really helped me through, and I will forever be thankful.

Arriving in Iraq was a challenge before I even got to the mission. I served as a government civilian (GS, or government schedule) in Iraq from 2009 through 2010. Iraq was a country at war and led by a dictator, Saddam Hussein, for years. I saw combat operations and the aftermath, Iraq's and ours.

My observations from my work in Iraq come from working with not only the multinational forces, but with the US military, the US embassy, Iraqi government personnel, Iraqi civilians, the US chain of command (CENTCOM), often outside of theater of operations, (meaning out of the country of Iraq), and personnel from the US that included military chain of command but also politicians and their responses to the American public. Suffice it to say there were many differing opinions, and the misperceptions were monumental.

Let's start with the first day just getting to Iraq. Over four hundred of us were on a military transport out of Fort Benning. We were all suited up with IBA (***Interceptor Body Armor)*** and helmets. My biggest concern was having to go to the bathroom while waiting in all these lines! Yeah, I was an older female civilian, so give me a break. I was at the end of this huge line and knew military aircraft were not customer friendly regarding bathrooms. I was getting desperate. I saw a porta potty off the tarmac. Could I make it? I was torn. This was the military, not so cushiony as today's, so I wrestled with myself. You have to go. So with this gear I was required to carry, I ran for the porta potty. Running was my plan, but with all this gear, it was impossible. But I made it. Getting in the stupid door was next to impossible.

I was undoing my pants on the fly. Then I had to button up to get back to the plane. All were on the plane, and I would be the last. I knew they would not wait. The plane was huge and yards away. The ramp was down, and stragglers were getting aboard. I ran as fast as my little 5'2" 115-pound body would go. No one paid any attention to me. The ramp was beginning to move. No one said anything or tried to help; I was a civilian in a military world, and I would experience this frequently on this venture. The lift gate was so high off the tarmac I could not make the step up, especially with all the heavy gear on, and it was closing! No one would help or even lend a hand. Hey, all were military, and I was one of the few civilians, and a female without a supporting contractor group. They were not going to help, nor would I let them defeat me. I literally flew myself onto the lift gate, probably looking like flying turtle with the IBA. I grabbed on to the metal rails and pulled myself in and eventually upright, feeling as though I would topple backward. What a chore, but it was the beginning of a long learning process about the military, how a female civilian would be treated, and how things were going to go once in Iraq, if I even got there.

Then to the job site. I arrived from Ali Al Salem Air Base in Kuwait in the middle of the night. The flights were secure by only flying at night, with no times posted. The pilots would take off and land in major vertical flight paths to avoid antiaircraft fire. It was disconcerting. The military airport, adjacent to Baghdad's International Airport, is a secure zone, and since I was a lone civilian, I had no support that would accompany military personnel and contractors. We could not call in our plane number, arrival time, or any information that the enemy could pick up on. It was almost like I was dropped off in the middle of a desert with no return air ticket back home in an emergency and no directions as to where to go, what to do, or whom to contact. No, not *like* that; it *was* that! My boss and the location I needed to get to was a colonel at Victory Base Complex, and it was nowhere near where we landed. There were few cell phones available at this time, not only due to the availability of an in-country Iraqi phone, but due to IEDs and security. A lieutenant colonel took pity on me and said, "You're going with us." She was a breath of fresh air, yet she was headed to the embassy, and I was headed to a forward operating base (FOB) and directed to be on-site the next morning. Traveling in a combat zone is…well, you just don't call a taxi or Uber. Through the lieutenant colonel, I eventually reached my colonel at two in the morning, and he was still at work! That should have told me something right there about what I would be facing.

The colonel (I will call him my first colonel to avoid names) sent a military driver to pick me up and get me on base. I still had to locate quarters and gear for the next day. I slept in a communal tent that evening in uniform and had to walk to find the building I was assigned to. It was dark, and I was stalked all the way in by a jackal. At the office (a square trailer placed on a slab of concrete), I was greeted by some of the military and the civilian contractors who would be working with me. All were very cordial and welcoming. I had been assigned as chief environmental engineer for the Multinational Forces Iraq (MNF-I) in theater, a heady position not without monumental challenges.

My first assignment prior to getting to Iraq was with JSOC, or Joint Operations Command, at FOB Balad Air Base, and my mission was to be taken out on night patrols by Blackhawk, dropped into villages to inoculate residents, check for disease, and then fly out. Totally weapons trained and ready. I finally reached someone at Balad and told him I thought they had the wrong person. The young marine said to me, "Well, you're not advising any generals out here." I was also assigned to a Provincial Reconstruction Team (PRT) that the US no longer supported. Thus those orders had to be changed as well. Thus, it was many more months, totaling eleven, before I knew somewhat where I would be heading in Iraq.

Within the same office at Victory Base was the Multinational Corps in Iraq (MNC-I), run by the Army Corps of Engineers. So right off the bat, one can see we have two armies here, and little did I realize at the time the conflicts that would create. A bit of "who's on first"!

Within minutes I could sense immense tension. As I later relayed to my sister, it was so thick you could cut it with a knife. I attempted to be that breath of fresh air I had met at the airport with the lieutenant colonel. The air needed space, not someone coming in and trying to control. So when I felt the colonel really wanted and asked for my help and guidance, that felt strange. Later it became apparent he was assigned way too much work and responsibility that no one could ever accomplish. He had been assigned a major position, and then another issue overrode that assignment, and he was tasked with both—definitely not unknown in the military. I learned that you did jobs whether that was your expertise or assigned or not. You just did it. His second assignment, which brought a chill to my heart, was being on a bases where the electrical wiring installed by contractors throughout the base was faulty. There had been a number of electrocutions, and soldiers died just taking a shower. You could not protect yourself from this fault. It was luck of the draw. Even just walking, which was the mode of transporting yourself around the base, with few to no vehicles, someone who stepped on the wrong wire was dead. This was our own version of IEDs (improvised explosive device, though this was electricity).

My colonel had been put in a lose-lose scenario, and the two lieutenant colonels working for him had total disdain for him. I might add they were

Common sandstorm in Iraq. What made them a major problem was air flights to sites. Sandstorms and helicopters and aircraft just don't mix well. Roos photo 2009.

army, and he was air force. We were all like that. I was "on loan" from the navy. It was a total joint operation, US wise, and multinational with other nations—many. I partook in some weighty military campaign planning with what I would call the best and the brightest people I had ever met. It was an honor to be in the presence of many of these military minds. Yet there were many more who were assigned and too scared to function or who were there for money or some other reason, and accomplishing the mission was not it. I met them all.

First off was finding out about the electrocutions and later how that effort impacted my boss. The first training I went through in theater, the very first day there, was suicide prevention. It was very real, and the recent victims at their own hand were mentioned and their friends interviewed. This was beyond very difficult.

Sleeping in a tent community, eventually to be moved into what was known as a CHU (containerized housing unit) was expected. The distance of the walk to the latrines and a separate walk to where showers were housed was problematic and not entirely expected. They were not even close to each other, let alone close to the housing quarters. You had to walk over huge gravel stones, placed to avoid the wet sands during the rainy season, and were surrounded by sixteen-foot T-walls (T-walls are huge concrete barriers to protect barracks from mortar and artillery attacks). They are more protective and installed as a more permanent barrier than the more common sand and barbed wired barriers. The problem was that I felt extremely closed in and could not detect if anyone was lurking around these walls. It was like a maze, only of tall concrete structures and not hedges. Then one of the female lieutenant colonels told me I needed to be very aware of my surroundings, especially at night due to all the current rapes. I was in a combat zone, surrounded with armed troops, and I was supposed to be concerned about rape? My concern was being caught, captured, and tortured by Iraqi militants. That we were trained for. I asked how Iraqis would get on base. No, she said, not Iraqis. Our own troops! That took a moment to sink in. I needed to be afraid of my own troops? (This situation was caused by the surge of American troops during the war to get more boots on the ground and troops were not screened as they had been. It was eventually corrected.)

So now my first two days were suicide prevention, potential for electrocution and rape, and a work environment that was as tense as a rattler ready to strike. I won't even talk about peeing in bottles and storing them until you could get to the latrines.

Within my first two months of being stationed at Victory Base, which was adjacent to several other FOBs, there was an emergency call out for all to be on high alert. A soldier on suicide watch at Camp Liberty (an adjacent base) had shot and killed five individuals. Three of them were doctors or medical staff trying to help him. Within the month, there was an alert that some militant Iraqis were making their way onto base to capture or kill troops or civilians. I was told that civilians were the target of choice. That week I was in a CHU shared with a colonel from the embassy. At two in the morning (why does everything happen at two in the morning?), there was a pounding on the trailer door. A deep voice yelling, "Dr. Roos, Dr. Roos." My roommate and I were on high alert. We both decided not to open the door for security reasons. Could be a tactic. The voice and pounding were nonstop. I finally yelled, "Yes, I am here." Had I just made a really big mistake? It was Lieutenant Kaz checking on me, as there had been a legitimate threat. Someone did access the base and tried to capture a ranking civilian. My command was checking on me. Of that, my roommate and I were both relieved.

Within several months, my own colonel was escorted back to the States, since he was considered a suicide risk or potentially a risk to others. He was caring a round in the chamber, and that was considered a sign and was also against rules in theater. Possibly it went against our security agreement with Iraq as well. That renegotiated agreement caused a great deal of heartburn. Obama had become president, and the world here in Iraq Theater of Operations changed. All military had their guns taken away, and transport equipment as well as air support to do our jobs was seriously impacted. We civilians were no longer allowed to carry weapons to defend ourselves and could no longer wear the military uniforms we were first required and issued to wear. Many of us didn't have other clothes, as we were told we were to always be in uniform. It was all very confusing, and the reason we civilians wore military uniforms was so we would not be easy targets for the militants. Now we were sitting ducks.

Midway in my service, I was on a mission to present my proposed Iraqi environmental protection goals to the minister of public health and environment. As we returned to the embassy, a report came through, unbeknownst to us, for our protection detail to be on the lookout for two female suicide bombers. Our drivers started driving very aggressively, like out of a *Bourne*

217

movie, over sidewalks and in the wrong direction. We had been successful in our talks with Iraqis and were celebratory until we discovered that those two women had made contact with a military patrol, killing three young soldiers. The last one died on the operating table upon our return. These

Author borrowing protective gear from a Colonel in much larger size to go on patrol. All identifications had to be removed first.

soldiers had been in the same vicinity as our return route. We went from high-fiving each other to attending the "Walk of the Angels" that evening when these young soldiers were to be airlifted back to the States. Two weeks later, my presentation colleague and friend from the embassy, Mageed Hussein, and CDR Wolfe (a highly respected navy civil engineer) were killed by an EFP (more explosive and dangerous than an IED) visiting a waste treatment facility we had constructed in Fallujah. He was scheduled the next day to return to Egypt to celebrate his daughter's fourth birthday. It changed my whole concept of war and the realities of life and death.

As my mission continued, another lieutenant colonel was sent home due to suicide prevention, as he had already served five tours and was considered very high risk. The tension grew between the MNF-I division and the MNC-I group. I was actually confronted by the lead lieutenant colonel of the MNC-I group and directed not to talk or even communicate in any way with his personnel. I politely asked him how we were going to get the job done without communicating, but he had told me he said what he was going to say. I will say that later, prior to his leaving, he apologized to me and told me he didn't realize all the efforts I had been making. It was a bit late, though, for the mission, and for my colonel, who had already been sent home. I worked numerous projects having major environmental implications of which I cannot address here. Suffice it to say there were major challenges. The aggression toward the civilians continued, and I seemed to bear the brunt. Well, I was in charge, and without a strong military leader, I was not in a good spot. This was after having five different directors within a five-month period. I had worked well with all of them (three air force colonels and two army lieutenant colonels acting), until our last colonel was assigned. It started off fine, but with all the baggage of the last eight months, this colonel coming in like she was going to change us all to her mold just didn't sit well with many, especially me. I saw her take down and seriously insult a very impressive army major. No one was more respected or worked harder to achieve what we were there to do. All the services and the multinational services respected this guy, and she challenged him every step of the way. I was her target now and more the brunt of her tactics, which I must confess were totally destructive to all involved.

So within a few months I experienced the realities of suicide, potential for electrocutions and rapes from our troops, murders of personnel trying to help suicide victims by our own troops, mortar and artillery attacks, our own troops shot in the back by Iraqi troops they had been training, my colonels and a lieutenant colonel being relieved of command and sent home due to being a suicide risk, a civilian mortared and killed in his CHU, high alerts of Iraqi infiltrations, *Rhino* (transport vehicle called a *Rhino* to make it look armored and protective yet it was not armored) trips to the embassy where a colonel wounded himself following discharge protocol and ongoing fear of IEDs, fast pursuit and escape tactics of military convoys and escorts to avoid IEDs and suicide bombers, the killings of four soldiers on patrol (where it easily could have been my patrol), an EPU attack killing my best friend and colleague and one of our CEC officers, and having to work for a colonel who was out to destroy my career and, at the time, I felt, for my health and life. I saw young troops actually terrified to be in the gun turrets of the MRAP (mine-resistant ambush protected) or jeep on our trips. They would swear and curse the Iraqis who got in our way. They were so frightened. It seemed a pathway to madness, and I finally did appreciate why soldiers would take their own lives. I must clarify the experienced Sergeants and military contractors exuded confidence and I felt much safer with them as compared to the young recruits. Within weeks of my leaving theater, yet another colleague, one of our young marines, committed suicide. He was handsome and charming. A good guy. I remember thinking of him as the breath of fresh air that I wanted to exude when I first came.

A couple of lights in the darkness were me reconnecting to my faith. I was so frightened and desperate with everything that was happening. I saw a Chaplin after Mageed died and when time permitted, it rarely did with 14-hour days, seven days a week, I attended mass. The Priest was wonderful. I recall him in military uniform with combat boots covered with the vestments. It was quite a sight. I was sad when he left and met him again in Ali Al Salem on his way to Afghanistan. I thanked him and pray for him and all the others I met in Iraq. Another light was my wanting to continue my yoga teaching. My OSD (Office of the Secretary of Defense) counterpart was supportive that I try to reach out to Iraqi women. That was when I was headed to

a Provincial Reconstruction Team that the US no longer supported. I decided to teach a class on the base. What was so rewarding was that my students back in the states joined together and purchased mats, straps and blocks and had them shipped to my location in Iraq. This required lots of logistics and effort, but it worked. Thanks to Karen, Jenneth and my best friend Bruce who orchestrated the effort. First day I had 80 soldiers, many in uniform, civilians and contractors doing yoga at 4:30 am. I can't even begin to share with you the response and thanks I received. Some told me before they returned to the states that I helped them make it through. It helped me as well.

Iraqi hospitality is amazing. I get what Vian (Chapter 10) stated about their traditions and culture. I also noted when one of our translators commented on US chickens and how tasteless they are, I said, "No, they're good. You just have to season them properly, and it depends on the chicken." He looked at me and said, "Wait until you eat an Iraq chicken."

From these photos (left and below), you can see the hospitality present itself. No need for words. And my Iraqi friend was correct. The chicken was the most delicious chicken I had ever eaten, as was the hummus. Nothing we have compares.

During my time in Iraq, I witnessed horrible and wonderful things. The most beautiful was the archaeological survey I was involved in of the Ziggurat of Ur, a neo-Sumerian ziggurat located in the once city of Ur near Nasiriyah. The history of a site over three thousand years old gives one pause. In short, it was the coalition forces who, based on their military rules of engagement, do not allow historic sites or structures to be attacked or damaged. Obviously,

there is argument about this, as many countries do not follow the same respect or guidance, and it can be used against troops in battle. Under the coalition, the US protection of the Ziggurat fared well, and little damage was incurred during my time there. In 2010, the site was turned back to the Iraqis. We, as representatives of the multinational forces, were invited to attend the ceremony turning the historical site back to Iraq. I was invited by my general, as I had performed in the site investigation and he wanted some knowledge along with him. It was the invitation of a lifetime, as was the survey. During the survey we researched all the restorations that had occurred since the 1950s and compared it to existing ancient structures and the different materials that had to be used due to the times. The Iraqi archaeologist (I will not provide names for protection purposes) and the State Department archeologists were extremely knowledgeable. We were guarded by special forces troops while there. The guys we were protected by had been with Blackwater in the past. I don't think I ever felt safer than with these guys when outside the wire. The turnover ceremony involved honoring Iraq's ancient moon goddess, Nanna. Music was performed by the Iraq's symphony orchestra, which as quite good. I was somewhat surprised

that in this heat, and with the ever-changing sand conditions, musical instruments could be maintained and stay in tune. The first of a couple of shocks to my system occurred when I was seated next to an Arab, the fourth governor of the province, during the ceremony. He offered to take me on a boat ride down the Euphrates with him, and he would feed me great food and show me how Iraqis grew their food. My general was listening to all this. My Arab friend continued to tell me he was not at all interested in this cultural resource "rubbish." It was not important, as he waved his hand. I asked what he did for a living, and he said he was a major dignitary of some district (I do not recall) and had a degree in nuclear physics. Many of the heads of all the ministries I met while in Iraq, from the minister of the environment and public health seemed to have degrees in nuclear physics. I thought this rather odd, especially with the minister of environmental protection, who was a female, and that surprised me as well.

When the ceremony was over, all the Iraqi troops started showing up in numerous trucks driving in at very high speed. This was a protected archaeological site, supposedly sacred to the Iraqis, and the drivers were driving doughnuts churning up all the sand around the Ziggurat. This was the location where our Iraqi archaeologist had picked up artifacts right off the ground earlier due to constantly shifting sands. The lack of respect really angered me, and my general said, "Let's get out of here."

The other sad event involved a special forces Iraqi soldier who was there to celebrate as well. They were in uniform and on duty but were having a good time. I was treated like a star, with all the Iraqis wanting to take their picture with me, mostly men but some women also. Lots of smiles, but some nerve-racking moments as well due to crowds where you could tell some did not like you; rather, they hated you. We were preparing to leave, and one of the very handsome special forces soldiers was being handcuffed by his own troops, and an officer was in his face. I came to find out he had been showing off his weapon, or he had taken it out for some reason, and it was misplaced. We all tried to find it, especially me, but my general said leave it alone; someone grabbed it as soon as they saw it. That gun is long gone, and so is this young man's career; maybe his life. That broke my heart, it was all so sudden. One misstep, and your career, your life is over. I just saw him being placed in the back of one of the army vehicles, handcuffed with his head down.

Iraqi art painted along Route Irish describing Iraqis' perception of the birth of man through evolution to man's ultimate adventure in space. Roos photo, 2010.

"Life, Liberty, Freedom" are terms easily touted and bantered about, yet few realize what they truly mean until they are threatened or lost. Many of the interviewees have shared their life experiences in either losing those freedoms or never having them until they arrived in America. Some never lost freedom and love their country of origin, yet they chose to be here. Most still cherish their heritage, but they cherish their freedom more. Don't be so sure of your opinions unless you have "walked in another's moccasins," to quote an old Indian proverb. ***And John Rich, country singer and song-writer and FOX host of* Pursuit *in an interview with Candace Owens, both stated, "Experience outweighs your opinion."***

I believe America matters, and from most in this compilation of immigrant stories, the people who came to his country agree. America is made up of good people coming from all walks of life, and many come from

an immigrant background. There are always exceptions everywhere, but when it comes to inviting immigrants into one's country, the US far exceeds any other nation in the world. When there are disasters anywhere in the world, it is the citizens of the United States who give the most and often bring in the most support.

Americans are a kind people and do care about one another and other peoples. Yet a select few are trying to tear this reality apart. Americans do care about illegals and the many attempting crossing borders illegally. And

Our team members changed frequently, and that made continuity of mission difficult. All outstanding people and ethics. A major coincidence was that one of my translators was someone I had met back in Orange County while working for CH2MHill. He managed a catering service at that time! Roos photo 2010.

please don't give me this "we are all equal in the eyes of God." That may be true, but countries must establish borders, or they are not a country! The irony is many supporting open borders are leftists who are agnostic or even atheist, so you really can't have it both ways. But right there is a rub. When one already chooses to violate a country's laws, it puts the citizenry of that country in danger. If you are one to say the law is wrong, then we have a system in place that can and does fix laws that do not work. It is a process, and it's why our founding fathers established our Declaration of Independence from a monarch and our US Constitution establishes three equal branches of government to provide balance and remedy our growth as a society in support of life, liberty, and the pursuit of happiness. The Constitution was

KATHLEEN S. ROOS PH.D.

amended over the years and became our nation's fundamental law. However, the broad language in the Constitution is illuminated by principles set forth in the Declaration, written eleven years earlier. The founding fathers realized that moral reasoning understandable to all, and not political will, is the basis of our political system. If reason is the foundation of the Fathers' vision, the method of how we justify our political order, and liberty is its aim; thus, the cardinal moral truths are these:

That all Men are created equal, that they are endowed by their Creator with certain unalienable Rights, that among these are Life, Liberty, and the Pursuit of Happiness. That to ensure these Rights, Governments are instituted among men, deriving their just powers from the Consent of the Governed (Cato Institute 2021).

The Founders continued to base their reasoning on "right reason" and outlined the moral foundation of a free society. Only then did they turn to government. We the people are to secure our rights, our natural rights we create to live our lives. The powers of the government must be derived from our consent. Thus, you can see the Founders limited government many times. They wanted to devise a government that was strong enough to secure our rights against domestic and foreign oppression, yet not be so extensive as to be oppressive itself. The Preamble itself states "We the people," for the purpose that ***all power comes from the people, not the government, not elected officials, and not lifelong bureaucrats and the media.*** Only certain powers were delegated by the people to the government, and those not delegated were reserved to the states. We the people wanted the power of government limited. In many writings, i.e., the Federalist Papers, the Founders intended the doctrine of enumerated powers to be our principal defense against overweening government. The Founding Fathers went beyond devising powers between the national and state governments, leaving most of the power with the states or with the people. They additionally separated powers within the national government into three branches, legislative, executive, and judicial, and then devised a series of checks and balances to further restrain those powers.

In the end no constitution can be self-enforcing. Government officials must fulfill their oaths to uphold the Constitution they were voted to defend. We the people must continue to be vigilant in seeing that they do.

America simply cannot practically, economically, or morally accept and assimilate all the peoples of the world who want to come here. No country can, nor is any other country asked to do something so frivolous. Whether that bothers your sensitivities or not, it is just not possible. And if we are as bad as George Soros and his minions tell you we are, then why are these thousands of people attempting to come here? I ask you, why? Is it right for Americans to be mandated to wear masks, not travel, be locked down, not visit family and friends, turn on each other, be mandated to take vaccines all at the same time hundreds of thousands of unvetted, unvaccinated, unmasked peoples from all over the world (not just Mexico or South America) come across our border and are moved into cities without their officials or citizenry even being notified? That is unconstitutional and totally ignored by the current administration that is actually driving this train, and it is morally wrong.

Allow me to clarify. I have traveled all over the world. It is the US Department of State and CDC requirements that we receive vaccines for yellow fever, tuberculosis, pertussis, measles, cholera, polio, small pox, and hepatitis A, B, and C, to name a few (I even had to get a rabies vaccine when I traveled to Iraq) when traveling to many places abroad, and all the immigrants coming across our borders are from these very same locations. It is immoral for our government to do that to our citizens.

Many issues require our attention about immigration and many other policies. But attempting to tear apart a system and a people that have demonstrated several hundred years of success, destroying our history and using the race card at every turn and calling us a racist country is dead wrong. Read through the common threads throughout this compilation about kindnesses shown by Americans to others. I will share two additional illustrative stories about who Americans are.

A man was heading cross-country early in his career for a job interview. He was driving with his teenage son and didn't have much money and really needed this job and could not afford to fly. They were headed for the Pacific Northwest from the East Coast. The son is relaying this story.

Our vehicle broke down en route, and we were in the middle of nowhere in the desert. The west looks very different from the easy access to thruways and cities of the east, what we were used to. Cell phone coverage was patchy at best. My father was frugal, and we were traveling with not much money. On the side of the road, with no cell service, my father was despondent, and we began to walk toward the closest town.

Along came a pickup truck, and it pulled over to offer assistance. The driver told us that all the service stations in town were closed, as it was Sunday. But he would give us a lift into town, about seven miles away, and ask his brother, who owned a shop, if he could help. All my father could see was dollar signs and that we couldn't afford this, but we were stuck.

We got to town and to the brother's house. He immediately sent out a tow truck and told my dad not to worry about it. Dad was really leery and not trusting. He told us we must be tired, thirsty, and hungry, so his wife offered to fix us a meal.

"I can't pay you for this," my father said.

"Don't worry about it."

They went out to the vehicle, and it was towed to the brother's service shop. Dad told them about the job interview the next day. They opened their shop and got to work. They didn't have the right parts. They contacted another friend in the neighboring town, and the part was brought over from twenty miles away. Dad was really starting to panic that this was going to cost and that he wouldn't have the money.

The original pickup truck driver took us to his home, where his wife had made us a meal. My father said no thanks, but they insisted. They told us to take a shower and cool off, as it was very hot in the desert. They give us a change of clothes so we would be more comfortable on the road. And when we come outside, our vehicle was parked out front, ready to go! We were in disbelief.

My father looked at me with this "now we are going to get ripped off to the max," a common phrase. This was how he felt.

He reluctantly asked, "So how much is this going to cost me?"

The truck driver just said, "Good luck with the job interview, and when you can, send us a check for the cost of the parts." And he handed him a note with an address and the cost of the parts.

Dad was speechless.

We got in the car, and my father did not say a word for the remainder of the trip. When we got to our destination, he said to me, "I want you to remember that this is what America is all about."

It made me remember.

And a recent story from friends about America's goodness. The following story is not from an immigrant but from someone who appreciates the goodness of Americans and has faith in God. The following is Stephanie's story taken from *Citizens Journal*.

Stephanie's story follows and describes a series of acts that confirms her belief that there is goodness left in the world. Depending on your viewpoint, did it all happen randomly by pure chance at the right time and place, or by divine intervention in answer to my prayers to God?

We had a family emergency to retrieve a relative's newborn baby who had many problems related to parental drug use. A 911 call was made because

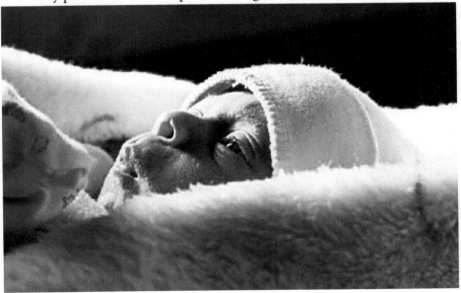

of domestic violence between the father and mother. They had been arguing outside, and it got violent, so neighbors called. When the police got there, it turned out they had left the baby in a swing that was rated for an older child. The baby was not even three weeks old. The police contacted child services, and the next day they came and assessed the situation. The mother persuaded child services to allow us to get the child instead of putting her into foster care. We got the call, and we agreed after speaking with child services. The baby and mother were supposed to stay with a neighbor until we could get there. Thus, we needed to make it across the country in three days, driving over 2,200 miles. Our neighbors jumped right in and took care of the mail, cleaned the house, and got rid of trash so we could get on the road first thing, as we did not know when we would be coming back. We got on the road that night and drove through Vegas and across Death Valley, up and down the Utah and Colorado mountains, through the cornfields of Nebraska, Iowa, and Illinois, and kept going east. We had a 2007 Ford Focus with standard transmission, referred to as a stick shift, that had over 274,000 miles. We were stuck in a traffic jam in Nevada when the temperature gauge starting rising, and suddenly the road cleared. We had no idea why. The next day, as we left our hotel in Colorado, we were told to check road reports, as mudslides had caused parts of I-70 to close. The pass opened that morning. As we traversed the mountains of Colorado on our way to Denver, we ran into road construction again at the top of approximately a 5 percent grade pass near Parshall, Colorado. Broken-down cars and trucks lined the side of the road everywhere. We had almost crested the top of the pass when our clutch overheated, not allowing us to shift into any gear. We could not move. We rolled the car to the side of the road as angry drivers sped past, showing no concern to allow us to get the car to the side of the road safely.

Once we got off to the side of the road, a motorcyclist stopped to help. He had a towing company. He was trying to call his shop as we were on the phone with our insurance company to get a tow. The next thing we knew, a tow truck with an SUV already on its bed stopped and picked us up, bypassing other cars. This tow truck driver helped call our insurance company to get approval as we were on the road. Our insurance company had the towing company take us west to Breckenridge instead of east to Golden. The boss of the towing company called our insurance company and directed us to a transmission shop that was located in the direction we needed to go and close enough that we did not have to pay extra towing charges. Our driver, Kyle, always had his dogs with him. That helped me, as I got to pet his dogs and calm down on the trip through the passes to Golden. What a great way to calm a distraught driver, especially if kids are involved.

We got to a transmission shop, but they were backed up, and the earliest they could get to us was the following day. The owner asked us what had happened. We told him about the baby, where we needed to be the next day, and why. He had his mechanics deal with the car, took it for a road test, and got us back on the road. He refused to charge us. We were able to drive straight through to our destination, through withering rainstorms in Nebraska and Iowa, and no more mountains. Before we began our return trip, we had taken the car to a shop to make sure there would be no issues on the return trip. Once we got to our destination, we took over the care of our granddaughter, and then, of course, we had other issues to solve. We found an Extended Stay America about thirty minutes from where we needed to go. The staff and residents saw the newborn and accepted us just like family. They even gave us a gift bag of baby stuff to help us out. They are still in contact with us. While eating at Shadow Brewing Company, a couple came in with a six-month-old baby in its car seat. I went to talk and ask them for pointers, and we got into a discussion on car seats. Her husband went out to our car and helped us adjust the seat. It turned out the car seat we were given had no adjustments, and the baby's head rocked. I had to hold her head while the car was in motion. We didn't know any better; we were in our sixties, and when we were kids, most cars did not have seat belts, and there were no car seats back then. The wife set us up with a 20 percent coupon and told us what store to go to that would help. We thanked them for their advice and told them we were going that evening to buy a new car seat, but the baby had a meltdown, so we went back to the hotel instead. When I opened the diaper bag, I found a note from the couple with $200 to buy a good safe car seat for our grandbaby. Are you seeing a pattern here?

We were in desperate need, and God put someone or something in place to take care of it.

The next day, to the baby store. The staff had us bring in our stroller and helped us pick out the best seat for our needs and set it up. They could have sold us a new stroller and car seat but made sure that we bought only what we needed. I then spoke with the manager and explained about the couple's generosity. He helped us set up a gift certificate in this couple's name for someone who really needed help. We took the northern route back to lessen the heat load on the car and us and to avoid the fires. There were great folks all along the way. We made reservations in Gillette, Wyoming, at the Arbuckle Lodge. The young lady who made our reservation stayed late and helped take care of the baby while we got our stuff moved in, and the hotel had free laundry, so we were able to have clean clothes. Now, that's service. We stopped for food and for the baby to have a break in Park City, Utah. A lady noticed that I was having trouble trying to feed the baby and hold on to the diaper bag and the baby while my husband was trying to find a parking spot. She offered to help. She was a nurse who worked with teenagers trying to get off drugs. She gave me some great tips on what to look for and resources for information. We stopped in Reno at Great Basin Brewery for food, and the waitstaff got us ice for the baby bottles and found out what highways were open and closed and helped us determine the best route around the fires to go home. Once we were home, our neighbors had filled our refrigerator with food. They came over daily to take the baby out in the stroller and to help with feedings and diaper changes. They provided us with all kinds of items needed, from a Pack 'n Play to a baby play station to a swing, but most important of all, support. One of our neighbors, a retired sheriff, told us about Tri-County Regional Center. We called and in less than a week, they scheduled an assessment and set up Early Start therapy to minimize any side effects from the drugs in the baby's system while in the womb. We located a great baby doctor, who got her records from the clinic and hospital so that we could get her immunization on track. This was no small feat. Everything fell in place to ensure that the baby would have the best chance she could have. Without our neighbors, I would still be looking for help. The baby is doing great. The "marina baby," as she is called, has a great support group. Keep in mind I have never changed a diaper in my life, and my husband's last child was thirty-five years ago. It is not as if we know anything about raising kids today, and apparently, many rules have changed. For everyone who helped us out and are still helping us, we want to say thank you. We could not raise the marina baby without your help. I took the car in for a checkup. Our local mechanic spent a while checking the vehicle, determined everything was good except maybe the clutch, and set us up with an appointment at a transmission shop for a free inspection. They spent hours going over it and said good to go. Considering everything our little two-door hatchback Focus went through, I believe someone definitely was looking out for it and us.

These are most of the major interactions that occurred during our trip. Along the way, we had all kinds of smaller acts of kindness. We stopped at mostly brewpubs and truck stops. Why? you may ask. Because usually the people who own and/or go to brewpubs and travel stops go out of their way to help and do not judge you. Those with kids know the look: Why are you traveling with a newborn? What a bad parent you are. You can believe that all these interactions were just random, but the chances of all these occurring at the right time and place is a bit much for me to believe that it was all just random occurrences. I pray that you may see that God is working in our world. He cannot stop bad things from happening but provides the opportunity for people to help deal with the bad. Will you choose to help others? Will you choose to believe? (End of Stephanie's story).

Some don't believe in God or in faith, whatever that may mean to you. That is your right, especially in this country. I have had a struggle through my life to where I stand and my time in Iraq helped me to reconnect. But I have to ask, why not? What do you lose by believing? I watched a TV documentary recently on a serial rape/murder investigation. A father was being interviewed. His daughter had been taken. In the interview, he states, "And here I am, a total atheist, praying to God to please bring my daughter back to me." The irony is plain to see.

Another instance was an experiment being conducted about cheating. In this experiment one group was asked prior to taking the test if they could state any of the Ten Commandments. Some knew one or two, and some knew none but did know what they represented. The other groups were just giving the test. Upon completion, only the group asked about the Ten Commandments, even if they did not know of them, specifically did not cheat. The other groups all had cheaters.

And finally, I looked up the quote "Do unto others as you would have them do unto you," otherwise known as the Golden Rule. When I looked up the basis of this quote, I found it in some version in every faith known on this planet! Some have asked me how I found immigrants and others to be interviewed and if this was a difficult undertaking. Many of these interviewees are my neighbors, friends, and/or local small business owners. Many are your neighbors; you just may not know it. It just shows how we don't get to know each other anymore, and maybe we need to try harder to get to know one another again. Sometimes interviews were difficult if there was a language barrier and I needed a translator, but most often I interviewed people privately face-to-face, and that was the best way to go. When others were invited in, the sessions devolved into an "ain't it awful" complaint session, or a social engagement. I had to learn to establish boundaries. Some who volunteered to be interviewed wanted to remain anonymous but then changed their mind and said, "No, this is too important, and I want to be identified." These are true heroes! I always conducted the interviews the old-fashioned way, by taking notes. I did not take the recommendation to record, and I think that was really the best way to go. When I did attempt recording, it was very difficult to hear people, and often a lot of their information was lost, so I had to go back and reinterview by taking notes again. On occasion an interviewee really wanted to be involved and then backed out due to fear of reprisals or impact on local business. On several occasions people would schedule a meeting with me and not show up. I gave them three times but then did not pursue them. I was left waiting for hours at times, and then sometimes I had no-shows, but overall, it was a labor of love and hope. I found it was a very rewarding adventure, and I learned so much from all these interviewees, even those I might not have agreed with or those who decided not to be interviewed.

My hope is that others will read this compilation and gain as much as I did by interviewing and getting to know these people. I feel we all made a connection. Once the installments were published in *Citizens Journal*, it seemed like a floodgate opened, and I was getting all sorts of requests from all over the country to be interviewed or people identifying others for interviews. Some of these had to be done over the phone and not in person, and that is why you will see questions in bold (from my questionnaire)—to make it a bit more organized and consistent. These are just some stories about the goodness of Americans. Again, it is my hope that in reading these stories, and those of immigrants who have come here and identified much of these kindnesses of Americans, you will recognize the pursuit of the American Dream is evident through these interviews. As you focus on the common threads running through these stories, you will become more informed. We are reminded that our government represents the people and that we elect representatives to do what they say they will do. Our founders relied on the wisdom of Americans to elect representatives that they can trust to honor their duty to represent our Constitution. It is our inalienable right to expect life, liberty, and the pursuit of happiness, and for us to foster our country's strengths to ensure a better future for all Americans.

I believe one can choose in this country to be a victim, a survivor, or a thriver. For many years I considered myself a survivor; now I choose thriver. America represents the best of us. It is a country of caring, often God-fearing people who demonstrate an unbridled generosity toward others in this world. It is a country of achievers and risk takers with the entrepreneurial attributes of creativity, inventiveness, craftsmanship, and hard work. "We the people" don't respond well to being told to lower our expectations. To accept less and become part of mediocrity is not why these people came to America. It is also the slippery slope to socialism. Read their stories. Be motivated, study history, and learn about what makes us proud to be American.

Freedom Is never more than one generation away from extinction. We didn't pass it to our children in the blood stream. It must be fought for, protected, and handed on for them to do the same, or one day we will spend our sunset years telling our children and our children's children what it was once like in the United States where men were free.
—**Ronald Reagan**

Why do our enemies see us as Americans and we Americans see each other as the enemy?
—**Kathleen Roos, PhD**

CHAPTER 24

If you believe a lie, even though it's a lie and not really true, it becomes true for you because that is what you believe.
—**Life Point via Joyce Meyers**

"Forsan et haec olim meminisse iuvabit"
(Maybe we will be laughing about even these things in the future).
—**Virgil**

THE FLEA'S STORY

There once was a flea who lived on a dog. We'll call him Our Flea! Our flea was free and able to jump from parts of the dog to other dogs with great ease. He was a very athletic flea, and jumping extreme distances was his nature. This flea could jump more than one hundred times his body length and almost two hundred times his body weight due to his God-given traits of very powerful hind legs.

Our flea was hunted and caught to be in a flea circus. His capturers wanted to train him for circus events, so he was placed in a jar with a lid to prevent his escape and so he could he could be trained.

Day after day he jumped with all his might. That was his nature, and he continued to hit his head on the jar lid. But he was a flea: strong and free and jumping was his nature. Our Flea continued to hit his head day after day and on and on. Little by little, he didn't jump as hard or as high, and he didn't hit his head. His capturer was pleased. He had stopped resisting and no longer tried to jump.

One day, the circus became obsolete, and Our Flea was set free to live among other fleas. He could not compete. He could no longer jump as far or as wide and soon died.

This story was relayed to me by Edmund Sonders (Chapter 21) in his description of how socialism and ultimately communism impacts one's soul. Lower your expectations; no need to be creative or be inventive. No need for entrepreneurs and risk takers; your government capturer will take care of you. Stay content in your jar.

I had heard this story years ago, but Edmund's description of how he felt in Soviet Latvia was moving. During his interview, he used a glass and put his hand over the top to illustrate the captured flea hitting his head repeatedly over time, then just giving up and not jumping as high.

Is this truly what Americans want? Think about it.

Why do our enemies see us as Americans and we Americans see each other as the enemy?
—Kathleen Roos, PhD

We don't let them have ideas. Why would we let them have guns?
—Joseph Stalin

INDEX AND NOTES

Identities changed; family records destroyed to avoid detection. Taking no documents or photos	1, 2, 3, 10
Being hunted or tracked	1, 2, 3, 10, 13
Avoiding minefields, IEDs, EPUs, Suicide bombers	1, 2, 23
Impacts of war	1, 2, 5, 10, 13, 23
Being silenced, not allowed to express opinions	1, 2, 3, 5, 6, 7, 8, 10, 13, 22, 23
Government dictates who you will marry, how many children you can have or keep. Government control of all personal behaviors	1, 2, 3, 5, 7, 10, 13
Bribery of officials / kickbacks / corruption	1, 2, 3, 5, 6, 7, 8, 10, 11, 13, 23
Child abandonment, abuse	4, 23
Survivors	1, 2, 3, 4, 5, 7, 8
Ungrateful Americans / Disregard of opportunities of those born in US	3, 4, 5, 7, 8, 13
Socialism	1, 2, 3, 6, 7, 8

Communism	1, 2, 3, 5, 6, 7, 8, 13, 22, 23
Dictatorship	1, 2, 3, 5, 10, 11, 13, 23
No rule of law. Criminal rule. Lawlessness	5, 6, 12, 13, 20, 21, 23
Burning cities, tires, buildings	5
No power/electricity	5, 7, 8, 10, 11
No clean water or running water	1, 2, 3, 4, 5, 7, 8, 10
Extreme poverty	1, 2, 3, 4, 5, 13
Blacklists	3, 5, 6
Helping others	6, 12
Mafia style, syndicate	6
Spies, being tracked	1, 5, 6, 13
Religious freedom, practice, destruction of places of worship	1, 2, 3, 7, 13, 23
Caste system	7, 16
Immigrants' contribution to America / work ethic	2, 3, 4, 5, 6, 7, 11, 12, 13, 21, 23
Family values	1, 2, 3, 4, 5, 6, 7, 8, 9, 10 , 11, 12, 22, 23

Agriculture	1, 2, 4, 7, 9, 21, 22, 23
Medical care (substandard) clinics / hospitals / wait times	6, 7, 8, 10, 11, 12
Education systems	6, 7, 8, 10, 11, 12, 13, 21, 23
Government breaking families apart	3, 8, 10, 13, 14
Pride in US citizenship	1, 2, 3, 6, 8, 9, 11
Opportunities in America: work, education, creativity	2, 5, 7, 9, 10, 11, 12, 13, 14, 15,16,17, 19, 20, 21, 22, 23
Racism	6, 11, 13, 11, 15
Border protection	6, 13
Choice of music / what you could listen to	13,14, 21
Free speech	All
Failing academic levels in US in comparisons	10, 12, 13, 19, 22,

ACKNOWLEDGMENTS

To all veterans who have made our freedom possible.

To those who provided their stories to make this publication happen. Many came to this country to find freedom from tyranny or to just make a better life for themselves and often their families. Many lost loved ones and endured horrors most of us could never conceive. Even their current families are often not aware of the ordeal they went through to come to the US. They also do not take their freedom for granted.

I have to thank Kyle, my colleague, who shared his story of being one of the original Vietnamese boat people to escape Vietnam. I have not been able to reach Kyle but will continue to try. He told me his story while we were working together and teaching Native American cultural resources and sensitivity training while with the US Navy. His story struck my core, and I felt I had to share his story and hopefully others like it. That was years ago, and it has taken me until now to go about the process of locating, interviewing, and consolidating these stories to publish them and get their stories out.

I recall Kyle saying his father had to fight adults on the boats who were trying to throw the younger children and weaker adults overboard to make space for themselves. Kyle as a young child saw many drown. He told me how they were starving with no water, and the sun just baked them for days in the boats (see Mark Lai's story). They prayed a ship would pick them up. When they finally did make it to a refugee camp, they struggled to stay alive. After a period of time, they were offered immigration status to either Germany or Australia. Kyle's father said no, even fighting his uncle who would eventually go to Germany. He said, "We wait to go to the US." They had to wait another six months.

Another mention is Emmerade "Simon" Sok and his wife Pavi, from Cambodia. There seemed just not enough time to get their interviews, though we tried.

243

I would also like to thank Mathew Connelly, a friend to my mother prior to her death, and also to me. He shared his stories of coming to America from Ireland. He emphasized that America matters! Mathew is another immigrant who loves his home country and heritage but is a proud American. Mathew Connelly, an Irish bagpiper on Uilleann pipes (Uilleann pipes are commonly referred to as union or Irish pipes), was one of the Irish Sandhogs who dug the underground tunnels for New York's subway system that created New York. Subways! Not only subways but sewer, water, train tunnels—the Irish built them all, from the Lincoln Tunnel to the Holland, Queens-Midtown, and Brooklyn-Battery Tunnels, as well as the foundations to most of the bridges.

Mathew, an Irish immigrant who loves his work and this country. I lost contact with Mathew after my mom died but did finally locate him and requested his interview. Mathew told me that his health is not good, and it would just be too much for him at this time.

To my teachers, professors, and mentors over the years, who were the best of the best. Dr. Earl Deubler and Dr. Merril Eisenbud greatly impacted me becoming an environmental scientist. Mr. Jesse Pollard made Latin and ancient history come alive. Mr. Rebe and Mr. Dion made physics and math exciting and understandable. Marine biologists Dr. Phyllis Kahn, one of the original shark researchers who studied with Eugenie Clark; Dr. Bernard Newman, marine scientist and forensic pathologist for Suffolk County Sheriff's Department; and Dr. Hugo Freudenthal. Mr. Creighton stimulated my interest in history, Captain Al Katz's ongoing support and many more whom I would love to mention.

I would also like to thank those at Citizens Journal: Johanna Ahim, a key interviewee in Coming to America; *Mark Caviezel; Dr. Greg and Anne Albaugh; and Douglas Batistic, who supported this effort. To get the information out to the world sooner, Citizen's Journal published chapters weekly.*

I cannot forget my sister, Mary Matera, her support and that of others who identified interviewees for inclusion in Coming to America, *including Stephanie Bond, Dodie Duffy, and David Littell.*

And to my friend Kay Armstrong, who encouraged me for years to write "my book." Though I am at work on my book, it was put into my heart to tell these immigrant stories.

To some who are now in a better place, who always encouraged me, I know they would have supported this effort: my mom, Mary Roos Morgan; and my dear friends Bruce Spangler, Art Garfield, Joe Snow, and Glenn Coates. Joe Snow educated me on every aspect of the US military services, their missions and platforms.

Additional thanks to Palmetto Publishing Company's Travis Crane and Katie Dahm for their support of this effort.

BIBLIOGRAPHY

Arnn, Larry in *Imprimis*. A publication of Hillsdale College November 2021 Volume 50, Number 11.

Baier, Bret, "The Unauthorized History of Socialism." FOX News Video. February 2020

Baykov, Alexander, The Development of the Soviet Economic System. New York: Macmillan, 1974.

The Declaration of Independence and the Constitution of the United States of America. In Cato Institute. 2021.

Etcheson, Craig, The Rise and Demise of Democratic Kampuchea. Boulder, Colorado: Westview Press, 1984.

Gillis, Gary M. Last Minute Productions at gary@lastminuteproductions. com. February 19, 2021.

Goerner H. G, *United States Socialist Republic*. The Liberal Marxists Machine and the Men, Method and Means to Fundamentality Transform America. Palmetto Publishing, 2020.

Hamilton, Alexander, Jay, John, and Madison, James. *The Federalist Papers*. (unabridged edition), William James, IAP 2019

Kostyal, K.M., *Founding Fathers. The Fight for Freedom and the Birth of American Liberty*. National Geographic Society 2014

Lee, Mike, *Our Lost Declaration, America's Fight Against Tyranny from King George to the Deep State*. Penguin Random House LLC 2019

Morton Heusuk, Rudolph, *Open Letter to all young people under 25 years age*. www.mortonplauenyoutheexcange.com

Levin, Mark R. *American Marxism*. Thresholds Editions. 2021.

McDonald, Forrest, *The American Presidency: An Intellectual History*. 1994

Nunes, Devin. C. *Countdown to Socialism*. Encounter Books. Encounter Broadsides, Special Edition. 2020.

Paine, Thomas, *Common Sense*. January 19, 1776

Schopenhauer, Arthur, *The Wisdom of Life*. 1851.